OPTIONS FOR
U.S. ENERGY POLICY

OPTIONS FOR U.S. ENERGY POLICY

Albert Carnesale
Stanley M. Greenfield
Fred S. Hoffman
Edward J. Mitchell
William R. Moffat
Richard Nehring
Robert S. Pindyck
Norman C. Rasmussen
David J. Rose
Henry S. Rowen
James L. Sweeney
Arthur W. Wright

Institute for Contemporary Studies
San Francisco, California

TABLE OF CONTENTS

CONTRIBUTORS

Albert Carnesale
Associate Director, Program for Science and International Affairs, Harvard University

Stanley M. Greenfield
President, Greenfield, Attaway & Tyler, Inc.

Fred S. Hoffman
Economist, The Rand Corporation

Edward J. Mitchell
Professor of Business Economics, University of Michigan

William R. Moffat
Director, Public Management Program, Graduate School of Business, Stanford University

Richard Nehring
Social Scientist, The Rand Corporation

Robert S. Pindyck
Associate Professor of Economics, Sloan School of Management, Massachusetts Institute of Technology

Norman C. Rasmussen
Head of the Department of Nuclear Engineering, Massachusetts Institute of Technology

David J. Rose
Professor, Department of Nuclear Engineering, Massachusetts Institute of Technology

Henry S. Rowen
Professor of Public Management, Graduate School of Business, Stanford University

James L. Sweeney
Associate Professor, Department of Engineering-Economic Systems, Stanford University

Arthur W. Wright
Associate Professor of Economics, Purdue University

PREFACE

In February 1975 the Institute published its first book, which was a critique of the Final Report of the Ford Foundation Energy Policy Project. Entitled NO TIME TO CONFUSE, the critique brought together ten economists and political scientists to examine what at the time was the central document in the public debate on national energy policy. It was thus fitting that the Institute response should have become the principal statement of what energy policy should *not* be.

Since NO TIME TO CONFUSE, the Institute has published nine other books on subjects ranging from land use planning to national health insurance to U.S. foreign and defense policy. During that time we have often been asked, having done the critique, when we would assemble a group of people to make a positive statement about the proper course for energy policy. The Carter energy proposals offered the opportunity this spring, and this book is the result. The occasion seems particularly fitting since the Carter proposals are largely a restatement of the Ford Project, and they were drafted with the assistance of the Ford Project director, S. David Freeman.

Now, in OPTIONS FOR U.S. ENERGY POLICY, we have asked twelve economists and engineers specializing in this field to examine energy problems related to national security, the environment, safety, and the general role of government as both proprietor and regulator of energy resources. We think the result presents a compelling agenda for the national energy policy.

H. Monroe Browne

President,
Institute for Contemporary Studies

San Francisco, California
September 1977

I

HENRY S. ROWEN

COMPREHENSIVE ENERGY POLICY: KING STORK?

Some relevant facts and predictions: the U. S. energy balance. Prices facing consumers and producers, rest of the world oil balance. The past: energy regulation as expression of domestic politics: Nixon and Ford. The Carter strategy. The Plan analyzed. Other doomsday predictions. How likely is the predicted crisis? An alternative strategy. Strategy over the longer run.

INTRODUCTION

Three administrations have searched four years for an energy policy to meet our national needs which also will be able to command essential political support. Two have, in essentials, failed. A third is now trying.

The felt need for a national energy policy was created by the 1973 oil crisis and the fourfold increase in oil prices imposed by the Organization of Petroleum Exporting Countries (OPEC). Before 1973 government intervention in fuels markets was far

from absent, but, World War II aside, nothing resembling a
national energy policy existed. After 1973 the Nixon administration opted for the goal of energy independence, a goal ill-defined
from the outset and modified substantially in the Ford administration. Despite the fact that many actions taken pointed in other
directions, reducing energy dependence—or at least halting increasing dependence—on the rest of the world has remained central to the declared policy of the government.

Limiting dependence is also at the heart of the Carter energy
plan (Plan 1977), although the reasons for doing so and the program proposed differ strikingly from those that have gone before.
The declared strategy of the Ford administration was to limit
imports by limiting the growth of demand and to stimulate supply
by allowing domestic energy prices to rise to the world level in
stages, by moving oil from Alaska, rapid leasing of the outer continental shelf lands, and resisting restrictive environmental regulations. By the time of President Carter's inauguration, however,
several years of maneuvering between Executive and Congress
had produced something quite different: a highly complex system
of energy regulations and an administrative structure to match.
There was not much of a consensus in the country on what should
be done—or even on what the problems were. Public confusion
reflected that of government; it is not surprising that the Congress
had failed to legislate strong actions towards independence when
half of the people polled in 1974 said they believed that the oil
companies had invented the crisis.

The Plan tells us that there is indeed an energy crisis, and its
cause is that the demand for oil and natural gas is growing while
supplies are shrinking. Unless we make large changes, our way of
life will be endangered; oil imports will rise steeply; our oil demand together with that of other countries will exceed supplies
from the oil-exporting countries by the late 1980s or early 1990s;
prices will rise; substitutes must be sought.

The proposed goals are 1) to reduce our vulnerability to supply
interruption, and to insulate ourselves against the coming world
oil shortage; and 2) to shift to renewable, inexhaustible energy
sources.

To attain these ends, an enormously complex program is proposed, one that is centered on taxes to reduce the growth in energy demand and to force consumers to pay the replacement cost of energy, and on price controls to prevent "windfall" profits to owners of energy properties. It is designed to shift consumption away from imports to domestic sources of energy, and away from oil and gas to coal and nuclear power.

The Plan posits as certain a possible event, a worldwide oil crunch in the 1980s, and offers a strategy poorly matched to its own diagnosis. The extraordinary assemblage of controls and taxes proposed will inflict large costs and inequities on the American people and will get in the way of the Plan's principal goal of reduced foreign dependence. Its emphasis on coal threatens more serious environmental damage than would a strategy less biased against gas or oil. By shifting attention to an unlikely 1980s crisis, it risks eroding support over time for the efforts proposed. We can do better than this.

A more appropriate set of goals—some of which are incorporated in the Plan and some not—would have us:

1. Meet our essential national security needs.

2. Reduce the large economic losses caused by government control in energy markets.

3. Protect the environment.

4. Carry out energy research and exploratory development.

To these four essential goals, we can add two more:

5. Seek to reduce the transfer of wealth imposed by the OPEC cartel, and

6. Insure against the *possibility* of an oil crisis in the 1980s.

A strategy to achieve these ends should recognize the large uncertainties that exist in future demands, supplies, the strength of OPEC, and technology. It should be an *adaptive strategy*, one based on making choices sequentially. Such a strategy would:

Meet our most urgent national security needs by rapidly building the strategic oil stockpile, as proposed earlier and, correctly, expanded in the Carter plan, possibly increasing it later on. Also, continue the Ford and Carter administration efforts to avoid premature commitment to aspects of nuclear power which are of doubtful economic benefit and which will bring many countries closer to being able to acquire nuclear explosives.

Recognize that the government has been a large part of the problem in impeding adjustment to changed energy prices and get it out of the way through phased deregulation of energy markets. Satisfy demands for a fairer society—or a more equal one, which is not the same thing—through broad fiscal and tax instruments, not through costly controls over particular fuels and efforts to prevent "windfall" profits.

Protect the environment, balancing environmental goals against other desired ends.

Carry out research and development on a very broad basis with particular emphasis on the research end of the scale, i.e., those activities in which the private sector underinvests because many of the benefits are not appropriable by firms.

Doing more than this makes sense if there are additional social costs from imports beyond the (reduced) level that would be produced by following this strategy. A strong case can be made that there are such costs. Today the world oil price is kept above its competitive price by OPEC; the position of the cartel may weaken in the next decade, and U.S. actions could help this process along. Alternatively, the world may, as the Plan asserts, experience the great oil shortage in the 1980s. In any case, heavy dependence on Middle East oil imposes international political costs and supply interruptions, even with an expanded strategic reserve. Therefore, we should value oil from OPEC, and especially from the turbulent Middle East, less than oil from elsewhere. It is not that imports of energy are bad *per se* any more than imports of other goods, but that imports from some regions have social costs not reflected adequately in prices. The best practical way to deal with this is to:

> Impose a tariff on imported oil so as to reflect its social costs and risks—with possible exemptions from the tariff for oil purchases in long-term contracts from secure sources.

In order to understand better where we should be going, we need to look at some of the relevant facts and estimates and to consider more closely the history of our efforts to grapple with these problems.

SOME RELEVANT FACTS AND PREDICTIONS

The U.S. Energy Balance

Table 1 shows U.S. consumption of fuels and sources of supply for three years—1960, 1972, and 1976—and the estimate for 1985 presented in the Carter plan.

Several trends emerge from Table 1: on the *demand* side, the growth in transportation use of energy, largely oil, changes into a nearly level demand from now to 1985; the rapid growth of electricity demand is also expected to continue, although at a lower rate. However, industrial demand is shown, surprisingly, as growing more rapidly in the future than in the past. In the aggregate, about a 30 percent growth in total energy consumption is predicted by 1985; adoption of the Plan is shown as reducing 1985 demand by only 4 percent in comparison with the level expected from current policies.

On the *supply* side, the rapid growth of oil and gas supply in the 1960s and early 1970s, includingh imports, is evident as well as the slow growth in coal output. For 1985, domestic supplies of oil are shown as little changed from the present, gas declines, nuclear power grows sharply (but is still producing less than 10 percent of our energy by 1985), and coal increases rapidly. Imports of oil are

shown as growing absolutely and as a share of total consumption
by 1985 without the Plan; with it, they are predicted as held about
constant.

Table 1

U.S. Consumption of Fuels
and Sources of Supply

				Fuel Balance by Sector (millions of barrels of oil equivalent per day)	
	1960	1972	1976	1985 (without Plan)	1985 (with Plan)
Demand	**22.0**	**35.3**	**37.0**	**48.3**	**46.4**
Residential & Commercial	6.5	13.0	13.8	16.1	15.2
Industry	10.0	13.1	13.7	21.4	20.6
Transportation	5.6	9.2	9.5	10.8	10.5
Electricity (included in other sectoral tables)	(4.0)	(9.0)	(10.5)	(16.3)	(15.5)
Supply	**22.0**	**35.3**	**37.0**	**48.5**	**46.4**
Domestic	**20.1**	**29.3**	**30.0**	**37.1**	**40.0**
Crude Oil	7.0	10.5	9.7	10.4	10.6
Natural Gas	6.5	10.5	9.5	8.2	8.8
Coal	5.1	7.5	7.9	12.2	14.5
Nuclear	–	.2	1.0	3.7	3.8
Other (including ref. gain)	1.5	.9	1.9	2.6	2.3
Imports/Exports (-)	**1.9**	**5.7**	**7.0**	**11.5**	**6.4**
Oil	1.8	6.0	7.3	11.5	7.0
Natural gas	0.5	0.5	0.5	1.2	.6
Coal	- 0.4	- 0.8	- 0.8	- 1.2	- 1.2

Sources: FEA (1976); Plan (1977).

Prices Facing Consumers and Producers

These changes have been and will be influenced powerfully by changing energy prices. Table 2 shows how energy prices facing consumers have changed over time (in 1976 dollars).

Table 2
Energy Prices*

	Gasoline (¢/gal. incl. tax)	Electricity ($/MM BTU)	Natural Gas ($/MM BTU)
1950	63.3	20.00	2.01
1960	59.9	13.92	1.92
1972	49.2	9.13	1.62
1976	59.5	10.23	1.98

*Data from Russell (1977).

The real cost of energy declined from 1950 to 1970 by 28 percent, a decline which accounts for much of the increase in energy consumption. The fourfold increase in world oil prices that occurred in 1973-1974, and increases in other fuels, is not fully perceived by consumers; the price of gasoline as seen by consumers, including taxes, in real terms today is only 21 percent more than in 1972 and less than the level of 1950. The average delivered price of natural gas has risen comparably, and is now at about the 1950 level. The average real price of electric power has .isen still less, and is only one-half the 1950 level.

The prices facing domestic producers have fluctuated more

widely. The real price of crude oil fell during the 1960s and early 1970s (in 1977 dollars) from around $6.10 in 1960 to $4.70 in 1972. With existing controls, producers face segmented prices, with so-called Lower Tier oil now priced at $5.25 and Upper Tier oil at $11.28. Under the Plan, price controls on already discovered oil will remain (but will be inflation indexed), but so-called "newly discovered" oil will be allowed gradually to rise to the 1977 world price level and kept there (but also indexed).

The price of interstate natural gas has long been held below its market clearing price. Between 1972 and 1977 the new contract wellhead price of gas increased from $0.33/MCF to $1.46/MCF. Increasing amounts of gas were sold in uncontrolled intrastate markets where most new contracts now range from $1.50 to $2.00/MCF (Pindyck, Chapter VI). Under the Plan, all natural gas, intrastate and interstate, would be controlled initially at a price of $1.75/MCF, increasing over time to the level BTU equivalent price of crude oil.

There would be an additional "wedge" driven between these prices facing producers and those facing consumers in the form of an array of taxes on already discovered oil and gas and on industrial users of these fuels.

Rest of the World Oil Balance

Table 3 shows the pattern of demand and supply of oil (not total energy) as estimated by the Central Intelligence Agency.

The CIA is forecasting that free world oil demand by 1985 will increase by 46 percent, an annual rate of increase of 4.4 percent. Also, the OPEC countries, today suppliers of about 65 percent of the free world's oil, will increase this share to 70 percent—assuming that they are willing to supply so much oil. This growing dominance, we are told, will exist despite the large projected increases in Europe (the North Sea) and the non-OPEC less-developed countries (principally Mexico). Particularly striking is the forecast that the Soviet Union will experience a net shift from imports to exports of about 5 million barrels per day (B/D). OPEC will, in this projection, be called upon to increase oil production by about

Table 3

World Oil Demand and Supply
(millions of barrels per day)

	1976	1985
Free World Oil Demand	48.4	68.3 - 72.6
United States	16.7	22.2 - 25.6
OECD Europe	13.6	15.8 - 18.2
Japan	5.2	8.1 - 8.8
Other developed countries	3.2	4.8 - 5.4
Non-OPEC LDCs	6.7	12.0
OPEC countries	2.1	4.0
Other	0.9	0
Non-OPEC Supply	17.5	20.4 - 22.4
United States	9.7	10.0 - 11.0
OECD Europe	.9	4.0 - 5.0
Japan	0	.1
Other Developed Countries	2.1	1.7 - 1.9
Non-OPEC LDCs	3.7	8.0 - 9.0
Net Communist trade		
USSR-Eastern Europe	.9	-3.5 - 4.5
China	.2	0
Required OPEC Production	30.9	46.7 - 51.2

Source: CIA (1977).

two-thirds by 1985; Saudi Arabia will have to more than double its production, from around 8 million B/D to around 20 million B/D, a development which the CIA and the Plan assert is by no means certain.

Similar, but somewhat less alarmist, prognostications have been published by the Workshop on Alternative Energy Strategies (WAES 1977) and by the OECD (1977). The message is: crisis looms, comprehensive national action is now urgent.

THE PAST: ENERGY REGULATION AS EXPRESSION OF DOMESTIC POLITICS

In the past, the U.S. government has influenced fuels markets in many ways: through public utility rate regulation of the electricity and natural gas industries, the famous oil depletion allowance provision of the tax code, foreign tax credits on foreign oil exploration, and individual state prorationing controls on oil production (Mead 1977). For example, the Texas Railroad Commission effectively controlled American oil prices—and strongly influenced world prices—before and for some years after World War II. Having large and monopoly-controlled quantities of low-cost oil, Texas performed the world price maintenance function that OPEC—and especially Saudi Arabia—does today. Several of these measures had opposing effects: the mandatory oil import quota system encouraged domestic development at the expense of foreign; the foreign tax credit, by stimulating production abroad, had the opposite effect (Mead 1977). They were simply the product of different political forces.

The importance of the federal government as an actor grew substantially in the 1950s: it played a central role in arranging for the participation of American independent oil firms in Iran after the overthrow of Premier Mossadegh, became a regulator of interstate natural gas prices in 1954, and controlled oil imports under executive order of President Eisenhower.

These interventions into fuel markets were largely the consequence of our political institutions performing a familiar role: allocating economic benefits to those groups able to muster the necessary arguments, money, and votes to persuade officials of the merits of not allowing market forces to continue to operate alone.

Although the oil import quota program, which produced large wealth transfers and social deadweight loss, was rationalized in terms of national security, there is little evidence that this argument was taken seriously. Indeed, one of the consequences of the quota, ironic in retrospect, was more rapid depletion of our low-cost oil by discouraging the importation of oil. (Under the Carter plan—as under the Nixon and Ford administrations—we will effectively be doing the opposite: discouraging domestic production and encouraging imports.) The alternative of building an oil stockpile as a cost-effective way of gaining protection against supply interruptions evidently was not seriously considered.

The regulation of natural gas had even worse consequences. The wasteful effects of price controls on interstate gas—which last year held the price at 25 percent of the BTU equivalent price of crude oil—although inevitable and predicted, were a long time in becoming painfully evident. Much gas was being produced in association with oil, and a modest revenue from its sale was a nice bonus for producers mainly investing in oil production. But by the late 1960s, although price controls on natural gas shipped between states were causing increasing amounts of gas to be shifted to the uncontrolled intrastate market, the federal government failed to act to forestall what was coming—increased gas shortages in the consuming states of the north. Only in recent years has it become evident (but not yet to about half the members of Congress) that, far from being benefited by these controls, a growing number of consumers are hurt; many face the prospect of having to pay for more costly imported gas or even more costly electricity.

In short, American prodigality in the use of energy is not only the product of an inherited frontier mentality and access to cheap fuel; it has been given a boost by government officials mindful of immediate constituent pressures but less mindful of the needs of the larger community over time. Indeed, it has become increasingly apparent that event he narrower interests of many constituents have not been well served.

With the oil shortages of 1973 and the quadrupling of OPEC prices within four months, political pressure mounted for a com-

prehensive energy policy, that is, for the shifting of many important choices on energy from the economic marketplace to the
political marketplace. This, despite the fact that no major market
failure in the domestic energy economy could be plausibly
blamed. There was indeed a massive market failure in the world
energy economy, but our response to this external threat was far
from adequate.

The Nixon and Ford Responses

The Nixon administration's response to the 1973 crisis was to
announce the goal of "Energy Independence." The goal of zero
oil imports for 1980 was soon abandoned, but was declared to be
attainable by 1985 at $11 per barrel (1973 dollars), assuming com-
plete decontrol and if additional conservation actions were taken
(FEA 1974). Emergency storage was proposed for protection
against sudden supply reductions. The zero import goal was rejected on the grounds that some imports were from secure sources
and emergency curtailment and storage could cope with some
reduction in supply. Indeed, prospects seemed sufficiently encouraging to generate concern that OPEC cohesion might erode,
oil prices fall, and imports into the United States surge. At a price
of $7 (1973 dollars), estimated imports would be around 12 mil-
lion B/D (6 million from "insecure" sources) and our vulnerability to a cut in supply high. These worries even produced proposals
that the importing countries should create a floor price for oil.
Despite this concern, implementation of the strategic oil reserve
moved very slowly.

   The new Federal Energy Administration (FEA) prudently expressed great uncertainty about the future price of oil as well as
about security of supply and examined several strategies to cope
with these uncertainties. It reported that at $11 a barrel, domestic
energy demand would grow slowly (2.7 percent per year to 1985,
but additional conservation measures could hold growth to 2
percent). At that price, domestic oil production could reach
13 million B/D (and with extra efforts including accelerated OCS
leasing, perhaps 17 million B/D). With natural gas deregulation,

production would rise from 22 trillion cubic feet (TCF) in 1972 to over 24 TCF by 1985 (FEA 1974).

A little more than a year later, FEA was less optimistic (FEA 1976). OPEC had succeeded in holding the real oil price roughly constant; the United States was spending over $30 billion on imported oil compared with about $3 billion in 1970, and estimates of oil and gas resources and future production rates had dropped. FEA now forecast that gradual deregulation of oil and gas could only keep oil imports at a level of 6 million B/D, about the same as in 1975. It still forecast that deregulation and OCS leasing could result in 12 million B/D of oil production, 22 TCF of gas production, and the production of perhaps over 1,000 million tons of coal. Particularly striking was FEA's estimate of the powerful effect of domestic policies on imports; at one extreme we might be able to reduce imports to 1 million B/D; at the other, if regulation continued, they might reach 13 million B/D.

Although FEA had concluded by 1976 that there was little possibility of a sharply lower OPEC real oil price level by 1980, it argued that proper importing country policies could exert downward price pressure. In reality, U.S. actions were at cross-purposes. Automobile efficiency standards had been enacted, an accelerated program of OCS leasing started, and the Alaska pipeline project was moving ahead; on the other hand, oil price controls had been extended by the Congress to include formerly uncontrolled "new" oil and the oil depletion allowance had been removed.

Despite the free-market rhetoric occasionally issuing from the Nixon administration, it had imposed general price controls in 1971 and subsequently, with powerful congressional encouragement, erected a complex and costly system of administrative controls. The Ford administration, although more opposed on doctrinal grounds to controls, found itself extending their reach. Not least among its bizarre aspects is the infamous "entitlement" system in which importers of oil receive a subsidy from domestic producers (cf. Sweeney, Chapter VII). Unlike the countries of Western Europe and Japan, the United States (also Canada), by protecting its consumers from the full impact of the changed oil price, was encouraging consumption, additional imports, and a strengthened OPEC.

By 1976 some acute worries had lessened. Immediately after the price increase in 1973-1974 there was serious concern about the stability of the international financial system in light of the sudden transfer of $100 billion a year of funds to the OPEC countries, the effect of larger trade deficits in encouraging protectionist sentiment, the net inflationary effect of much more costly energy, and fears that the Arab OPEC members might use the new financial power in a manner similar to the wielding of the "oil weapon." Although the worst of these possibilities have not been realized, some of these concerns were justified; the economic consequences have been severe. The large resource transfer, together with heightened concerns about inflation, has undoubtedly contributed to a slowing of world economic growth. Moreover, the future stability of Western economies now experiencing 6 percent or more inflation rates remains uncertain. A slide into a prolonged period of "stagflation" cannot be ruled out.

Not only did the goal of energy independence fade during the Nixon and Ford administrations, it never received a clear definition. As the 1974 Project Independence Report pointed out, independence could mean zero imports, an achievable but costly goal, or it could mean permitting imports from secure sources, or even from insecure sources so long as compensating actions were taken. The essential task of defining independence and expressing it in concrete terms that could be understood by Congress and public and thus provide a focal point for public support was not done. The responsibility for this failure rests on the Nixon and Ford administrations; the Congress, as is usually true, was occupied with its diverse interests.

Why did these administrations do so badly? The Nixon administration was in its last throes in the critical period of late 1973 and early 1974. But intellectual confusion helped. The State Department and White House in the early 1970s, insofar as they were paying any attention to international oil developments, were complacent in the face of growing evidence of greater OPEC effectiveness and were extraordinarily inept.[1] After the 1973 crisis, the government faced a conflict between two foreign policy objectives: a policy of confronting the cartel—arguably necessary if the American people were to be mobilized in support of a vigorous energy program—was in conflict with the U.S. role as peacemaker between Israel and the Arabs. Secretary Kissinger and two presidents put the peacemaking goal over trying to counter OPEC and its Arab members in particular. The strength of domestic interests in the oil crisis also helped to weaken our response. If players in the domestic energy industries had no substantial role in precipitating the crisis, some no doubt could perceive benefits in it (Vernon 1974).

The upshot is that U.S. oil consumption, which reached a level of 17 million B/D in 1973, will be more than 18 million B/D in 1977. Imports, then at 6 million B/D, will be over 7 million B/D. Natural gas consumption peaked at 23 TCF in 1973 and is now around 19 TCF. Coal production has risen only slowly. Even so, in 1977, in the midst of a strong economic recovery, we will be consuming only about 3.5 percent more energy than in 1973 with a real GNP about 8 percent higher. Even the modest increases in real prices that consumers face are having their effect.

THE CARTER STRATEGY

Now it is President Carter's turn. His first priority has been the creation of a Department of Energy with far-reaching powers over the country's energy sector. This department, starting with 20,000 employees and a budget of over $10 billion, will exercise enormous influence over the energy sector and therefore the entire economy. We also have a Plan, one that rests on a set of ten principles (Plan 1977):

1. The need for a comprehensive strategy and for a public ready to make sacrifices;
2. Continued economic growth;
3. Protection of the environment;
4. Reduced vulnerability to supply interruptions;
5. Equity among regions, sectors, and income groups;

6. Restrained demand through conservation and efficiency;
7. Prices that reflect replacement costs of fuels consumed;
8. Stable government policies;
9. A shift from fuels in short supply to those abundant; and
10. Expanded use of non-conventional energy sources.

The Plan goes on to describe the three "overriding" energy objectives mentioned earlier: reducing dependence on foreign oil and vulnerability to supply interruptions; keeping imports low so as to weather the period when world oil production approaches capacity limits; and having renewable, nearly inexhaustible energy supplies for the long term. Specific goals associated with these objectives are:

Reducing annual energy demand growth to under 2 percent.

Cutting oil imports from a potential level, under current policies, of 16 million B/D to 6 million B/D, and gasoline use 10 percent below the 1977 level.

Expanding the strategic oil reserve.

Almost doubling coal production by 1985.

Bringing 90 percent of homes and all new buildings to minimum energy efficiency standards and using solar heating in over 2.5 million homes.

Among the legislative actions proposed are the following:

A graduated tax on "gas guzzling" automobiles with an offsetting rebate for small cars.

Tax credits for household insulation and solar heating measures.

Modified price controls through the definition of yet another category of oil, in effect "new, new" oil, whose price would be allowed to rise to the world level over three years; current price controls would be maintained on already discovered oil (but indexed for general inflation); an "equalization tax" would be imposed on these other oil categories to bring the price up to the world level with the revenues collected being returned to consumers.

The creation of a billion barrel oil reserve.

Control of intrastate gas along with interstate gas; the price of "new" gas would remain controlled (but tied to the crude oil price and inflation indexed).

Prohibition of burning oil or gas in new industrial or utility boilers.

A universal requirement for using "best available" coal pollution technology no matter how low the sulfur content of the coal used.

A complicated set of taxes on industrial and industry uses of oil and gas.

The Plan Analyzed

Consider first the principles. *Principle Number One* states that the energy problem can be effectively addressed only by a government that can deal with it comprehensively and by a public willing to make necessary sacrifices. This is an unselfconscious assertion of the power of the state over the individual. It asserts as a matter of principle the near total politicizing of this sector of economic life, in contrast to the past incomplete and haphazard politicization. It assumes, contrary to the record, that government can effectively perform in the public interest in this domain.

Consider also *Principle Number Eight,* that of providing stable government policies. There is proposed the creation of a large new government department, a legislative program with over 100 items for action in 1977 alone, including the extension of controls on natural gas, changes in definitions of oil categories, new taxes, rebates, and the like. Surely this prospect generates wide skepticism about this principle. Consider as an unparalleled source of uncertainty, the Plan's proposal for a *standby* gasoline tax! No wonder Mobil Oil has decided to invest in land development and retail merchandising, and other oil companies are contemplating similar diversification!

Or contemplate the *Overriding Objective* of "reducing dependence on foreign oil and vulnerability to supply interruptions." An important distinction, present in Project Independence, is lacking—that between secure and insecure sources of supply. Implicit is the sequence that imports means imports from OPEC, means imports from the insecure Middle East, and that imports are bad. But not all oil imports are from OPEC; exceptions include Canada and Mexico. Not all OPEC producers are in the Middle East and prone to supply interruptions; for example, Venezuela, Indonesia, and Nigeria. Imports might be preferred if the source is secure, the price is competitive, less environmental damage is caused, or the economic advancement of less-developed countries is promoted.

Supply interruption, given the experience of 1973, we can understand, and this threat needs to be met. To do more, to treat imports as bad *per se,* is to indulge in a kind of mercantilism, that discredited doctrine which, phoenixlike, arises.

The question raised here is whether it is possible and useful to segment the oil market along a line other than domestic vs. foreign. What this boils down to is the possibility and usefulness of adopting a discriminating policy against the Middle East producers, those who continue to wield the ''oil weapon'' as a threat, are the price leaders in OPEC, and cannot assure us a secure supply of oil in any case.

But, reducing dependence is not the only or even perhaps the principal reason for holding down imports. Instead, the Plan introduces the prospect of a looming world oil shortage. World demand is growing worldwide more rapidly than supply. To meet this demand, as shown in Table 3, OPEC by 1985 might have to produce over 50 million barrels per day. (This is a large increase over the 1974 Project Independence estimate of a 1985 world demand for OPEC's oil of only 28 million B/D at about today's real oil price.) But most OPEC countries cannot increase production and some will experience declines; OPEC can only come close to meeting this ''requirement'' if Saudi Arabia increases its output to about 20 million B/D. Even if it does so, it cannot meet the even higher demands of the late 1980s and early 1990s. So there will be a sharp price increase unless world demand growth is held down.

In case the world somehow escapes a struggle for oil in the 1980s, it will soon thereafter because it is pressing on ultimate limits to oil resources. Proven oil reserves in the United States, only about 30 billion barrels, are falling, and are only equivalent to ten years of current production. The prospect is not much better worldwide. Current proven crude reserves are 600 billion barrels, and ultimate recoverable reserves are estimated at around 2,000 billion barrels. Consumption, now at 22 billion barrels a year, has been growing at 6.6 percent since 1940. The Plan tells us that if it were to grow in the future at only 3 percent, total remaining recoverable oil reserves would be exhausted by 2020; at a growth rate of 5 percent the oil would be gone by 2010. In reality, increasingly costly production methods will cause prices to rise making oil prohibitively costly for most energy users (Plan 1977: 15). This prospect is imminent, not remote.

The Plan holds out little hope that natural gas can save us. American production peaked in 1973 and is declining to a predicted level of 16.5 TCF in 1985; consumption will remain at 19 TCF, the difference being made up by imports. Although the Plan observes that interstate price controls were set at a level which priced gas at only one-fourth of the price of imported oil on a BTU basis and caused severe market distortions, it holds that "it is doubtful that even large price increases could do much to arrest the decline in gas production" (Plan 1977:18). New gas sources— Alaska, OCS, deep tight formations, geopressured methane—are held not likely to contribute much gas until after the mid-1980s.

The upshot is a future—absent vigorous action and necessary sacrifices—that holds in store supply disruptions, sharp price increases, damage to the environment, a disproportionate share of capital devoted to energy, enormous foreign payments for oil (possibly as much as $175 billion in 1985) or an incapacity to buy it at all, regional disputes within the United States, further constraints on U.S. foreign policy leadership already hampered by increased dependence on Mid-East oil, and economic depression.

Other Doomsday Predictions

Similar forecasts are to be found outside of the government, for example, in the WAES report. It concludes that the "supply of oil will fail to meet increasing demand before the year 2000, most probably between 1985 and 1995 even if energy prices rise 50 percent in real terms''; demand will continue to grow even if governments adopt rigorous conservation policies; alternatives need vigorously to be developed now. But "even with prompt action the margin between success and failure in the 1985-2000 period is slim" (WAES 1977: 3-5). Time is running out. The critical problem is, once again, the growing gap between supply and demand, that between oil imports "desired" by consuming countries and "maximum" exports available from exporting countries. For a range of cases in which economic growth, energy prices, and other parameters vary, the prospective gap in the year 2000 varies from 15 to 20 million B/D (WAES 1977: 9).

WAES is, however, less determinedly pessimistic than CIA and the Plan; it even anticipates the possibility of a world oil surplus in the mid-1980s if OPEC sets the oil price as high as $17.24 per barrel (in 1975 dollars). Crisis comes early only if there is high economic growth, a falling oil price, and a "restrained policy response." This crisis, which in oil will amount to 26-28 percent of total potential production, can be met by a massive shift to nuclear power and coal. But more will be needed; vigorous conservation efforts and higher prices to induce alternative production methods (the higher prices will be tolerable if the rise is steady and predictable, damaging if rapid). The basic danger is that the gap "could become critical before it seems serious." Like the CIA, WAES also focuses on Saudi Arabia's willingness to expand production as crucial. If the crunch comes early in the 1980s, the resulting price rise might trigger a world recession—and confrontation and conflict.

These prognostications are only the most recent in a growing body of pessimistic publications on resources including *A Time to Choose* (Ford 1974), the summary volume of the Energy Policy Project of the Ford Foundation, and *The Limits to Growth* (Meadows et al. 1972), the celebrated collection of model projections that show that the world economy may collapse within the next 100-200 years from population growth, exhaustion of raw materials, pollution, or some combination of these. *A Time to*

Choose presented themes echoed in the Carter plan, perhaps not accidentally in view of the fact that the director of the EPP, S. David Freeman, also participated in the Plan's preparation. It announced that we have entered a new age of energy, that energy has become a fourth essential of life along with food, clothing, and shelter. It deplored the absence of a coherent national policy, lamented our extravagance in energy consumption, and called for vigorous government action to produce more efficiency in energy use through technical substitutions and even to move us to a zero energy growth track. Such a goal, proposed as an end in itself, should be accomplished by government control over the energy sector.

These doomsday analyses, including the Plan, have several common characteristics:

Excessive Confidence in Predicting the Future. Despite saving remarks about "optimistic," "most likely," and "pessimistic" possibilities, only a small range of variation of demand, supply, prices, the behavior of OPEC, new technology or new energy sources, is incorporated in most of these analyses.

The actual record of prediction in energy resources, in other resources, or in much else in life, does not inspire high confidence in these forecasts. The cheery 1974 FEA predictions have rapidly been succeeded by less optimistic ones. This is not a new phenomenon. Wildly wrong predictions of resources are legion. In 1891 the U.S. Geological Survey estimated that there was no oil in Texas; in 1914 the Bureau of Mines estimated total future U.S. production at 6 billion barrels. A consensus of eleven U.S. oil companies' forecasts for 1980 made in 1962 was already exceeded in 1972 (Mitchell 1974). A review of past energy consumption projections of the 1960s showed large errors even for the consumption in that decade (Darmstadter and Landsberg 1974)! Official predictions for installed U.S. nuclear power in 1985 have fluctuated by over a factor of three in the past seven years (Wohlstetter 1977).

The difficulty of energy prediction was exhibited strikingly in the report of the Cabinet Task Force on Oil Import Control in 1970 (Cabinet Task Force 1970). It concluded that

> the world market seems likely to be more competitive in the future than in the past because the growing number and diversity of producing countries and companies makes it more difficult to organize and enforce a cartel.... These reasons support the conclusion that the landed price of foreign crude by 1980 may well decline and will in any event not experience a substantial increase.

The difficulty in long range resource forecasting is also evidenced by comparing predictions in the 1952 Paley Commission report with actual outcomes.[2] This report estimated the consumption by 1975 of twenty-four commodities (ferrous and nonferrous metals and nonmetallic minerals including oil, gas, and coal). From 1950 to the 1972-1974 period, actual increases for ten commodities exceeded predicted ones with a median difference of 32 percent; predicted increases exceeded the actual for thirteen commodities with a median difference of 43 percent. For energy, the estimate for coal was 44 percent too high, oil almost exactly right, and for natural gas the actual increase was 136 percent greater than the predicted increase. Moreover, the U.S. economy grew at an average real rate of about 3.6 percent per annum rather than the 2.5 percent assumed by the commission, which meant that the economy was about 30 percent larger than assumed and should have absorbed many more resources than estimated by the commission (Cooper 1974).

Uncertainties in economic growth, changing tastes of consumers, substitution possibilities in production and consumption, and geological accident are inherent difficulties in resource forecasting. Their existence has a major implication for energy policy; we should adopt an energy strategy which takes explicit account of them.

A Preference for Government Controls over Market Forces. Implicit is the conviction that millions of individual consumers and producers do not know as much about what is in their true interests as bureaucrats, legislators, or energy analysts. Only the government can determine the ''right'' price for natural gas, the price differential that should exist among scores of grades of crude oil, the miles per gallon the average car should have, and so on and so on.

Those who believe that they know best what people "need" are not willing to allow these decisions to be left to individual choices because, they hold, consumers are energy hogs, ignorant, exploited by oligopolistic oil firms; moreover, allowing the market to work would cause undeserving "windfall" gains and impose an inequitable burden on users.[3]

Not only does this (perhaps sometimes unconscious) authoritarianism substitute the values of centralized bureaucracies for individuals, it is costly to operate and risks causing the wrong price signals to be sent to consumers and producers. People faced with price signals, especially ones they judge stable, more or less consciously adjust their behavior to these signals in ways appropriate to their particular situation. To many people the signals are to put insulation in houses, increase drilling for oil and gas, and buy smaller cars—despite the muffling effect of government controls. These adjustments do not take place instantaneously; some consumers—and producers—are slow in receiving the message, but in the aggregate they move in the directions indicated; they would move more rapidly, however, if the signals were clearer. Government bureaucrats cannot do as well in making these decisions. They have an impossible burden of acquiring information relevant to large numbers of transactions carried out in many different market settings. The results are sometimes perverse.

A striking example of perversity caused by regulation is the effect of utility rate regulation. In the state of Washington, cheap hydropower is being sold to many customers at the historical accounting cost of about .9¢ per kwh. However, good hydropower sites are exhausted, additions to electric capacity must now be nuclear or coal; these, in today's dollars, produce electricity at a cost of about 3.5¢/kwh. This is the socially relevant cost of consumption of an additional kwh of electricity. But the consumer faces a regulated price of one-fourth as much. So it is not surprising that he demands more and more of it at this low rate, forcing the utilities to add capacity at a cost over four times the price charged. It is not surprising to discover that some firms in that region are considering using electricity as a boiler fuel to make steam! This is a clear case for the application of *Principle Number Seven* that energy prices should reflect the true replacement costs of energy.[4]

The view that the government should take over from the market is argued on the grounds that markets are imperfect, that cartels exist, that oil markets have long been influenced by oil trusts and industry-dominated Texas Railroad Commissions. In short, that because the girl is no longer a virgin we might as well treat her as a whore. Evidence that fuels markets are fairly competitive on the one hand, and the amply demonstrated inperfections in the government management of the energy sector on the other, are given little weight.

Errors of "Gapology." Several of these reports are replete with references to energy "gaps." It is a favorite concept of those of a technocratic bent. A gap exists when more is desired of a given commodity than is produced; its opposite is a surplus. Short-term gaps and surpluses are common enough phenomena in life—for example, when an opera company plays to an empty house or an airline oversells tickets for a flight. The discovery of oil in East Texas in the 1930s, together with a depression, drove the price of a barrel of oil down to 10¢ a barrel. Speaking loosely, one can say that there then was a surplus of oil. OPEC's production cuts in 1973-1974 caused a short-lived shortage, or gap. But usually, if markets do not clear through price changes, it is because government action has prevented it.

As a rule, dealers in "gaps" are either ignorant of the working of the market forces or are pushing some nostrum. As Alchian has pointed out, the concept of a "gap" is intellectually bankrupt, and anyone who accepts it deserves the resulting political control over consumers' use of resources by allocation, rationing, or political pressures in order to influence behavior towards politically approved "needs."[5]

The concept of "gap" follows naturally from the assumption that there are consumer "needs" that can be determined politically. These are often represented as fixed; in less extreme form the assumption is that demand is nearly invariant in relation to prices. Cited in support is the fact that the increased price of oil has not caused a sharp reduction in its consumption but, as the data in Table 2 show, real energy prices facing consumers after costs of refining, transportation, and taxes, have risen only moderately; in real terms, 1977 average consumer prices are only about 25 percent higher than in 1972.[6] The supposed nonresponsiveness of consumers is an illusion.

A Small-World Perspective. Little has attracted many technocrats, well-to-do liberals, and environmentalists more than the Malthusian view of the world as finite, small, and about to be exhausted. The many predictions mentioned above on the imminent exhaustion of resources show the vitality of this belief.

Associated with many of the modern as well as ancient versions of the limits-to-growth doctrine is a fascination with exponential growth rates. How much more attention-grabbing it is to observe that estimated world recoverable oil will be exhausted in thirty-three years at an exponential growth rate of 5 percent than to observe that at a constant rate it would be exhausted in about 100 years, or that at an exponentially declining rate of 5 percent a year it would never be exhausted. But differences in these times makes a large difference in the costs of transition to substitute resources.

A failure to understand the scope of possible substitutions is often joined to a failure to understand the possibilities of new technology. Predictions about energy supplies and demands in the year 2025 are now commonplace, yet predictions made in 1929 about today would hardly have included nuclear power and would probably have underestimated the importance today of natural gas (as did the Paley Commission twenty-three years later).[7] Limits-to-growth analyses typically assume rising real costs of resources, yet the record of the past 100 years shows that technological progress has about offset depletion for many raw materials—to the distress of many raw material producing countries.

Should we assume then that technology will save us from having to find alternatives in the next few decades to relatively cheap oil and gas? It would be risky to do so; nature offers no guarantees in this regard. It is especially dangerous to assume that technology will provide near-term fixes. But over the longer run, there will be many new choices.

The small-world perspective is also often associated with a tendency to have a static view of time. To those who know that some good—or evil—is going to occur in the 21st century (e.g., from using, or not using, the liquid metal fast-breeder reactor, or expanding coal output), it is tempting to treat the event as occurring now. Yet the value of resources in alternative uses, together with revealed time preference of consumers, requires us to value the future less than the present (although it has not produced a single consensus number to use, in part because of the wedge driven by taxes between the return on savings and on investment). Few people who stop to think about the matter would argue that the time rate of discount should be zero. The implication for energy is that, with substantial investment in basic and exploratory research, we need not be too worried about how the world will get its energy in the 21st century.

Still, there is the problem of getting from here to there, and the laws of nature do not exclude the possibility of resources being distributed in such a way that the supply of resource has a sharp kink in it; i.e., that a resource is plentiful and cheap up to a point and then there is no more except a little bit available only at a very high cost. The assumption in the Plan is that demand inexorably grows, suddenly to face the "cliff" of no more oil. The implicit pattern is shown in Figure 1. It can be used to explain both the fact of low (indeed, declining) oil prices from the early 1950s to the early 1970s (implicitly assuming that oil property owners or speculators are blind to the coming exhaustion of resources), as well as the prediction that prices will skyrocket in the future, or even that the United States might not be able to purchase all the oil it "needs."

Short-run supply schedules of resources—for example, oil and gas—often have a shape approximating that of Figure 1, and this fact can produce short-term dislocations. But long-run supply functions are very unlikely to take this form.[8] Even if some resource has a geological distribution which would produce such a kinked long-run supply schedule, substitutes will be developed as the anticipated shortage of the depleting resource comes closer in time and prices rise. Only if a sudden discontinuity occurs (usually in wartime) does the problem of needing and developing substitutes—or doing without—become urgent.

Figure 1

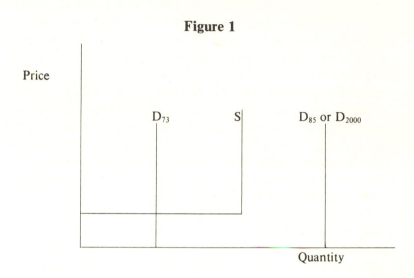

A Pressing Concern with Equality. The Plan can reasonably be viewed as a massive income-redistribution scheme: away from oil refiners,[9] against those who favor large cars, and in favor of those with large gas-heated swimming pools; in favor of residential uses of oil and gas and opposed to industrial use; in favor of the northeast versus the southwest; in favor of coal miners and owners in the east (which has high-sulfur coal) and opposed to those in the (low-sulfur) west; in favor of those who have delayed insulating their homes (who can now receive money for what it pays them to do anyway); and away from people who live far from the job and drive to work. All in the name of fairness. The blue-collar worker with a large family who lives in a rural area and whose principal recreation is hunting and fishing might think himself unfairly treated by "gas-guzzling" taxes. So also might a prudent oil man who, anticipating a future increase in the price of oil and believing the government when it decontrolled "new" oil in 1973, put his money at risk, found some oil, and then found its price controlled in 1975. Now he might invest in real estate instead.

In our age the pursuit of equity increasingly is interpreted as requiring the pursuit of equality. Everyone should be induced or coerced into driving small cars, using appliances and buildings with stipulated efficiencies, and receive equal rebates from energy taxes. But because the circumstances of individuals differ enormously, rules which aim at equality often have a far from equal effect. This is the case for those householders who have been able to get natural gas hook-ups because politicians in earlier years had decided that they should not allow owners of gas properties, some of whom are workers who have invested via their pension funds, to get rich at the expense of homeowners—some of whom own (natural) gas-guzzling houses.[10]

Examples abound, but are these quibbles? Isn't rough justice all that is possible in these matters? If nature, or government, causes changes in welfare, it is natural to expect pressure for compensation from those affected or to feel that fairness requires it. But neither the roughness of the justice nor the costs should be underestimated. Attempting to prevent "windfall" gains penalizes not only the lucky but the farsighted and the entrepreneurial, the most productive members of society. And compensation to some leaves others out in the cold who have an equally felt claim to justice. But if compensation is deemed warranted, it should leave those affected with the maximum freedom of choice, i.e., be in the form of money rather than gas, food, housing, etc. (A similar proposition applied to taxes argues for excess profit taxes on energy producers—despite its complications—rather than the taxes on oil and gas as proposed in the Plan.) However, placing a high value on individual choices is contrary to the reformer's predilections for imposing his tastes on others, and contrary to the politician's preference for having a government so complex that he is in the happy position of being an essential intermediary in providing particular services to his constituents.

The principle of expanding the realm of choice also suggests that the scope of income maintenance reform perhaps should not proceed independently of energy welfare considerations. And also that regional income distribution which enters prominently into energy policy bargaining should be examined in a wider context.

HOW LIKELY IS THE PREDICTED CRISIS?

The CIA has the world energy "gap" opening up in the early 1980s (with an upward "price break" indicated for 1983). To WAES, this is the earliest date for the crisis; it suggests that the crunch is more likely to come in the late 1980s or 1990s.

Not only is this crisis unlikely, but a condition of slack in energy markets could develop by the 1980s sufficient to undermine OPEC's strength to set prices. The two principal reasons for questioning the likelihood of this crisis are slower demand and larger supply than it is now fashionable to assume.

Slower demand growth and stronger price responses than widely predicted. Demand growth is likely to be slower than predicted because of slowed economic growth in the United States and in the rest of the world. The Plan assumes 4 percent per year real average growth in the U.S. and asserts that previous policies would cause energy consumption to grow at 3 percent annually, but the higher prices in the Plan will cause growth to be under 2 percent. The assumption of an average 4 percent per year real GNP growth to 1985 is optimistic; real growth in the American economy in the past decade averaged only 2 percent per year, well down from the postwar average of about 3.6 percent. Moreover, a high level of inflation is likely to produce restraints on growth. Allowing for a more slowly growing work force makes an average growth rate closer to 3 percent per year more plausible than 4 percent.[11]

The other main effect limiting demand is the cumulative effect of rising prices. The United States uses about twice as much energy per unit of GNP as the countries of northern and Western Europe and Japan. A careful analysis of Swedish versus U.S.

energy consumption, adjusted for the differences in climate and industrial composition, shows that Sweden uses per capita 30 percent less energy (Schipper and Lichtenberg 1976). Much of this difference reflects the fact that gasoline is taxed at a low level in the United States, our natural gas resources have been extensively developed and distributed at a controlled price, and coal is relatively cheap in the United States. There is no reason to believe that, given time for adjustment, Americans faced with similar prices as Europeans would consume energy very differently.

We are now inexorably being faced more nearly with similar prices (although resistance to gasoline taxes on a European level remains powerful). Real energy prices facing consumers are predicted to rise by about 30 percent by 1985 from today. Adjustment more nearly to a European scale of energy consumption will take place through changes in capital stock, insulation efforts, and the like over the course of the next decade or two. During this process, economic growth will exert offsetting upward pressure on energy consumption; the net will probably be less than 2 percent energy growth in the next decades; this is likely in the absence of the Plan being implemented.

As for the rest of the world, the CIA predicts that energy growth in the non-U.S. OECD countries will be around 4 percent per year. Yet *economic* growth rates among these countries are unlikely to be much higher than this. With a slowed growth rate in the non-U.S. OECD countries, together with an estimated moderate consumer response to higher energy prices (and a continuation of world oil prices at today's real level), estimated energy consumption increases of around 3 percent annually seem plausible for these countries.

Although none of these estimates should be taken too seriously, the use of more plausible economic growth rates and allowing for the effect of price increases that have occurred suggests around 8 million B/D less energy demand in 1985 from the OECD countries than estimated by CIA. Much of this difference can be interpreted as reduced demand for oil. Similarly, economic growth in the less-developed countries is being retarded both by slower growth in the developed countries and by higher energy prices.

In sum, it seems likely that non-Communist world oil demand at today's real price of oil, instead of being around 70 million B/D in 1985, is more likely to be around 60 million B/D or less.[13]

A Larger Oil and Gas Supply than Widely Predicted. The CIA estimates the 1985 oil supply outside of the OPEC countries, including net trade with Eastern Europe, the Soviets, and China, at about 21 million B/D. Despite increased exploration efforts, there is assumed only a 4 million B/D increase in oil supply in these countries between 1977 and 1985. One reason is that the Soviet Union is assumed to move from exporting around 1 million B/D to importing around 4 million B/D. This leaves "required" OPEC production at around 50 million B/D.

This projection is very dubious. The United States has been punched full of holes by wildcatters, but most of the rest of the world has not. Moreover, a substantial part of the nearly 2,000 billion barrels of recoverable oil that geologists now say were originally in place are supposed to be located in non-OPEC countries or in continental shelves adjoining them. And some important discoveries are being made. By 1985 Mexican output may be around 5 million B/D, a level that would place it in the class of Iran and Iraq as producers. Another "Mexico" (or "North Sea") may be found by then and be well under development by 1985. Not only are the lesser-developed countries now exporting small quantities of oil such as Mexico likely to become major exporters, but many LDCs now importing oil (at the rate of 3.5 million B/D) have developable oil resources. If they can acquire the necessary capital from international lending agencies and private sources, this group of countries, around 70 in total, might become nearly self-sufficient in the aggregate by the mid-1980s. The net increment to world oil production from these countries over the current level could be as much as 4 million B/D.

It is useful to keep in mind that oil production does not necessarily have to take place in the United States in order to help either security of supply or to weaken OPEC's hold. The latter only requires that the new resource be located in countries with a powerful incentive to produce. This suggests measures which encourage oil exploration and development in countries with more favorable geological prospects than the United States and that are likely to encourage rapid development of new discoveries.[14] These might include financial help through international lending agencies, or special access to U.S. markets—for example, exemption from a tariff on imports.

The Soviet Union and China. Assessing the future role of the Soviet Union and China in world energy markets is exceptionally difficult. The Soviet Union has been a principal supplier of oil to Eastern Europe, and in the last few years it has become an increasing supplier of oil to the West; its Western exports between 1975 and 1976 increased from .8 to 1.6 million B/D. The Soviet incentive to sell oil and gas abroad is strong, its success in selling manufactured goods abroad has been poor, its financial credit in the West is stretched to the limit, its economic growth rate is declining, and imported technology is even more valuable than in the past. Nevertheless, the CIA has estimated that it will shift from being a net exporter of oil today to a net importer of oil by the mid-1980s, perhaps on a large scale. This conclusion is based on the expected declining productivity of its fields and the high costs of developing Siberian fields (CIA 1977). The pattern predicted for Soviet oil production is striking: perhaps as much as a 25 percent increase in oil production from 1975 to 1980, followed by almost as great a decline by 1985.

A good deal of evidence is offered in support, including poor Soviet petroleum technology, and oil production practices which maximize short-run output at the expense of greater total recovery. Still, for the Soviet Union to shift from being a net exporter to the West of over 1 million B/D to an importer on a much larger scale would mean a swing of about $20 billion per year in Soviet foreign exchange expenditures by the mid-1980s. This would require a formidable adjustment for that economy. One response would be to employ its enormous military power in order to get more favorable terms of trade from Middle Eastern countries. Another, less risky, would be for it to make a series of marginal adjustments to avoid the crisis: conservation efforts, an increased effort to import advanced Western oil technology, an accelerated shift towards the use of coal in place of oil, and greater dependence on natural gas both for domestic use and for export.[15] The marginal value of Soviet oil and gas sold abroad for hard currency is likely to be much greater than its use inside the Soviet Union. The export of the equivalent of 1.8 million B/D in the form of oil and gas now earns around $8 billion a year, and earnings of at least this scale will continue to be valued very highly by the Soviets.

None of this will be easy, if the CIA is right in its predictions of a sharp decline in oil production by the early or mid-1980s. But if the Soviet economy slows as markedly in the years ahead as the CIA predicts, so will the demand for energy. Instead of having domestic energy consumption growing at 5 percent to 6 percent a year, the stated intention of Soviet officials, an economy growing at around 3 percent a year could tolerate a comparable energy growth rate. It can probably muddle through on energy without becoming a big oil importer—or even while remaining a small net exporter.

Prospects in China are even more obscure. Since Mao's death, the regime is giving much higher priority to economic develop-ment, a course which will increase the demand for energy. China has large reserves of oil and, doubtless, of gas. What is in most question is the pace of development of these reserves, the extent to which the Chinese will obtain Western technology, and the alloca-tion of oil to export markets. The CIA estimates that internal needs will result in no net oil exports by 1985. Such a choice would not be rational. As in the Soviet Union, the marginal value of exported oil is likely to be much greater than consumption at home. Mid-1980s Chinese production might be around 4.5 million B/D versus today's estimated rate of around 1.7 B/D. The possibility of Chinese exports at the level of 1 million B/D or more by the mid-1980s should not be excluded.

Natural Gas Usage Worldwide. The natural gas potential in many regions is substantial and may have been underestimated. This fuel is used much less outside of the United States and Canada than in these countries, and it is clear that gas use will rise rapidly. However, most known deposits of gas are located far from the main unexploited markets in Western Europe and

Japan. Costs of transportation are high whether through pipeline or liquefaction (and 25 percent of the gas is lost in transit in the latter method).[16] According to WAES, in 1985 Western Europe could produce around 7 TCF (around 75 percent more than it is now), as well as import an additional 2.5 TCF. Japan, according to WAES, will continue to produce virtually none and might be importing around 3 TCF. (The CIA forecasts a larger production of gas than WAES both in Western Europe, 10 TCF, and Japan, 1 TCF.)

This substantially expanded use of gas in Western Europe and elsewhere will partly offset the demand for oil. The significance of possible additional gas production worldwide amounting to the equivalent of 5-10 million B/D is not entirely clear, given the fact that the OPEC countries will be an important source of this fuel. But, together with the prospect of slowed demand growth, expanded gas supplies might make a large contribution to moderating oil prices through the 1980s.

There is probably also a larger potential for natural gas in the United States than is recognized in the Plan. In 1976 the FEA forecast 1985 production of 22 TCF with the "new" gas deregulated and 25 TCF with additional steps to encourage development. Now the Plan says that only around 17 TCF can be produced even with large price increases. (Despite this heightened supply pessimism, the Plan proposes a price for new gas discoveries below that for imported oil.)

Part of this supply pessimism is evidently a result of less emphasis on OCS development. Part also reflects the assumption in the Plan that freeing the price of natural gas will not induce more supply than holding the price at $1.75/MCF. How can anyone really be confident of the gas resources that exist at this or a higher price, given that until very recently there was little reason to invest money in finding higher cost gas? Very large amounts of gas remain in the United States, although there is a good deal of controversy about the cost at which it could profitably be produced. There are several analyses which concluded that a good deal of gas would be produced between the Plan's proposed price of $1.75 and $2.50-$3.00/MCF.[17] If the gas economically recoverable in the United States at a price of, say, $3.00/MCF is several times the 200 TCF of proven reserves, then the predicted energy crisis of the next decade or two can easily be averted. But we can find out only if impediments to developing these resources are removed.

In sum, assuming a constant real world price of oil, non-Communist consumption by the mid-1980s, excluding the Soviet Union and China, may grow only moderately from this year's level of around 50 million B/D (62 million B/D including the Communist countries), perhaps to around 60 million B/D rather than the 70 million B/D or so implied by the CIA, the Carter plan, and the higher of the WAES projections. If so, the OPEC countries would probably find a market for no more than 35-40 million B/D. Since they could easily then have a production capacity of 45 million B/D, they would face the familiar cartel problem of allocating production. They might succeed in doing so, but their power to move prices to a higher level would be weakened. Moreover, virtually all of the OPEC members, even Saudi Arabia, by then would have developed a large demand for imports. Although this does not mean that the cartel would collapse, because OPEC oil is regarded by most consuming countries as a residual source of fuel, OPEC may be providing no more than half of the world's oil by the mid-1980s, under 40 percent of its combined oil and natural gas supply, and about one-fourth of total energy supplies. As marginal producers, the impact of energy developments elsewhere have an amplified impact on the cartel in general and on Saudi Arabia in particular. If non-OPEC government policies are inept or producers elsewhere have bad luck, the cartel will flourish; but this is a conclusion that should not be taken for granted.[18]

AN ALTERNATIVE STRATEGY

The principles of an alternative strategy are suggested by the preceding discussion: they are to take out insurance against unfavorable developments that could damage our security, to seek to limit the role of government to essential functions, to adopt an adaptive strategy which explicitly recognizes the large uncertainties which exist, to develop a diverse mean of technologies, and seek to smooth the transition from heavy dependence on oil to other fuels over time.

An important inadequacy of the Plan is that, even if it works, on its own analysis it simply defers the crisis for a short time. In 1985 energy demand is only 2 million B/D less and domestic energy production is only 2 million B/D more than without it. Yet timing is all important. What would be a very costly transition to make suddenly in 1985 would still hurt in 1990 and yet be easily managed if stretched out until, say, 2010. It should be a central object of policy to assist and not to interfere with the longer-term shift as well as to guard against the contingency of nearer crisis.

The interruption of fuel supplies can cause enormous economic dislocations in peacetime, and in wartime cause still worse damage. The costs even of the former are by no means trivial, as OPEC has taught us; the rents being extracted by it from the United States annually are now perhaps around $16 billion per years, and from the OECD countries altogether around $50 billion.[19] Different methods are appropriate for dealing with these two distinct problems although they have been confused in much of the governmental and public discussions of this subject.

In addition to stockpiling, security of supply can be sought through having greater control over resources and through diversification.[20] Fuels in one's own territory are under one's control, although their consumption reduces their availability for crises. Control may not be assured but might be enhanced through long-term contracts and through foreign investments in fuels in the right countries. One way government policy might promote these objectives is through a discriminating tariff imposed on oil imports. Exempted might be oil from secure sources and from exporters willing to expand production.[21]

Diversification can take several forms: political diversity means seeking energy supplies from a number of independent political entities, especially those not likely to behave against one's interest. Regional diversity tries to avoid supply interruptions caused by possible conflicts centered in a region, e.g., the Middle East. Product diversity means emphasizing the development of substitutes, e.g., natural or synthetic gas or oil from shale for imported oil. R&D diversity means working on a wide measure of new technologies. Even where supplies are relatively assured, as with coal and uranium in the United States, the principle of diversity is valuable. A heavy commitment to coal risks environmental damage and exposure to labor disruption; a heavy commitment to nuclear power risks widespread popular reaction against this form of power from possible nuclear accidents, terrorist acquisition, and use of nuclear explosives or nuclear war anywhere in the world.

Inducing a more vigorous supply response than is provided in the Plan is an essential part of such a strategy. The requirements for inducing such a response are evident: phasing out price controls (permitting some "windfalls" to domestic interests rather than OPEC), accelerated OCS leasing, perhaps encouragement for exploration abroad outside of OPEC countries through international financial institutions or government tax and other financial incentives. As we learn more, the strategy can be altered. If the pessimists are right and oil imports continue to rise, then the planned stockpile could be increased to 2 or 3 billion barrels. (A 3 billion barrel stockpile would cost only about $5 billion a year—or less if the real price of oil rises steadily.) If this price increase is reflected in domestic prices, new technologies and resources will be exploited. If, on the other hand, the real price declines, the prospect that seemed worrisome in 1974—the issue of how much import dependence to allow—would revive, but many domestic interests would volunteer suggestions on how to cope with this problem.

What should we do with the time available? Allow the private sector to continue the process of transforming the stock of capital and consumer goods in response to higher energy costs, and conduct a large and diverse program of energy R&D. And stop trying to pretend that we know what will happen in 1985 or the year 2000.

STRATEGY OVER THE LONGER RUN

Several of the forecasts mentioned above predict a crisis in resources within the next quarter-century or longer. This is essentially a technocratic fallacy. It is *not* a fallacy to observe the finite-
ness of the earth and the gradual running down of the universe. In
the end, entropy will grow enough, the sun will cool enough, that
life will not be quite the same. But the time scale suggested by the
doomsters is rather shorter than this process suggests. Most focus
on the 21st century, including global effects that might impose
severe constraints on fuel consumption, such as the CO_2 "greenhouse" effect.

The need for an early transition away from oil is widely argued
as imminent. The history of forecasts about resources—including
energy, as we have seen—should make us cautious about the estimates of recoverable resources.[22] The problem clearly is one of
adaptation to changing relative availabilities, and the important
changes that have occurred have been in technological capacity
and in capital accumulation. Substitutes exist or, given time, can
be created. For example, Pennsylvania rock oil for whale oil, coal
for wood, nitrogen from the atmosphere for nitrates, reinforced
concrete for structural steel, and so on. It appears that the world
will, in fact, have to make a transition away from oil in the next
half-century, but this analysis suggests that it will not have to be a
traumatic shift. Several recent analyses show that the economy
can easily adapt, and at low cost over the long run, to large
changes in energy costs (Hogan and Manne 1977).

Some adaptations, however, are likely to have higher social
costs than others. Most of today's energy forecasters say that we
should make a transition towards an economy heavily based on
electricity, coal- and nuclear-based, for the next several decades;
then nuclear, increasingly using the breeder reactor, a technology
which could be used for hundreds of years. Nuclear fusion might
become competitive after the turn of the century, or a break-
through might be made in solar electric power. But the main line
of development, we are told, is clear: electrification and the
breeder. Therefore, most nuclear enthusiasts not only deplore the

delay in installing the current generation of light water reactors, but would also have us move as quickly as possible to adopt the breeder, with its famous potential for extracting thirty times or more energy value from a given amount of uranium.

Recent trends in nuclear power have not been encouraging. Installed 1985 nuclear capacity in the United States will be around 100 GWe, only one-third that predicted by the AEC (now ERDA) in 1970; for the year 2000, the official estimate is now around 380 GWe, also one-third the 1970 projection. Similar shrinkage has been taking place elsewhere in the world. It now appears that the total amount of nuclear power installed in the world in 1985 will not be much over 200 GWe, a level far below the 1975 estimate of 500 GWe made by OECD/IAEA (1975). The sources of this decline are reduced growth of demand for electricity, delays in constructing plants, and sharp increases in real nuclear power costs. Moreover, nuclear power is not economic outside of the countries with large electric power grids and with relatively cheap capital, i.e., advanced industrial countries. There is also growing awareness of the dangers of the spread of nuclear weapons through the spread of civilian nuclear technology. Reducing these dangers by modifying the most troublesome aspects of the nuclear fuel cycle with present types of reactors is technically feasible, and probably at no economic penalty.[23] However, the dangers of the plutonium breeder, which necessarily requires the circulation of large quantities of a nuclear explosive material, are greater, and its economics are uncertain. It is important to avoid premature commitment to that technology, which in any case cannot be employed commercially on a significant scale until the 21st century. There is adequate low-cost uranium to see the world well into that century. Moreover, alternative technologies can be developed which can save on uranium.

We will be living for the indefinite future with a comprehensive energy policy. It is a prospect that brings to mind a certain fable:

> The Frogs were living happily in a swamp, caring for nobody and nobody troubling them. But some of them thought that was not right, that they should have a king and a proper constitution. So

they petitioned Jove to send them a King to rule and to keep order. "Mighty Jove," they cried, "send unto us a King that will rule over us and help us keep order." Jove laughed and threw down into the swamp a huge Log, kersplash. The Frogs were frightened out of their lives by the commotion but after a time, seeing that it did not move, one or two of the boldest of them ventured out toward the Log. Then the greatest hero of the Frogs jumped upon the Log and commenced dancing up and down on it. Thereupon all the Frogs came and did the same. Soon the Frogs paid not the slightest notice to King Log. So they sent another petition to Jove asking for a real King, one that would really rule over them.

This made Jove really angry so he sent them a Stork that soon set to work gobbling them all up. Then the Frogs repented but it was too late.

MORAL: Better no rule than cruel rule.

Aesop, "The Frogs Desiring a King"

II

ARTHUR W. WRIGHT

ENERGY INDEPENDENCE: INSURING AGAINST DISRUPTIONS OF SUPPLY

Understanding the problem. The five components of a successful independence program. Existing policies and current proposals. A recommended independence policy: a tariff and tax on crude oil; a buffer stock and import-sharing; two measures to weaken the cartel; capital loss guarantees; contingency policy for supply interruptions.

The Arab embargo of 1973 focused attention on the "independence" of oil supplies in the United States, Western Europe, and Japan. But after four years of heated debate the issue has still not been resolved—witness its prominence in the supporting rhetoric of the Carter energy proposals. The failure to settle the independence question is unfortunate, for it makes the other energy problems facing the United States and its allies seem more difficult than they are.

One reason for that failure is the fog of misunderstanding and emotion that surrounds the independence question. Happily, the fog can be dissipated: the problem of independence in energy is not only tractable, but susceptible of a relatively straightforward solution.

A complete solution to the problem of independence in energy —effectively, in oil—must deal with five important issues, three of them general and two specific to oil under present conditions. General issues concern not just the quantities imported, but the appropriate prices of crude oil and refined products; arrangements for buffer stocks and emergency import-sharing in case normal supplies are disrupted; and a contingency plan for coping with a supply disruption. Specific issues relate to policies towards the world cartel of major oil-exporting countries, and to uncertainty about future oil prices because of the excess producing capacity held by cartel members. Both existing energy policies and the Carter proposals are deficient on four of the five counts.

UNDERSTANDING THE PROBLEM

The problem of independence arises from the sudden, unexpected disruption of normal supplies. This can happen from a variety of causes, but perhaps most common is a significant interruption of imports. Sudden supply disruptions, whatever the cause, impose costs on a society—one of which, for many goods, is impairment of military power. But the societal costs inflicted by a sharp reduction in normal supplies may extend beyond "national security." By upsetting established routines of producers and consumers, a sudden supply reduction can cause losses of ouptut and individual well-being throughout a society.

One way to avoid, or at least to mitigate, these costs is to create an emergency buffer stock. Another is to reduce demand (misnamed "conservation" in the parlance of U.S. energy policy debates) in hopes of either reducing imports or discouraging some uses that would suffer if a part of normal supplies were cut off. Such steps of course entail costs of their own that must be balanced against the costs of disruption. Independence in a good therefore will usually be a matter of degree; complete self-sufficiency will almost always be too costly to pursue.

To focus solely on quantitites of imports, buffer stocks, or total use, however, is to ignore a central aspect of the independence problem. The very fact that costs are involved suggests that independence policy should be concerned with *price* as well as quantity. Specifically, the costs suffered as a result of a supply interruption should be counted as part of the total cost of supplying a good; and people who value a secure supply of the good should cover the costs of providing the security

To appreciate this point, it is useful to think of the independence problem as posing a risk. A society faces a certain expected extra cost of using a good which is subject to sudden supply disruptions. That expected cost is equal to the losses inflicted if a disruption occurs, multiplied by the probability that it will occur. The question is whether the risk is insurable. That is, can the society pay a premium of some kind in order to avoid at least the most serious losses that would result from a sudden reduction in the availability of the good?

Markets routinely handle many risks. Insurance policies protect people against the loss of income caused by illness or death, against the loss of property caused by bad weather or fire, and against the loss of solvency caused by large hospital bills. Buyers and sellers of agricultural and mineral commodities commonly hedge their market positions to protect against price movements large enough to wipe them out. To insure against financial ruin, oil and gas drillers avoid staking everything on one or two prospects; instead, they participate in large drilling programs involving many "wildcats." The costs of handling such risks are, of course, incorporated into the market prices of the goods and services.

The risk posed by the independence problems, however, is another matter. Sudden supply disruptions tend to be large scale and infrequent, and they may well be politically motivated. Thus they fall into the category of low-probability, high-loss events, along with earthquakes and nuclear reactor accidents—events that even a well-organized set of primary and secondary markets cannot cope with. As a result, for goods subject to sudden disruptions of supply, expected disruption costs are not included in the market-determined price. Failing to include such costs produces inefficiency: the market price is less than the social cost, and therefore too much of the good is produced and consumed. An analagous inefficiency occurs in allocating "environmental quality." Use of the air, for example, cannot be priced on the market because of the prohibitive costs of defining and enforcing property rights to air. Hence the price of air is too low (zero) and people tend to overuse it, resulting in what is called air pollution.

In effect, markets omit a risk premium that should be included in the price of any good susceptible to abrupt reductions in normal supplies. One task of independence policy, then, is to do what markets will not do—namely, see that an independence premium is included in the price of a good where economic efficiency warrants it. The risk premium must, of course, apply to *all* units sold, not just to the portion subject to supply disruption, because the actual occurrence of a disruption will raise the scarcity value of all remaining units in the market.[1]

For parallel reasons, private decision makers find it profitable to hold inventories or other reserve stocks in order to be able to respond to fluctuations in demand or supply. As a rule, however, it is not in their interest to hold buffer stocks against a low-probability, high-loss event such as an embargo. Even though such stocks would be extremely valuable if a disruption occurred, it is generally too expensive for private individuals or firms to hold them. This is especially true as governments are prone, during emergencies, to requisition stocks of critical goods, to suspend normal market operations, and to resort to physical allocations. Thus a second task of independence policy is to build up and maintain buffer stocks of goods subject to sudden disruptions. The means of financing such stocks is discussed later.

In terms of the foregoing discussion, few people would need to be persuaded that the United States and the other industrialized oil-importing nations have an independence problem in energy. More specifically, they have an independence problem in oil. All of them use oil products widely in consumption and at the various stages of production; hence a sudden disruption of normal oil supplies could impose heavy losses on their economies. In addition, all import substantial shares of the oil they use. In the United States, the import share rose sharply between 1971 and 1973—the three years immediately preceding the Arab embargo of October 1973—although the effect was exaggerated because of the oil import quota in effect during the 1960s.[2] Since then, American oil imports have continued to climb, both absolutely and as a percentage of total U.S. oil consumption; as of this writing, the latter figure is approaching 50 percent. As we shall see, present U.S. energy policies further raise the percentage share of imports in total oil use.

Beyond importing significant amounts of an important basic commodity, the United States and its principal allies today face a higher probability than previously of an import disruption. The coalescing of the cartel of major oil-exporting countries in the early 1970s greatly increased the probability of a serious and successful embargo of foreign oil shipments. The direct cause of reductions in Western Europe's oil imports in 1956 and 1967 was the closing of the Suez Canal, not the ineffectual attempts to limit shipments. In 1973, however, the closing of the canal played only a minor role; the growing power of the cartel and its machinery for limiting output was what made it possible for Saudi Arabia and other Arab countries to reduce production and attempt to withhold shipments selectively from certain Western nations.

THE ELEMENTS OF A SUCCESSFUL INDEPENDENCE PROGRAM

It is clear, then, that the governments of the industrially advanced oil-importing nations need a policy that will achieve independence in oil. Such a policy should contain the three general components we have just identified:

1. *Prices to include risks of disruption.* The first and most critical component is a program to ensure that the prices of crude oil and refined products include a premium reflecting the expected cost of a sudden cutoff of imported oil.

2. *Creation of buffer stocks.* Importing governments (singly or together) should be building and maintaining buffer stocks of oil against an embargo of foreign shipments.

3. *Program to weaken the cartel.* The importing governments should be making a concerted effort to weaken—and if possible, to break up—the monopoly power of the cartel.

Two additional aspects of the problem of oil independence affect the losses that would be inflicted by a disruption of oil imports:

4. *Insuring downside oil price risks.* This problem concerns the ability of an economy to adapt flexibly to new conditions—in the present case, the increases in the prices of oil and other forms of energy since 1970. Adaptability is in part a function of the degree to which producers and consumers have adjusted their habits and facilities to the higher relative prices of energy. The more fully adjusted the economy, the more flexibly it can respond to adversities such as an import embargo, and the smaller the resulting losses of output and personal well-being.

In oil and energy, the adjustment to higher prices has been impeded by the distinct possibility that oil prices, and with them other energy prices, could fall. That possibility is a direct outgrowth of the excess producing capacity being held by Saudi Arabia and the other members of the cartel. It is the existence of such excess capacity and the resulting temptation to cheat on one's fellow cartelists that makes all cartels inherently unstable. The current risk that oil prices may fall is not one that private investors can handle through markets. As a result, investment projects are being postponed that would otherwise be initiated at current prices. Hence a fourth component of independence policy in oil should be government measures to help private decision makers handle the downside price risk.[3]

5. *Contingency measures to minimize losses.* The second additional aspect of oil independence concerns the reaction of the victim to an embargo. The magnitude of the losses inflicted by an embargo can vary widely, depending on how governments react to the event itself. The reactions to the Arab embargo of 1973-1974 ranged from calm (e.g., the Netherlands) to panicky (e.g., the United States); as a result, the losses ranged from painful but bearable to unnecessarily severe and debilitating. Yet a fifth component of an independence policy for oil, then, should be a set of contingency measures designed to minimize losses due to the response rather than to the supply disruption itself. This component is important not only for reducing the expected cost of a disruption to the victim, but also for reducing the attractiveness of a disruption as a policy option to would-be perpetrators.

The discussion thus far has been devoted to analyzing in the abstract the problem of independence, and in concrete terms as it applies to oil. We have identified five components that an independence policy should include. Three of them are general: an independence premium in prices; reserve stocks and other measures to offset at least part of the interrupted supplies; and a contingency plan for responding to a disruption to supply. The other two components are peculiar to oil: the heightened probability of an embargo, and the risk of a decline in oil prices—both attributable to the existence of the world oil cartel.

In the next two sections I shall apply the above analysis to existing and proposed policies, and then to a preferable substitute policy for achieving independence in oil. For reasons of space, the bulk of the discussion will deal with U.S. policies and policy options. The points in the argument where U.S. developments impinge in the choices of its major allies will be noted as we proceed.

EXISTING POLICIES AND CURRENT PROPOSALS

Both existing energy policies and those currently proposed to replace them have a pronounced patchwork or grab-bag quality
about them where oil independence is concerned. In part this
quality is traceable to conflicts with other goals of policy—primarily equity concerns about windfall profits and higher consumer prices which have followed the increase in world crude oil
prices. But existing and proposed policies also have a grab-bag
quality because of the lack of a unifying theme, indicating a dis-
turbing failure to grasp the basic issues involved. In particular,
existing and proposed policies reflect a preoccupation with the
quantity of imported oil, or with the share of imports in total
domestic oil use. There is no evidence of a concern to incorporate
into the market prices of crude oil and refined products the expected cost of an import disruption. In the one or two cases where
price is the main policy instrument, the central focus of the policy
is on reducing the quantity of imports, curbing the total quantity
of oil used, or both.

1960s to Early 1970s

Intellectually, the patchwork quality of oil policies in general, and
of independence policies in particular, harks back to the decade of
the 1960s. The overall tone of oil policy in that decade was set by
the import quota, discussed earlier (note 2). Under the protection
of the quota, the major oil-producing states restricted production
through "market-demand prorationing" in order to support the
price of oil above what it would have been in the absence of production restrictions (McDonald 1971). At the same time, federal
tax policy subsidized the development and production of domestic crude oil through the percentage depletion allowance and the
option to expense (rather than capitalize and depreciate) "intan-
gible" drilling costs and "dry hole" costs (Agria 1969). The entire
grab bag of the import quota, market-demand prorationing, and
the federal tax subsidies was defended on pseudo-independence
grounds: a "strong oil industry" was needed, the argument ran,

to protect the "national security" (American Petroleum Institute 1974).

A major difference between the policies of the 1960s and those of the 1970s is in their effects on oil prices in the U.S. market. Whereas the former policies resulted (on balance) in prices higher than free-market equilibrium levels, the latter policies have been designed expressly to hold prices below market-clearing levels. This difference has prompted one experienced observer to contrast the era of "surplus" policies (the 1960s) with the era of "shortage policies" (the 1970s) (Mitchell 1974*a*).

After the 1973 Oil Embargo:
Price Controls and the Entitlement Program

In spite of all the talk about "Project Independence" that followed the Arab embargo, the principal set of existing policies towards oil—the price controls on crude oil and the accompanying entitlements program—is directed at equity goals, not independence. There are programs (discussed below) for creating an emergency buffer stock of oil and for sharing available imports with other industrialized countries in the event of another embargo. In addition, the joint participation program of the Energy Research and Development Administration (ERDA) can be interpreted as a response to the risk of a sharp decline in oil prices. But existing policies totally ignore the matter of a risk premium in oil prices to cover expected disruption costs, and policies towards the world oil cartel consist at best of lame proposals to discuss disagreements and of efforts to deflect Arab resentment over U.S. foreign policy towards Israel. Further, as argued in the next section, the ERDA program that offsets the downside price risk appears to be overly costly.

The price controls on part of domestic U.S. crude oil production began life as part of the general price controls imposed by the Nixon administration in August 1971. When most other controls ended in 1974, however, the crude oil controls assumed a life and evolution of their own. The purpose of putting price ceilings on "old" oil was and remains to prevent "windfall profits" from accruing to owners of productive capacity that was in existence before crude oil prices began to increase in 1972. Because the controls are selective, it has been necessary to supplement them with a program to allocate equitably among petroleum refiners the rights to low-priced regulated crude oil. That is the purpose of the current "entitlements" program, which each month takes the income expropriated from producers of regulated crude oil to divvy up among refiners in proportion to their shares in total industry "throughput" of crude oil. Although it is still a controversial question, it appears that the operation of the entitlements program leads refiners to refine more oil than they otherwise would. As a result, the prices of some refined products are lower than they would be without the controls and entitlements. To the extent this is so, consumers share in the subsidy from crude oil producers to oil refiners in the form of a lower product prices (Montgomery 1977; Cox and Wright 1977).[4]

That the primary intention of crude oil price controls and entitlements is to serve equity objectives does not mean that they have no effect on independence. The controls reduce domestic crude oil output compared to the free-market case. In the current situation—with the United States a price taker in the world crude oil market and the U.S. government pursuing essentially a policy of free trade in oil—this means increased imports of crude oil. Thus one cost of preventing windfall profits to domestic crude oil producers is a greater exposure to a possible disruption of imports. To the extent the entitlements program increases total U.S. refinery throughput, of course, it reduces imports of refined products; but (where domestic U.S. product prices are reduced) it also encourages the overuse of oil. This is just the reverse of the effect of adding an independence premium to prices.

Dealing with the Quantity Problem

Existing U.S. oil policies do include two noteworthy attempts to deal at least with the quantity (if not the price) aspect of the independence problem. The Federal Energy Administration has begun to implement the "Strategic Petroleum Reserve" program, under which the U.S. government will store oil at various spots around the country for use in case of a supply disruption. The initial target of the program was 500 million barrels in place by 1982; subsequently, more ambitious targets of 500 million barrels by 1980 and 1 billion barrels by 1983 have been substituted. (For reference, at present rates of consumption a reserve of 500 million barrels would last about 25 days if *all* imports, plus *all* domestic production, were cut off. A total cutoff is unlikely, of course, so the 25 days would be an absolute minimum.) The reserve is being funded from general tax revenues; thus taxpayers generally, not oil users specifically, will pay for the added security of supply provided by the program.

The other attempt to cope with a possible cutoff of oil imports is an agreement (under the umbrella of the International Energy Agency or IEA) to share available oil imports in the event a portion of world shipments is reduced or embargoed. Of the nineteen parties to the agreement, virtually all major U.S. allies are included except Australia and France. The sharing arrangement, which is still being fleshed out, would be triggered if one or more of the participant countries suffered a shortfall of deliveries amounting to 7 percent or more below current consumption levels. When that happened, each participant would be obligated to reduce total consumption by 7 percent, and to contribute its resulting extra imports to a common pool for sharing with the other participants. There is no provision for dipping into domestic crude oil reserves or outout (e.g., in the United States or the United Kingdom) or into any participant's special emergency buffer stock (such as the American "Special Strategic Reserve"). Interestingly, the *price* terms on which the sharing would take place have not yet been settled or even discussed to any great extent.

The Carter Proposals

In marked contrast to existing policies, independence in oil is the foremost objective of the Carter administration's "National Energy Plan." For all the emphasis on independence, though, there are good reasons to doubt that, if adopted, the plan will achieve as much independence in oil as its advocates predict. In part this is because the administration evidently felt constrained not to sacrifice the equity objectives that are so conspicuous in existing policies. But the reasons also include deficiencies in conception and design.

The independence objective is stated in the National Energy Plan in the form of a target quantity of oil imports. The stated target is 7 million barrels a day by 1985, in contrast to a level of about 9 million barrels a day attained in early 1977. Even the target of 7 million barrels a day by 1985—which would be a reduction of far more than 2 million barrels, assuming continued growth of oil use and imports—is not viewed as enough by the administration. According to the National Energy Plan document, "additional steps" will be necessary to reduce imports well below 6 million barrels a day to achieve independence. The means to achieve the target is a bewildering phalanx of special taxes, subsidies, and regulations—113 measures in all—designed to promote the "conservation" (reduced use) of energy in general and of oil in particular. With one exception,[5] the conservation is to be effected without raising any energy price higher than its free-market equilibrium level, and in fact leaving some prices below that level.

The denial of windfall profits to domestic crude oil producers is to be carried one step further than in existing policies by adding a new category of regulated production, "frontier oil." The effect of this measure will be to retard the development of domestic crude oil production and thus to hinder the other efforts in the Carter plan to reduce oil imports. The existing transfer of crude oil income to refiners and consumers through price controls and entitlements will be replaced by a differentiated tax on crude oil, which will equate the purchase price of all domestic crude oil with the prevailing delivered price of imported oil. By taking an existing subsidy away from oil refiners, this measure should raise the prices of some refined oil products; to the extent that happens, the administration's objective of increased "conservation" will be furthered.

The Carter administration's National Energy Plan can be and has been faulted for its overemphasis on reducing oil use, for its lack of consistency with other programs (e.g., strip-mining and air-quality standards), and for its sheer complexity and seeming gimmickry. In the present frame of reference, however, the basic fault of the plan is that it lacks four of the five components I argued above were essential to achieving independence in oil. The Strategic Petroleum Reserve and the import-sharing agreement through the IEA have, happily, been retained. But the plan itself contains no provision for incorporating into oil prices the expected cost of a supply disruption; no provision (other than reduced demand) for seeking to weaken the world oil cartel; no new provision for handling the downside price risk created by cartel excess capacity; and no provision for contingency policies that would go into effect if and when a supply disruption occurred. Judging from recent news accounts, the Carter administration would respond to another embargo largely as the Nixon administration did to the last one—*de facto* nationalization of petroleum distribution, allocations of products by region and by class of user, and "standby" rationing. This may reassure Arab governments looking to widen their foreign policy options, but it should not reassure U.S. citizens.

A RECOMMENDED INDEPENDENCE POLICY FOR OIL

The following independence policy for oil covers all five of the requisite components and is also relatively compact, especially as compared to the 100-plus measures in the Carter administration's program.

1. A combined tariff and tax on crude oil, to incorporate an independence premium into oil prices.

2. A buffer stock like the Strategic Petroleum Reserve, and an import-sharing agreement like that being developed by the IEA.

3. Two measures designed to weaken the world oil cartel.

4. Capital-loss guarantees for investments in the new energy production capacity, to handle the downside price risk due to cartel excess capacity.

5. A contingency policy for responding to a supply disruption, combining the use of emergency stocks and import sharing, market-clearing prices, and consumer rebates and payments in lieu of windfall profits taxes through the federal income tax system.

Let me now briefly discuss each measure in turn.

A Tariff and Tax on Crude Oil[6]

This policy measure would incorporate in oil prices the premium reflecting the expected cost of a supply disruption that should be the key component of any policy for independence in oil. At present, the U.S. (uncontrolled) market price of crude oil is determined by the delivered cost of imports. Hence imposing a tariff on imported crude oil would raise the U.S. market price by the amount of the tariff. A corresponding excise tax on domestically produced oil[7] would also be required because, as was pointed out earlier, the independence premium applies to *all* oil used in the United States, regardless of source. Applying just a tariff and not an excise tax on domestic output would give the classic case of tariff protection, with its familiar inefficiency of the overuse of domestic production. In effect, a tariff-only policy would yield more independence (fewer imports) than would be economically efficient. With a matching excise tax, however, domestic production would be the same as before the tariff and tax policy was introduced. The increase in the market price of crude oil would reduce the total quantity of oil consumed in the United States; with domestic output the same, therefore, oil imports would be reduced by the same amount. With the tariff and the tax set at the expected cost per barrel of a supply disruption, the resulting level of imports would represent the optimal level, *inclusive* of the independene premium.

The increase in the price of crude oil in the United States would raise oil refiners' costs, which would in turn raise the prices of those refined products where domestic supplies determine market prices. Separate tariffs would have to be imposed on products (such as residual fuel oil in the east and Gulf Coast markets) the prices of which are determined by the delivered costs of imports. Buyers of refined oil products would then have a market incentive, corrected for independence costs, to economize on their use. As a result, we would no longer need the myriad devices in the Carter plan for inducing or forcing people to "conserve" energy —e.g., compulsory conversions by electric utilities from oil to coal, intricate tax rebate schemes geared to auto mileage standards, and special tax credits for home insulation.

The tariff and tax on crude oil proposed here would, of course, yield the Treasury revenues equal to the total quantity of oil sold times the dollar amount per barrel of the tariff or tax. On the one hand, economic efficiency considerations might suggest using the revenues to finance the Strategic Petroleum Reserve, on grounds that the people paying the independence premium would be purchasing the added security provided by the buffer stock. On the other hand, equity considerations might suggest rebating the revenues to taxpayers through the federal income tax in order to reduce the burden on them of higher oil prices. A mixture of the two uses of the revenues is not only a possible but also a politically probable compromise, were the present proposal to be adopted.

A Buffer Stock and Import-Sharing

The Strategic Petroleum Reserve and the import-sharing agreement, the latter worked out through the IEA, are basically sound in conception. I have nothing to add that would materially improve either measure, except to urge that (if possible) the price terms for shared imports be settled before rather than after the next embargo begins.

Two Measures to Weaken the Cartel

M.A. Adelman of MIT has suggested two specific steps for weakening the world oil cartel. They stand some chance—which is more than the zero chance of the other measures attempted or proposed to date—of succeeding, and therefore warrant a trial.

One of Adelman's suggestions would place a limit on U.S. oil imports and then allocate the rights to supply those imports through sealed bids based on low price. (This suggestion need not, of course, be limited to the United States. Indeed, the effectiveness of the device would increase with the number of oil-importing countries that used it—preferably in league with one another. The limit placed on imports could be determined in conjunction with the premium to be added to oil prices through the tariff and tax scheme outlined above.) The idea is to encourage cutting price to increase profits at the expense of other cartel members—an inherent tendency in any cartel. Imposing the limit on U.S. imports would intensify rivalry for shares of sales to the United States.

Adelman's other suggestion is to attempt to change the marketing arrangements used by cartel members to sell their oil. At present, the cartel countries find it convenient to have the large international oil companies market the bulk of their oil shipments. This makes it relatively easy to monitor both production levels and terms of sale. Compelling the cartel governments themselves to organize the distribution of oil would enhance the prospects for price cutting (Adelman 1972-1973).

Neither of the above steps would guarantee the break up, or even a substantial weakening, of the cartel. They would, however, be a start in an important area where no start has yet been made.

Capital-Loss Guarantees for New Energy Investments

As explained earlier, the risk of a decline in the price of oil has a chilling effect on investment projects that would be profitable at today's energy prices but not at lower prices. Lagging investment, however, retards the adjustment of the economy, particularly the energy-producing industries, to the relatively higher energy prices of the 1970s. The delay in adjustment in turn imparts a rigidity to market operations that makes responses to changes in demand or supply more volatile than otherwise.

This problem has been recognized for some time. Thus far, however, the only actual response to it has been government subsidies or "joint participation" in investment projects involving mainly new or exotic forms of energy. In 1974 and 1975 the U.S. government attempted without success to gain support for an energy price floor of $8.00 a barrel of oil-equivalent. Other proposals have included guaranteed rates of return, cost-plus pricing on government contracts, and capital-loss guarantees.

There are precedents for all of these proposals. Subsidies and joint participation have been used for decades in the nuclear power industry. (It is no surprise, then, that ERDA is the leading advocate of this approach.) Price floors have been the linchpin of agricultural policy for about half a century. Guaranteed rates of return and cost-plus pricing have been widely used in utility regulation and government procurement. Capital-loss guarantees were employed in building defense plants during World War II.

All but the last of these measures have the signal disadvantage of inducing greater supply than would otherwise be forthcoming, *exclusive* of the problem of the downside risk. Only the capital-loss guarantees address the price risk without inducing inefficient levels of production.[8] On these grounds, I would prefer the loss guarantees to any of the other possibilities.

A Contingency Policy for Responding to Supply Interruptions

A sudden disruption of normal supplies of a good invites panicky calls to "do something." Politicians wisely choose to make at least a show of doing something, even if they believe it is not necessary, because of the difficulty of reasoning with panicky voters. Panic is also a problem in institutional fires, aerial bombings, and traffic accidents involving injuries. The proper way to deal with this problem has long been recognized: prepare an orderly plan in advance and (if it cannot be tried out) at least publicize it well. People who know what to do in the crisis will feel less helpless and not succumb so readily to panic.

The Arab embargo of 1973 created panic in the United States, in important part because there was no contingency plan for coping with such an event. Unfortunately, when the U.S. government finally got around to "doing something," it only made matters worse. With the distribution of oil placed under the control of a fledgling agency,* there was widespread queuing for gasoline and No. 2 heating oil in the eastern part of the country; at the same time, storage tanks were filling up—to the point where tankers had to queue up to offload (Mancke 1975). The embargo sparked concerns for equity, as sharp price changes in the world oil market created the spectre of huge windfall profits for oil companies and heavy burdens on consumers.

The case for a contingency plan thus seems clear. The elements of such a plan are straightforward. It should, of course, include bringing into use the buffer stock and the import-sharing arrangement. It should also include a clearly worded standing policy that, in the event normal supplies are disrupted, prices will be permitted to rise if necessary to clear the market—that is, to the extent the reserves cannot replace the missing supplies; such increases would help the United States meet its obligation to reduce domestic oil use temporarily during the emergency under the IEA import-sharing agreement. Finally, a standby consumer rebate mechanism should be created in the federal income tax system, and an agreement should be worked out between the Internal Revenue Service and the oil companies for payments in lieu of windfall profits taxes based on the size of the price increases that occur. Note that the existence of a contingency plan would obviate the need to "do something" if a disruption actually occurred. Hence the role of the government could be limited to performing pre-arranged tasks—tapping the buffer stock, implementing the import-sharing agreement, arranging for consumer rebates, and

---

*One official of the agency (the Federal Energy Office) characterized its staff as a "bunch of ex-postal clerks." The characterization is surely wide of the mark: ex-postal clerks would not have made such a mess of the oil distribution network.

receiving payments in place of windfall profits taxes. No more instant agencies staffed by ex-postal clerks.

This five-part policy spans the range of issues that make up the problem of independence in oil. Four of the parts have not yet been effectively introduced, either into existing policies or into the Carter administration's ambitious National Energy Plan. Yet the recommended policy that does deal with those four components is far simpler and easier to comprehend in its effects than the president's plan. The simplicity derives from an analysis of the independence problem that enables one to see it in its essentials and thus to recognize the issues that require attention. Not to look for essentials and basic issues invites policies that are needlessly complex and probably expensive. This would seem to be the case with the National Energy Plan. One hopes the presumptuous title will not stifle further debate on the question of U.S. independence in oil.

III

ALBERT CARNESALE

NUCLEAR POWER AND NUCLEAR PROLIFERATION

Nonproliferation policies, 1946-1968. Recent policies: before Carter. The Nonproliferation Treaty (NPT). The "London Suppliers Club." Mounting proliferation. The Carter policy: criticisms and responses. A comprehensive nonproliferation policy.

> ...and they shall beat their swords into plowshares, and their spears into pruninghooks...
>
> (Isaiah 2:4)

The history of nuclear energy has in some ways fulfilled this Biblical prophecy. The invention of nuclear weapons (the swords and spears) led to establishment of civilian nuclear power programs (plowshares and pruninghooks) in the decades after World War II. But in recent years, unfortunately, it has become clear that the transformation is reversible: the technologies, facilities, and materials associated with nuclear power can be used to make nuclear weapons, and the expansion of nuclear power worldwide is therefore expanding the capability to make bombs. About fifty countries now have nuclear power reactors either operating, under construction, or planned. As a result, nuclear proliferation has become an important concern of both nuclear energy policy and energy policy in general.

NONPROLIFERATION POLICIES, 1946-1968

Concern about the link between nuclear power and nuclear proliferation has increased greatly in recent years, but it has been a subject of concern over a much longer period. On 24 January 1946—less than a year after the first successful test of a nuclear weapon and only two weeks after the first meeting of the United Nations General Assembly—a unanimous resolution established the United Nations Atomic Energy Commission and authorized it to "make specific proposals...for control of atomic energy to... ensure its use only for peaceful purposes" (Keesing 1972:44). At the commission's first meeting (14 June 1946), U.S. representative Bernard Baruch presented a proposal for internationalizing the nuclear fuel cycle (U.S. Senate 1956:190). The Baruch Plan called for creation of an International Atomic Development Authority which would own all nuclear materials, including all uranium and thorium ore deposits and mines; manage all fuel cycle operations; inspect all nuclear facilities to detect diversion of materials or unauthorized research activities; judge whether violations had been committed; and determine what would constitute "condign punishment." For various reasons the plan was unacceptable to the world community, and especially to the Soviet Union.

With the failure of the Baruch Plan, U.S. nonproliferation policy emphasized protection of the "secret" of the bomb—a strategy doomed to eventual failure.

In 1953 President Eisenhower's "Atoms for Peace" program shifted American policy to cooperation in and active promotion of civilian nuclear power abroad. In announcing the program Eisenhower proposed the creation of an International Atomic Energy Agency (IAEA), which became a reality four years later.

RECENT POLICIES: BEFORE CARTER

The Technical Problem

The problem of nuclear proliferation must be understood in light of the combination of ingredients, knowledge, personnel, and equipment necessary to make nuclear weapons. An essential ingredient of any nuclear weapon is "fissile" material (i.e., material in which nuclear fission can be induced by low-energy neutrons). Among all materials found in nature in significant quantities, only the isotope uranium-235 has this quality, but its concentration in natural uranium is insufficient for use in a weapon. Uranium-235 constitutes only 0.7 percent of natural uranium, with the remainder being the non-fissile isotope uranium-238 and a trace of uranium-234. To be usable in a weapon, uranium must be "enriched" to at least 20 percent uranium-235, and bomb designers prefer something over 90 percent. The uranium used as fuel in today's power reactors (of the light-water type, which dominate the industry) is enriched to about 3 percent, and therefore neither natural nor low-enriched reactor fuel can be used directly for weapons.

Although building a bomb requires more than just suitable fissile material, for most countries lack of access to weapons-usable fissile material has been and is the major technological obstacle to the production of nuclear weapons, and it is likely to remain so for some time. Uranium enrichment is a high-technology operation.[1]

While uranium-235 is the only fissile material which occurs in nature in significant quantities, other fissile materials can be produced artificially by exposing "fertile" materials to the neutrons in nuclear reactors. Important among fertile materials are the naturally abundant isotopes uranium-238 and thorium-232, which can be converted into the fissile isotopes plutonium-239 and uranium-233, respectively. In some ways, the artificially created fissile materials, especially plutonium, pose the greatest proliferation threat. Plutonium can be separated from uranium by relatively straight-forward chemical means and, when separated, can be used directly in the manufacture of weapons. No isotope separation is required. And plutonium is produced in large quantities in power reactors from the uranium-238 which constitutes about 97 percent of the uranium fuel. Indeed, the spent fuel removed annually from a typical 1000 Mwe nuclear power plant contains about 250 kilograms of plutonium—enough for tens of bombs. Before it can be used in bombs, though, the plutonium must be separated from the remainder of the spent fuel, an operation referred to as "reprocessing." Breeder reactors, which produce more fissile material than they consume, would yield still more plutonium.[2]

There are a number of ways in which a nation might go about getting fissile material for weapons. The material might be received as a gift or on loan; it might be stolen; it might be bought on an open, black, or gray market. The route favored in the past has been to construct facilities designed specifically for the production of nuclear weapons materials; a variation would be to build the same facilities but to use the term "peaceful nuclear explosives" to describe the explosive devices produced through their use. Another approach would be to use equipment and facilities ostensibly designated for nuclear research. A final path would be to use materials and/or facilities associated with a nuclear power program. This path is clearly the one related most directly to energy policy considerations; it is also complicated, costly, and as yet untaken. But, with the current and anticipated global spread of nuclear power, in the future it could be of vital importance. This expanding potential for producing nuclear weapons underlies the movement of nonproliferation policy over the past decade.

The Nonproliferation Treaty [NPT]

The principal international legal instrument governing nonproliferation is the Treaty on the Nonproliferation of Nuclear Weapons (NPT), which was negotiated in the mid-1960s. The NPT was concluded in 1968, entered into force in 1970, and at this writing has been joined by 102 states. Under the treaty, non-nuclear-weapon states agree not to manufacture nuclear explosive devices, and to submit their peaceful nuclear installations to international safe-guards—applied by the IAEA—against diversion to military uses. In return, the nuclear weapons states agree not to transfer nuclear explosive devices, while acknowledging the right of all parties to participate in exchanges of equipment, materials, and scientific and technological information relating to peaceful uses of nuclear energy. Among the more important non-members of the NPT are China, France, Argentina, Brazil, Egypt, India, Israel, Pakistan, South Africa, and Spain.

The "London Suppliers Club"

With the oil crisis of 1973, much of the world looked to nuclear power for eventual relief from energy-related economic woes. But India's explosion of a so-called "peaceful nuclear device" in May 1974 brought the proliferation problem back into focus. Responding to a U.S. initiative in late 1974, the major suppliers of nuclear materials and equipment—Canada, England, France, Japan, the Soviet Union, West Germany, and the United States—began a series of meetings in London. After more than a year of talks—during which West Germany sold to Brazil a complete nuclear fuel cycle package, including reactors, an enrichment facility, and a reprocessing plant—the "London Suppliers Club" finally agreed on a common set of principles designed to inhibit the further spread of nuclear weapons, without impeding the peaceful use of nuclear energy. Henceforth all recipient states were to accept IAEA safeguards on all nuclear imports; to provide assurances not to use these imports to make nuclear explosives for any purpose, peaceful or otherwise; to protect imported facilities and materials against theft and sabotage; and to demand the same conditions on any re-transfers to third countries. The screws were being tightened on would-be nuclear importers.

Why all the fuss? What had happened to terminate so abruptly the complacency which had come with the signing of the NPT? The Indian "peaceful bomb" and the German-Brazilian deal might have been reasons enough. But there were more.

Mounting Proliferation

Nuclear power was expanding rapidly. By early 1976 eighteen countries had power reactors in operation, and twenty-seven more had them under construction, ordered, or planned (see Table 1). Gaseous diffusion enrichment plants were operating in each of the five nuclear weapons states (China, England, France, the Soviet Union, and the United States); centrifuge plants operated in England and Holland and were under development elsewhere; the jet nozzle process had been demonstrated in West Germany and sold to Brazil; and it had been reported that an aerodynamic enrichment pilot plant was operating in South Africa. Reprocessing plants for separating plutonium from spent reactor fuel either had operated, were operating, or were expected soon to operate in (other than the weapons states) Argentina, Belgium, India, Italy, Japan, Spain, West Germany, and Yugoslavia; a French-designed plant had been sold to Pakistan and a German-designed plant to Brazil; it was assumed by almost everyone that Israel had been separating plutonium for some time. There were indications that still more countries, including South Korea and Taiwan, were actively seeking to acquire their own reprocessing plants.

The new dimension of the proliferation problem was the incipient global spread of the "sensitive" fuel cycle technologies—enrichment and reprocessing. Reactors themselves were not the problem, for neither the fresh fuel they are fed nor the spent fuel they discharge can be used to make bombs. Reactors and their fuel, fresh and spent, pose no real military threats. But stockpiles of plutonium, or facilities capable of producing weapons-usable materials, are another matter. Once a nation has these items in hand, the lead-time to weapons could be reduced to months, weeks, or even days, depending upon how much had been accomplished in advance toward preparing those portions of the weapons other than the fissile material. And this shortened lead-time could, in times of international crisis, lower the threshold of the political decision to acquire nuclear weapons. Weapons-usable materials from a civilian program might be diverted clandestinely

Table 1

Survey of Nuclear Power Reactors

Country	Operating	Under Construction	Ordered	Planned	Total
Argentina	1	1	3	0	5
Austria	0	1	0	1	2
Belgium	3	2	2	0	7
Brazil	0	3	0	6	9
Bulgaria	2	1	1	4	8
Canada	7	10	4	5	26
China (Taiwan)	0	4	2	0	6
Czechoslovakia	1	4	0	16	21
Denmark	0	0	0	6	6
Egypt	0	0	0	5	5
Finland	0	4	0	0	4
France	10	17	12	8	47
Ger. Dem. Rep.	3	0	2	0	5
Ger. Federal Rep.	7	12	8	4	31
Hong Kong	0	0	0	1	1
Hungary	0	1	1	0	2
India	3	5	0	0	8
Indonesia	0	0	0	3	3
Iran	0	0	4	1	5
Ireland	0	0	0	1	1
Israel	0	0	0	1	1
Italy	3	2	4	16	25
Japan	10	14	0	5	29
Korea (South)	0	1	1	8	10
Luxembourg	0	0	1	0	1
Mexico	0	2	0	7	9
Netherlands	2	0	0	3	5
Pakistan	1	0	0	1	2
Phillipines	0	0	2	8	10
Poland	0	0	0	2	2
Portugal	0	0	0	4	4
Rumania	0	0	1	2	3
South Africa	0	0	2	0	2
Spain	3	7	7	21	38
Sweden	5	6	0	3	14
Switzerland	3	1	3	2	9
Thailand	0	0	0	3	3
Turkey	0	0	0	1	1
USSR	19	8	0	10	37
United Kingdom	29	10	0	7	46
Yugoslavia	0	1	0	1	2
Cuba ⎤	0	0	0	8	8
Kuwait ⎟ *	0	0	0	2	2
Libya ⎟	0	0	0	2	2
New Caledonia ⎦	0	0	0	2	2
45 Countries	112	117	60	180	469

Source: Walske (1977:97). Data provided by the Atomic Industrial Forum.

*No details are available on the implementation of the planned nuclear power programs for these countries.

to weapons use, either without detection, or with detection coming too late to provide timely warning to parties seeking to prevent the use of the materials in weapons; there might be overt transfers of materials to weapons use in the absence of, after withdrawal from, or in violation of any international agreements to the contrary; or the materials or sensitive facilities might be seized by sub-national groups.

In an important sense, the mere possession of an enrichment or reprocessing plant "elevates" the possessor to the status of a nuclear weapons state. The fact that bombs *might* rapidly be made leads prudent adversaries and potential adversaries to act as if bombs had been made. Israel, with a nuclear weapons policy of "fostered ambiguity," serves to illustrate the point—and it has not even been demonstrated that Israel has a reprocessing facility, let alone separated plutonium or assembled nuclear weapons.

THE CARTER POLICY

Presidential candidate Jimmy Carter brought the proliferation issue into the 1976 campaign. Recognizing that "danger lies in the spread of facilities for enrichment of uranium and the reprocessing of spent reactor fuel" (Carter 1976*a*), candidate Carter claimed that, as president, he would "call upon all nations to adopt a voluntary moratorium on the national sale or purchase of enrichment or reprocessing plants... [and] seek to withhold authority for domestic commercial reprocessing until the need for, the economics, and the safety of this technology is clearly demonstrated" (Carter 1976*b*). Less than a week before the election, President Ford responded to Carter's initiatives and to increased congressional interest in proliferation by announcing his decisions to suspend transfers of reprocessing and enrichment technology and facilities for at least three years, and to defer domestic commercial processing (Ford 1976).

Increasing awareness of the nuclear power/nuclear proliferation linkage was not confined to the American political arena. An influential report prepared for the U.S. Arms Control and Disarmament Agency (1976) answered in the affirmative the question which served as its title: "Moving toward life in a nuclear armed crowd?" A British Royal Commission (1976:204), examining environmental impacts of nuclear energy, concluded that: "The dangers of the creation of plutonium in large quantities in conditions of increasing world unrest are genuine and serious. We should not rely for energy supply on a process that produces such a hazardous substance as plutonium unless there is no reasonable alternative." Similar concerns had been expressed by a special commission studying development of Australian uranium deposits (Ranger 1976: 178), and by an independent American study group (Nuclear Energy 1977:22).

On taking office, President Carter ordered a review of nuclear power policy, and on 7 April 1977 he announced seven decisions which comprise the heart of his program:

First, we will defer indefinitely the commercial reprocessing and recycling of the plutonium produced in the U.S. nuclear power programs. From our own experience we have concluded that a viable and economic nuclear power program can be sustained without such reprocessing and recycling. The plant at Barnwell, South Carolina, will receive neither federal encouragement or funding for its completion as a reprocessing facility.

Second, we will restructure the U.S. breeder reactor program to give greater priority to alternative designs of the breeder, and to defer the date when breeder reactors would be put into commercial use.

Third, we will redirect funding of U.S. nuclear research and development programs to accelerate our research into alternative nuclear fuel cycles which do not involve direct access to materials useable in nuclear weapons.

Fourth, we will increase U.S. production capacity for enriched uranium to provide adequate and timely supply of nuclear fuels for domestic and foreign needs.

Fifth, we will propose the necessary legislative steps to permit the U.S. to offer nuclear fuel supply contracts and guarantee delivery of such nuclear fuel to other countries.

Sixth, we will continue to embargo the export of equipment or technology that would permit uranium enrichment and chemical reprocessing.

Seventh, we will continue discussions with supplying and recipient countries alike, of a wide range of international approaches and frameworks that will permit all nations to achieve their energy objectives while reducing the spread of nuclear explosive capability. Among other things, we will explore the establishment of an international nuclear fuel cycle evaluation program aimed at developing alternative fuel cycles and a variety of international and U.S. measures to assure access to nuclear fuel supplies and spent fuel storage for nations sharing common non-proliferation objectives (Carter 1977).

The Carter program is consistent with the following propositions:

——The world (or at least the U.S.) would be better served by halting the further spread of the capability to produce weapons.

——Current international safeguards and other controls provide inadequate protection against misuse of weapons-usable materials and enrichment and reprocessing facilities.

——Neither the U.S. nor others need to rush ahead into a "plutonium economy" in which weapons-usable materials are widespread as articles of commerce.

——Measures taken in the interest of nonproliferation should neither prevent any nation from meeting its energy needs nor provide any nation with a commercial advantage.

While few observers would disagree seriously with these propositions, the reception provided the seven-point program was more "hot" than "warm."

Criticism: Constructive and Otherwise

Reactions to the Carter decisions ranged from condemnation to kudos and from despair to delight. Summarized below are the principal objections and responses for each of the seven points.[3]

1. Defer commercial reprocessing:

Criticism: By foregoing the 20-25 percent savings in consumption of fresh uranium ore achievable by recycling and reprocessing, the U.S. would increase the demand for and the price of uranium, thereby strengthening the case of those in other countries who argue in favor of reprocessing and recycling.

> *Response:* A U.S. decision not to reprocess would have only a small effect on the worldwide uranium market in this century. Uranium ore deposits in the U.S. alone are sufficient to fuel its growing nuclear power program until well into the 21st Century without reprocessing and recycling; indeed, any economic benefit of reprocessing would be marginal at most (1-2 percent of the cost of the electricity generated) and could be negative.

Criticism: Rather than deferring reprocessing, the U.S. could provide this service to others in order to reduce their incentives to acquire their own reprocessing plants.

> *Response:* American involvement in commercial reprocessing would contribute to the spread of weapons-usable materials, would be cited as evidence of a legitimate role for commercial reprocessing, and could stimulate the spread of reprocessing facilities.

Criticism: Because far more research and development has been performed on disposal of radioactive wastes from reprocessing than on disposal of unreprocessed spent fuel, one can be more confident that reprocessed waste can be disposed of safely.

> *Response:* There is no reason to believe that spent fuel cannot be disposed of as safely as reprocessed waste, and spent fuel can be held safely in retrievable storage until a safe disposal technique has been demonstrated (or until the reprocessing deferment ends).

Criticism: Recycling plutonium and "burning" it as reactor fuel diminishes the amount of plutonium for disposal, thus reducing proliferation (and other) hazards.

> *Response:* For the U.S. to ask others to defer reprocessing while, at the same time, it proceeds with its own domestic commercial reprocessing program, would be viewed as inconsistent and possibly disingenuous.

Criticism: The Barnwell facility, if completed, could serve as a laboratory for the testing of effective safeguards.

> *Response:* No promising technique for safeguarding a reprocessing plant has been proposed, and any small incremental benefit of using Barnwell as a laboratory would be outweighed by the political and economic costs of U.S. Government involvement in a reprocessing venture.

Criticism: The U.S. decision not to reprocess may be of little relevance to the decisions of other states.

> *Response:* For the U.S. to ask others to defer reprocessing while, at the same time, it proceeds with its own domestic commercial reprocessing program, would be viewed as inconsistent and possibly disingenuous.

2. Restructure the breeder program and defer commercialization:

Criticism: The plutonium breeder reactor has in the past been selected over many alternative breeder designs, hence it is unlikely that a more attractive alternative will be found.

> *Response:* In the past, nonproliferation objectives were not considered as important factors in the design of breeder reactors.

Criticism: Deferment of the breeder may entail too high a risk of its not being available when needed to meet U.S. energy needs.

> *Response:* Breeders may eventually be needed; however, to postpone their introduction by a decade or two would pose little risk because there is enough uranium available to fuel a nuclear power industry based on light-water reactors (LWRs) until well into the next century.

Criticism: Deferment of the breeder would increase U.S. uranium consumption, thereby increasing the incentives for others to acquire their own uranium-conserving reprocessing plants and breeders.

> *Response:* Deferment of the breeder will have no effect on uranium consumption through the remainder of this century and only a small effect in the first decades of the next century.

Criticism: Because others (including France, Japan, West Germany, and the Soviet Union) already have programs for development of the plutonium breeder, the U.S. decision may be of little relevance to the decisions of additional states.

> *Response:* By practicing what it preaches, the U.S. enhances the credibility and acceptability of its claim that breeder commercialization can and should be deferred, and prompts others, including those with active breeder programs, to reconsider their breeder plans.

3. Accelerate research on alternative fuel cycles:

Criticism: The uranium-plutonium fuel cycle has been selected over alternative fuel cycles, hence some consider it unlikely that a more attractive alternative will be found.

> *Response:* In the past, nonproliferation objectives were not considered as important factors in the selection and development of nuclear fuel cycles.

4. Increase U.S. enrichment capacity:

Criticism: To those countries seeking to avoid dependence upon the U.S. for essential enrichment services, expansion of the American near-monopoly in this field is of little comfort.

> *Response:* Countries are more likely to be willing to forego indigenous enrichment facilities if the U.S. has enough enrichment capacity to meet their needs as well as its own.

5. Guarantee nuclear fuel supplies to other countries:

Criticism: The credibility of American guarantees is not what it once was, and this decline applies *a fortiori* in the case of nuclear fuel supplies.

> *Response:* By acknowledging the importance of U.S. guarantees for nuclear fuel supplies and by proposing legislation to permit them, the president has enhanced their credibility, and the U.S. is prepared to augment its own guarantees by participating in international arrangements for fuel assurance.

Criticism: By guaranteeing fuel supplies, the U.S. would forego future use of its principal means for applying political and economic leverage in the field of nuclear power; viz., the threatened or actual withholding of such fuel.

> *Response:* U.S. guarantees would be offered only to countries undertaking appropriate nonproliferation obligations, and could be terminated if those obligations were not met.

6. Embargo the export of enrichment and reprocessing technologies:

Criticism: An embargo on enrichment and reprocessing technologies could be considered as inconsistent with the obligation assumed under the NPT "to participate in the fullest possible exchange of equipment, materials, and scientific and technological information for the peaceful uses of nuclear energy."

> *Response:* An embargo on the export of sensitive technologies is inconsistent with the competing and overriding NPT obligation "not in any way to assist, encourage, or induce any non-nuclear-weapon State to manufacture or otherwise acquire nuclear weapons or other nuclear explosive devices."

Criticism: Attempting to deny to others access to the "sensitive" technologies could induce them to acquire them from other suppliers or to develop indigenous facilities which might not be subject to effective international control.

> *Response:* The international controls currently practiced cannot protect against possible misuse of sensitive facilities, and all of the supplier nations now share the view that inhibiting the spread of these facilities should receive higher priority than subjecting them to safeguards.

7. Establish an international fuel cycle evaluation program:

Criticism: It would take years to conduct comprehensive analyses and evaluations of alternative fuel cycles, of measures to assure access to nuclear fuel supplies, and of international mechanisms for storing and disposing of spent fuel; and additional years to implement the results. Some countries would not be willing to accept such a delay in preparing to meet future energy needs.

Response: Only the plutonium economy would be deferred during the evaluation program; worldwide demand for nuclear power could be met through the use of LWRs (without reprocessing).

The arguments supporting the president's decisions have merit, but so too do those of the critics. And the persuasive power of either case can be strengthened by elucidation. For some measures, the balance of pros and cons appears to tip only slightly in favor or against, and the side to which it appears to tip depends strongly on the perspective of the observer.

Observers differ in the relative values they assign to nuclear power objectives and to nonproliferation objectives. Included among the interested parties are: those who support nuclear power without qualification and who are prepared to accept (or to deny the existence of) any proliferation risks associated with the use of that energy source; those who oppose nuclear power for safety, environmental, or other reasons unrelated to nuclear weapons, and who are sympathetic to any arguments, including nonproliferation arguments, which discourage the growth of nuclear power; those who believe nuclear weapons proliferation constitutes a grave threat to world order and human survival, and who are willing to forego any benefits of nuclear power in order to inhibit even slightly the spread of nuclear weapons; those who view proliferation as a political-military matter which is virtually unrelated to nuclear power; and those who see conflict between the goal of expanding the use of nuclear power to meet energy needs and the goal of halting the proliferation of nuclear weapons, and who seek a coherent policy in which neither goal is subordinated any more than is necessary.

The gap of disagreement between Carter and most of his critics can be narrowed somewhat if the president's policy statements are taken literally; that is, if the critics take the president at his word. For then to *"defer indefinitely"* commercial reprocessing means to *postpone* this practice *for a period of time which remains to be determined.* This period could turn out to be a year, a decade, a century, or forever; only time will tell. Similarly, to *"defer the date"* of breeder commercialization means to *postpone to a later date the day on which it takes place.* To *"continue"* an embargo is to *maintain it for now;* hardly a permanent commitment. And a promise to *"explore"* alternatives is a promise to *examine* them; it is not a promise to adopt them.

In this light, Carter's program calls for a pause in the spread of weapons-usable materials and the facilities for making them. During this pause, the U.S. is to keep its domestic nuclear power policy in line with the nonproliferation dimensions of its foreign policy, and is to join with others in searching more thoroughly than ever before for ways to meet world energy needs while reducing to acceptable levels the proliferation dangers of the global use of nuclear power.

A COMPREHENSIVE NONPROLIFERATION POLICY

In addition to issues related directly to civilian nuclear power, a comprehensive nonproliferation policy must include a number of measures having little or nothing to do with nuclear power. These non-energy-related measures interact with the energy-related ones, and are no less important.

Many political-military measures could reduce the incentives of other countries to acquire nuclear weapons of their own. Among them are: maintain and strengthen alliance commitments and other forms of security guarantees; pledge not to use nuclear weapons against any non-nuclear-weapons states except where there is aggression in concert with a nuclear-weapons state; promote and support the establishment of nuclear-weapons-free zones; enhance the stability of regional military balances through transfers of conventional (i.e., non-nuclear) weapons; prepare to impose sanctions (economic, political, or military) against countries which violate international nonproliferation commitments; reduce the importance of nuclear weapons by reducing the level of the rhetoric associated with them; complete a comprehensive test ban prohibiting all nuclear explosions, peaceful or otherwise; and demonstrate meaningful progress toward controlling and eventually eliminating those nuclear arsenals which already exist (cf. Epstein 1977; Nacht 1977).

One might wish that it were possible to identify a combination of measures which would halt proliferation now and forever, but it is not. There is no perfect nonproliferation policy. (Even if there were, it is likely that such a policy would be inconsistent with other national goals.) An action that prevents one state from "going nuclear" might make it possible for another, and that which appears as a disincentive to one might look like an incentive to another.

There is only one realistic choice: to recognize that any nonproliferation policy involves tradeoffs among conflicting objectives and that there is no comprehensive nonproliferation policy which can assure success; to develop and pursue mixes of strategies and measures tailored specifically to the objectives and the times; to minimize inconsistencies between nuclear power policy and nonproliferation policy, and between nonproliferation policy and other dimensions of foreign policy; to avoid irreversible errors; and to acknowledge and correct the reversible ones. To students and practitioners of policy formulation, it should come as no surprise that flexibility wins again.

IV

STANLEY M. GREENFIELD

ENVIRONMENTAL PROBLEMS WITH FOSSIL FUELS

Environmental impacts from current use of fossil fuels. Problems related to future synthetic fuels: oil shale, coal gasification and liquefaction. Uncertainty in the available data base. Global environmental problems: increased rainfall acidity, atmospheric CO_2. Conclusion.

From its first use, fossil fuel has been accompanied by the obvious presence of noxious pollutants. The man who first discovered that a torch dipped in naturally occurring pools of tar would burn brighter and longer could not help but observe the odor and smoke that accompanied those benefits. The industrial revolution requiring, as it did, the ever-increasing use of available fossil fuel was symbolized by the factory chimney. The belching smokestacks and the smoke-grimed industrial towns became the hallmark of the successful technologically based society.

While the overt societal consequences of fossil fuel use have long been present, the apparent acceptance of these consequences suggest they were felt to be a small price to pay for the benefits that accrued to an economically growing society. Thus there was a continuing tendency to overlook the increased gaseous and particulate concentrations that enveloped our urban areas. In addition, there was little understanding of the potential direct and indirect environmental consequences of our increasing dependence on fossil energy (and in particular, oil and gas) as the mainstay of our continued economic growth and development.

In this chapter we examine the potential environmental problems associated with the current and projected future use of fossil energy. We have focused on total impact, from extraction to end use, and conclude that although the use of fossil energy may produce significant environmental problems, many of them can probably be controlled or avoided by astute planning in a comprehensive energy strategy. Overriding all of these conclusions is the surprising fact that the current state of knowledge makes it very difficult quantitatively to assess the environmental problems associated with fossil fuel either singly or in the integrated manner suggested. But to do less invites unwarranted limitations on the use of this important resource.

ENVIRONMENTAL IMPACTS RESULTING FROM CURRENT USE OF FOSSIL FUELS

The Marshaling of Public Interest

As often happens when society feels a sudden concern with the consequences of an action, the awakening results from a disaster than cannot be ignored. In the case of fossil energy, one such disaster occurred in London in the early 1950s, when several days of stagnant air trapped the products resulting from the burning of soft coals. Since this fossil fuel is high in both ash content and sulfur, the result was a thick smoke blanket over London—and a large increase in human deaths, primarily among the elderly and among those afflicted with various respiratory diseases. These increased deaths, estimated to number in the thousands, strongly focused public attention on the potentially burgeoning problems associated with the use of this form of fossil energy. This incident was followed by similar incidents in England and in other industrialized countries, and it stirred growing public concerns about fossil-energy induced pollution. The result has been a growing body of regulatory laws addressing the problem.

As with coal-related incidents, visible evidence of air pollution associated with the processing and/or use of petroleum-based products, particularly in the Los Angeles basin, has produced considerable public and official concern. Studies have traced the source of this pollution to the hydrocarbon and oxides of nitrogen resulting primarily from gasoline and oil use. These studies have led in turn to environmental regulations aimed at controlling emissions.

Fossil Energy Extraction Problems

Besides their use, it is also clear that the extraction, transport, storage, and processing of fossil fuels can impact the environment strongly. This is particularly true of coal extraction in surface mining, a process which removes the land overburden covering a coal seam near the surface and allows the coal to be stripped away. While a highly efficient process for extracting coal, the resulting environmental impact is extensive unless the land is reclaimed. Unreclaimed strip mines do not improve with time; the impact grows and extends spatially because of erosion and runoff.

Underground mining produces other effects resulting primarily from subsidence and surface disturbances that are secondary results of underground workings. In addition, some effects result from the disposal needs for mine, mill, and processing wastes. Here, too, runoff can significantly increase the geographic extent of the impacts, primarily by changes in stream and river ecological systems. A follow-on environmental impact frequently occurs from draining low pH (high acidity) waters from abandoned mines, with an impact on water ecological systems that can be locally quite devastating if not arrested.

Table 1 shows the magnitude of the land reclamation problem associated with coal extraction. It should be noted that these data are from the period 1930 to 1971, when underground mining predominated. There has been an increasing emphasis on strip mining in the last decade, driven primarily by cost factors and the

Table 1

Land Uses for Mining of Fossil Fuels by Function, 1930-1971
(excludes oil and gas)

Type of Use	Utilized (in acres)	Reclaimed (in acres)
Surface area mined (area of excavation only)	966,000	716,000
Area used for disposal of overburden and other mine waste from surface mining	320,000	268,000
Surface area subsided or disturbed as a result of underground workings	87,000	4,000
Surface area used for disposal of underground mine waste	166,000	20,000
Surface area used for disposal of mill or processing waste	31,900	6,480
Total	1,571,800	1,014,400

Source: U.S. Bureau of Mines (1974*a*).

desire to utilize the near-surface, low-sulfur coals in the Western United States (see Table 2). Note that surface-mined coal increased from 35 percent of the total in 1966 to 48 percent in 1972. Furthermore, Western surface coals accounted for 9 percent of the total stripped in 1966 and 18 percent in 1972. The implications are clear: at least in the near future, surface extraction will increase in importance as the primary source of coal. (In 1973 surface-mined coal passed the 50 percent point.) Thus, land reclamation, and the impact of widespread surface mining, will continue to be a major growing environmental issue.

Table 2

Distribution of U.S. Coal Production by Region and Mining Method for 1966 and 1972
(units: thousands of tons)

Year and Method	Eastern	% of Total	Midwest	% of Total	West	% of Total	Total
1966							
Underground	284,640	84	44,224	13	9,659	3	338,523
Surface	81,679	45	83,499	46	14,878	9	180,056
Total	336,319	70	127,723	25	24,537	5	518,579[a]
1972							
Underground	242,598	80	52,066	17	9,438	3	304,102
Surface	129,234	46	98,277	36	48,271	18	275,782
Total	371,832	64	150,343	26	57,709	10	579,884[b]

Source: U.S. Bureau of Mines (1966; 1972).
[a]Does not include auger mining production (1,702,330 tons).
[b]Does not include auger mining production (15,544,000 tons).

As with coal in the last decade, oil extraction has emerged as a major environmental issue. In this case we include exploration as well as production and transport of crude oil. A major impetus for this concern has been the accelerated attempt to exploit the potentially rich offshore oil fields, and the increasing requirements for tanker transport—including the related development of the Alaskan North Slope oil fields, and the extensive pipeline required to bring the crude to the Gulf of Alaska. Tanker and drilling accidents have resulted in oil spills around the world and have focused public attention on serious environmental concerns. The environmental questions concern the impact on ocean ecological systems, particularly the nearshore and estuarine areas which are essential to the viability of ocean life, and which are especially vulnerable to oil either spilled directly or carried toward the shore from accidental ocean spills.

Public reactions to real and/or imagined environmental degradation has been apparent and intense. Reactions such as that in the late 1960s to the oil spill in the Santa Barbara channel have institutionalized restrictive regulations. That particular incident, in fact, played a significant role in obtaining passage of the 1969 National Environmental Protection Act, which mandated Environmental Impact Statements (EIS) for every major federal action. This requirement forces consideration of environmental issues *prior* to major federal actions such as granting of oil leases on the outer continental shelf or coal leases on federal land.

In using fossil energy such as coal and oil, it is clear that potential environmental problems exist at every stage from extraction to end use. For each stage, these problems have produced some forms of regulatory response, which, taken together, are potentially restrictive to the use of fossil energy.

At the extraction end, local regulations on strip mining and the EIS requirements have delayed coal-source development in many parts of the country. The recently signed federal law on strip mining will help insure reclamation of mined areas and thereby lessen the impact argument and delays, but will increase the fuel cost. Similarly, local and federal (EIS) concerns with the potential environmental impacts have affected development of offshore oil fields.

More significant in both impact and public reaction is the transport and off-loading of petroleum from offshore and foreign sources. This problem concerns both the potential for spillage during transport and transfer, and the air emissions during storage and transfer. Local and state agencies in California, for example, have expressed concern about the potential for increased hydrocarbon emissions into an already impacted region from the storage and transfer of oil from the Alaskan North Slope. To date, these concerns have delayed the use of Long Beach, California, as one terminus of a pipeline to carry this oil to refineries in Texas.

Although not currently subject to regulation, the potential impact on groundwater resources of extracting fossil fuels is emerging as an important issue. This potential has particular relevance for coal extraction, especially western coal, because the major near-surface coal seams that are suitable for stripping are frequently also the major groundwater aquifers. In addition, vast quantities of water are required to reclaim stripped land. In regions of sparse water resources, destruction and extensive use of groundwater can be particularly harmful. Moreover, this region of the country possesses other potentially developable fossil resources such as oil shale, which are competitors for the same water. We shall return to this presently. Without careful concern for these environmental considerations, we may be limited in our ability to develop fully the vast fossil-energy resources in the Rocky Mountain region.

Source Developments Resulting from Pollution Control Requirements

In considering development of the western coal resources, it is important to examine why this source of fossil energy is in growing demand. The demand is especially interesting when one realizes that, in general, western coal is unimpressive in heat content (Btu per pound), and therefore possesses an ash problem that must be dealt with in combustion and disposal. The reason for the demand, however, starts with the fact that coal in general contains a variety of organic and inorganic substances and, as a result of combustion and processing, can be the source of considerable quantities of air pollutants. Table 3 lists the minor elements in coal as well as the trace elements for which data were available at the time of writing. Table 4 provides a similar list for crude oil where the trace elements are considered potential environmental pollutants. Of current major importance are those pollutants for which National Ambient Air Quality Standards (NAAQS) were promulgated as one of the first federal actions under the Clean Air Act of 1970. These include SO_2 (sulfur dioxide), NO_2 (nitrogen dioxide), HC (unburned hydrocarbons), CO (carbon monoxide), and TSP (total suspended particulates). SO_2, NO_2, and CO are the direct result of combustion (with CO primarily occurring from gasoline engine exhaust). HC can result from in-

Table 3

Minor and Trace Elements in Coal

Minor Elements (about 1% or more, on ash)	Trace Elements (about 0.1% or less, on ash)	
Pollutant	**Named as Hazardous**	
Sulfur	Beryllium	
Nitrogen	Fluorine	
	Arsenic	
Ash-forming	Selenium	
	Cadmium	
Sodium	Mercury	
Potassium	Lead	
Iron		
Calcium		
Magnesium	**Others Analyzed**	
Silica	**Coal Basis**	**Ash Basis**
Alumina		
Titania	Boron	Lithium
	Vanadium	Scandium
	Chromium	Manganese
	Cobalt	Strontium
	Nickel	Zirconium
	Copper	Barium
	Zinc	Ytterbium
	Gallium	Bismuth
	Germanium	
	Tin	
	Yttrium	
	Lanthanum	
	Uranium	

complete combustion of oil products, or as evaporative losses during storage and processing. Oxidant is a secondary pollutant derived from photochemical reactions in atmospheric mixtures of HC and oxides of nitrogen.

Obviously these are not the only pollutants produced by using fossil energy, but they are currently the only ones for which national ambient standards have been established. An exception is the fact that three substances (beryllium, mercury, and asbestos) have been designated hazardous air pollutants, and emissions

Table 4

Minor and Trace Elements in Petroleum

Minor Constituents	Trace Elements	
Sulfur	Vanadium	Antimony
Nitrogen	Nickel	Barium
	Iron	Chromium
	Arsenic	Lead
	Beryllium	Manganese
	Cadmium	Molybdenum
	Mercury	Tellurium
	Selenium	Tin

standards have been established for specific activities (none directly related to the use of fossil fuels). While it is clear that other substances (as listed in Tables 3 and 4) may ultimately contribute to establishment of limitations on fossil energy use, the six listed above constitute the major currently recognized problems.[1]

Despite the importance of TSP in environmental controls on coal usage, and of CO, HC, NO_2, and oxidants on emissions from petroleum-using activities, SO_2 has been the single most important pollutant in overall impact on the use of this resource. This is peculiar in itself since SO_2, as a single pollutant, is not an impactor of human health at levels considerably above the current primary ambient standards (.14 ppm/24 hrs.). Nevertheless, SO_2 has been identified as a major pollutant for which controls are required, even though historically it has always been used as an indicator pollutant (i.e., a general indicator of air pollution). This oddity has imposed a demand for stringent emission controls and/or use of low-sulfur fuels on most major combustion sources. As concern with petroleum availability has grown in recent years, in particular with the availability of low-sulfur imported crudes, the demand for low-sulfur coals has increased. If one examines the distribution of coal from the standpoint of sulfur content and mineability, a major reason for the growth of western surface-mining activities becomes apparent (see Figure 1).[2]

Figure 1

U.S. East-West Coal Reserve Base,
Surface vs. Underground
(billions of tons)

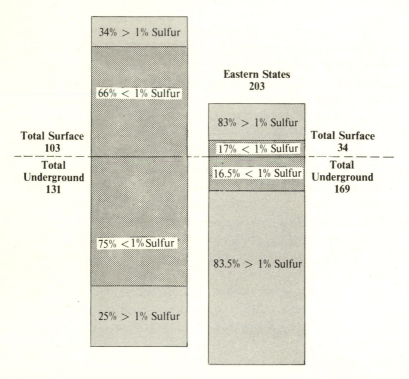

Source: U.S. Bureau of Mines (1974*a*).

Refined Approach to Pollution Control Emission Standards

This discussion on implementation of the SO_2 standard is relevant to other federally established pollutant standards as well. There is little question that using fossil fuel in the forms currently available may cause harmful environmental effects. How they do so, however, is exceedingly complex. The dangers range from local emission of a single toxic pollutant which must be controlled, to emission of substances which can produce a problem pollutant only in the presence of solar radiation and/or other airborne materials. These effects can be produced locally by single sources of individual pollutants, or by the complex interaction of multiple sources over long times and distances.

Effective approaches to avoid these potential problems are as complex as the pollutant mix itself. Setting single pollutant standards, which are enforced as if they existed and acted in isolation from the rest of the air contaminants, can produce the appearance of a vigorous environmental program without necessarily producing a real benefit to society.

Such complexity arose when addressing the question of controlling photochemical oxidants. The formation of photochemical oxidants is a very complex problem in atmospheric chemistry, involving competing reactions among the varying mix of hydrocarbons, oxides of nitrogen, and ozone in the presence of sunlight. Attempts have been made to specify the control level for NO_x hydrocarbons to meet a specified threshold concentration of oxidant. This approach to ambient air quality control has been a continuous problem, primarily because there still exists considerable controversy about the effect of the ratio of NO_x to hydrocarbon concentrations on the formation rate of photochemical oxidants.

A similar problem has been encountered in determining the required ambient concentrations of SO_2 and particulate matter that would be protective of human health. Here, as indicated in the criteria documents issued in 1969 (HEW 1969), the observed health effects of ambient SO_2 were observed *only with the simultaneous presence of substantial concentrations of particulate matter.* It was on this basis that the ambient air quality standards were established for each of these pollutants. It is interesting to note, however, that in enforcing these standards to date, they are viewed as if SO_2 and particulate matter existed as *non-interacting pollutants with independent impacts.*

After setting these standards, a large, nationwide epidemiological study was undertaken to obtain better information on pollutant adverse health effects thresholds, and to remove admitted uncertainties in the data underlying present federal standards. The summary results of this study have been widely circulated, and maintain two basic conclusions relating to SO_2. First, no evidence. exists at present to strengthen SO_2 standards. Second, observed effects in the presence of SO_2 concentrations lower than the current 24-hour ambient standards may be due to another pollutant. At the time the hypothetical causative pollutant chosen by EPA was sulfates.

At present EPA has not set a standard for sulfate because of the admitted lack of sufficient evidence. Nevertheless, arguments continue to be made about the need for more stringent SO_2 emission standards, which, although admittedly based on assumptions that are currently unsupportable, would impose a rigid costly control strategy on the nation. The major proponents of more stringent controls assume that the primary source of harmful sulfates available to the public must be the utility industry. The result has been a reaction in many states increasing control of SO_2 and thereby making it increasingly difficult for electric utilities to meet growing demands for power with available fossil fuels.

One might assume that in the early life of the National Environmental Protection Act, the Environmental Protection Agency needed to move quickly and forcefully to give credence to the federal intent. However, as problems become more complex, costs of implementation escalate, energy problems increase, and priorities and social impacts change, it becomes even more important to assure that we are acting from a base of knowledge and understanding, and that actions taken are rational and defensible in their total benefits to society. This can only be accomplished with sufficient understanding of the processes involved, the effects produced, and the available control strategies and their impacts. This problem is particularly important as we move from the simplistic world of single pollutants which can be addressed individually and independently, to the complex world of interacting pollutant subsets of varying reactivities under varying ambient conditions.

It is clear that the use of fossil fuels in the forms presently available creates a host of potential environmental problems. These problems are complex both in form and solution, and if addressed simplistically can seriously inhibit the continued use of fossil energy. Solutions are available, however, but they require development of integrated assessments and energy use strategies that weigh the benefits and costs of various options.

The most basic limitation of analysis lies in difficulties quantifying potential environmental impacts. While the data available are not impressive, this should not deter society from approaching the problem in an integrated manner, while modifying perceptions and strategies with time as more information becomes available. To do less would force undue restrictions on an available energy resource. The problem can be approached in this manner while retaining full determination to protect the environment.

THE PROBLEMS OF FUTURE SYNTHETIC FUELS

As indicated by the subject of this book, in a very few years this nation has evolved from one secure in its presumption of available energy resources into one with concern for immediate or projected shortages. This concern has given rise to demands for new sources or new technologies.

The demand for increased energy occurs at a time when society is showing an intense concern for environmental pollution and protection, and a remarkable willingness to accept social limitations to improve the environment. This concern has had a particularly strong impact on the energy industry which, as a whole, represents perhaps the nation's most pervasive source of potential environmental impact. In addition, however, particularly in the fossil energy area, the energy industry is burdened by the fact that energy conversion is an old and rather inflexible process, and at best the available environmental controls represent a cumbersome add-on technology.

In developing new technologies, one would like to address simultaneously their environmental impacts in a way as to achieve practical, efficient, economical, effective long-term solutions. In this respect it is important to examine potential impacts of a technology during development stages in a manner that permits "fixes" to be found expeditiously (or to eliminate intractable technologies from further development).

One class of "new" technologies that may extend the availability of fossil energy is production of synthetic fuels. These include coal conversion (i.e., the gasification and liquefaction of coal), and extraction of petroleum from oil shale or tar sands. In the former case, the coal can be gasified at high temperatures and pressures and used either directly as a low Btu fuel, or upgraded or methanated (by the addition of hydrogen) to a high Btu or "pipeline quality" gas. Coal can also be liquefied in the presence of a catalyst, or dissolved in a solvent to produce a crude suitable for refining into a variety of petroleum products. It can also be reconstituted into a "clean" solid fuel. In the latter case, the hydrocarbons are bound quite tightly into the shale or tar formation, and are removed by retorting the mined material at high temperatures.

As with all fossil fuels, none of these approaches escapes the problems associated with producing a total environmental impact that extends from extraction to end use. Figure 2 shows that in considering the use of fossil energy environmentally, all modules must be dealt with in almost all cases.

Oil Shale

In the case of oil shale,[3] the major developmental work to date has involved stripping the shale by surface mining techniques, and retorting for oil recovery. While known environmental problems exist with the crude oil extraction process concerning the emissions of the regulated pollutants, these are controllable in general.

Figure 2
Combined Modules for Coal Gasification

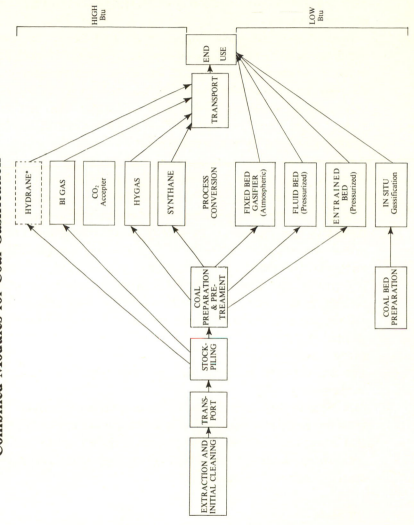

What is currently not well known is the extent of potential environmental impact that would result from the presence of toxic trace materials in the synthetic crude or the resulting products that are unique to shale hydrocarbons, the extraction process, or both. Let me hasten to state that this *does not mean that this problem is known to exist—rather that we do not know enough to eliminate the suspicion that such toxics do exist.*

Given these limitations of knowledge, we must exercise caution in developing this resource, and undertake an adequate program to determine the extent of the problem by characterizing products and effluent streams. With respect to shale extraction, the act of grinding and retorting the mined material produces a residue that is 20 to 30 percent greater in volume than the original extracted material. This poses a disposal and reclamation problem requiring both large quantities of water and considerably greater land area than the original strip mines.

A second approach to oil shale development involves *in situ* retorting. In this case, the shale is not stripped from the surface, but rather is prepared for underground retorting. Some below-ground extraction is required for this purpose, but it is minimal. The formation is then fractured and sustained heat is applied to retort the hydrocarbon and bring it to the surface. While it is clear that waste disposal and reclamation problems are thus essentially eliminated, the same cautionary note as above must still be applied to the crude oil produced. Potential environmental impacts attendant to the extraction process for *in situ* retorting concern the effect of fracturing on groundwater aquifers and possible subsurface migration of retorted liquids.

Coal Gasification and Liquefaction [4]

While there are a number of different processes available for coal gasification and liquefaction, all involve a high-temperature, high-pressure system for gasification with possibly a stage of methanation to produce high Btu gas, or a carbonization process for production of various forms of liquid fuel. All fuels produced by these methods involved process steps in which potentially harmful chemicals are available either as effluent streams and/or fugitive emissions, or are possibly passed along in the product stream.

It is amazing at this stage of our technology development to realize how limited our data base is for characterizing effluent streams from coal gasification and liquefaction. Data have been collected primarily from small pilot plant and "bench scale" units which have been sampled intermittently and represent operating characteristics somewhat similar to those that will be encountered with commercialization. The argument that present product streams are representative of those expected from large-scale operations may hold more for gasification than for liquefaction. It should be noted, however, that processes do change during development, and that apparent potential current problems can be absent in the final evolved system. Interestingly enough, this is all the more reason for examining these potential problems early in the development cycle. With this perspective on data limitations we may examine several sets of results, which will allow inferences about compound types to which the work space and the general environment might be exposed.

We assume that the gasification technologies foreseeable in the near future have basically similar effluent characteristics, and that a laboratory SYNTHANE gasifier under development in the U.S. is representative of those technologies at commercial scale. Table 5 indicates that the gasifier gas components vary markedly in concentration with the type of coal and its sulfur content.

It should be noted that sulfur containing compounds (H_2S, thiophene series, etc.) and benzene must be removed prior to upgrading by methanation, and it is expected that most of these constituents will be removed from the final product stream.

Table 6 presents a representative elemental analysis for the several coals displayed in Table 5. The amount of H_2S produced is seen to be a function of the initial sulfur content of the coal, and the aromatic products seem to be associated with the rank of the coal. Further, the production of thiophene and its derivatives is related to the organic bound sulfur in the coal.

Table 5

Components in Gasifier Gas (ppm)

	Illinois No. 6 Coal	Illinois Char	Wyoming Subbituminous Coal	Western Kentucky Coal	North Dakota Lignite	Pittsburgh Seam Coal
H₂S	9,800	186	2,480	2,530	1,750	860
COS	150	2	32	119	65	11
Thiophene	31	.4	10	5	13	42
Methylthiophene	10	.4	-	-	-	7
Dimethylthiophene	10	.5	-	-	11	6
Benzene	340	10	434	100	1,727	1,050
Toluene	94	3	59	22	167	185
C₈ aromatics	24	2	27	4	73	27
SO₂	10	1	6	2	10	10
CS₂	10	-	-	-	-	-
Methyl mercaptan	60	.1	.4	33	10	8

Table 6

Representative Analyses of Coals (weight percent)

Coals:	Illinois No. 6 Coal	Western Kentucky Coal	Wyoming Subbituminous Coal	North Dakota Lignite	Pittsburgh Seam Coal
Moisture	8.3	4.3	18.1	20.6	2.5
Volatile matter	37.5	34.6	31.9	32.9	30.9
Fixed carbon	43.0	44.5	32.0	38.2	51.5
Ash	11.2	16.6	18.0	8.3	15.1
Hydrogen	5.3	4.7	5.4	5.7	4.7
Oxygen	15.9	10.9	30.3	32.6	9.3
Carbon	63.0	62.7	45.2	51.5	68.4
Nitrogen	1.1	1.2	.6	.7	1.2
Sulfur	3.5	3.9	.5	1.2	1.3

Source: Forney et al. (1974).

Substantial coal tar and char are formed as part of the initial gasification process. For economic reasons this tar will most likely be burned to supply energy for steam production when the process goes commercial. Similar tars to those expected in a commercial process have been analyzed and have been found to contain more than 38 structural types, of which two were polycyclic aromatic hydrocarbons and five were nitrogen containing heterocyclics. Data on the characterization of tars is limited to those constituents which volatize below 300° C. The analyses presented in Table 7 may be considered representative of compound types to be found in tars produced by coal gasification.

A major potential source of hazard, both environmental and occupational, relates to the condensation of unused steam during the primary gasification step. The organic content of this recovered water ranged from 0.6 to 2.4 percent by weight, and over 60 percent of this organic material was phenolic in nature. Qualitatively, the mix of contaminants was found to be similar regardless of the kind of coal which was gasified. Again, Table 8 presents data for test results obtained from a single laboratory-scale SYNTHANE gasification unit, utilizing six different coals. The actual concentration of phenolic components ranged between 2,000 and 7,000 ppm depending on the type of coal used.

Clearly the disposal of condensate water presents a major potential environmental and health problem. At the same time it should be noted that results reported in these tables are preliminary and may not represent the complete spectrum of material which might be present. Data pertaining to analysis of water, tars, chars, and gases is subject to modification, depending on the solvent system used to extract organic constituents from the effluent. Also, while one might expect the final product gas to be relatively free of these toxic compounds, this is not as yet completely certain.

Chemical characterization of the product stream from various coal liquefaction processes has been limited to gross elemental analysis in most cases. This contrasts with the sophisticated mass spectrometric data (however limited) that is available for gasification technologies. It is important to note that the elemental analysis data has been collected primarily as a support activity to the

Table 7

Summary of Data Derived from Mass Spectrometer Analyses of Products from High-Temperature Carbonization of Coal

	Naphthalene oil	Anthracene oil	Heavy creosote	A	Pitch Sample B	C
Boiling range °C	220-230	300-360	360	-	-	-
Softening point °C	-	-	- 1	80-85	100-110	140-150
Average molecular weight	134	195	218	242	252	267
Aromaticity (f_a)	-	-	-	-	-	-
Analysis, percent:						
1 aromatic ring	39.6	.9	-	-	-	-
2 aromatic rings	53.9	18.2	2.0	2.2	.9	.6
3 aromatic rings	3.4	46.3	27.6	14.9	8.3	4.8
4 aromatic rings	.5	19.5	30.8	21.0	23.3	14.3
5 aromatic rings	-	-	.3	1.5	.9	1.6
6 aromatic rings	-	-	1.8	7.0	9.3	10.9
7 aromatic rings	-	-	.3	1.5	.9	1.6
Oxygen, sulfur and nitrogen compounds	2.6	8.2	21.6	12.7	12.3	10.4
Residue	-	5.7	9.3	29.1	28.6	42.0

Resource: Bureau of Mines (1967).

Table 8

Contaminants in Product Water from Coal Gasification

	Illinois	No. 6	Wyom.	W. Ky.	Pgh.	N. Dak.	Montana
Phenol	3,400	2,660	4,050	2,040	1,880	2,790	3,160
Cresols	2,840	2,610	2,090	1,910	2,000	1,730	870
C_2-phenols	1,090	780	440	620	760	450	240
C_3-phenols	110	100	50	60	130	60	30
Dihydrics	250	540	530	280	130	70	130
Benzofuranols	70	100	100	50	70	60	80
Indanols	150	100	110	90	120	110	140
Acetophenones Hydroxy-benzaldehyde	60	110	60	50	80	40	-
Benzoic acids Naphthols	160	110	80	160	170	140	160
Idenols	90	90	60	80	20	50	70
Benzofurans	-	-	-	-	110	10	10
Dibenzofurans	-	-	-	-	-	-	-
Bephenols	40	20	40	20	60	-	-
Benzothiophenols	110	60	20	70	20	10	-
Pyridines	-	60	120	30	540	220	270
Quinolines	-	-	-	-	10	10	20
Indoles	-	20	20	40	40	30	70

Source: Bureau of Mines (1974*b*).

engineering aspects of the liquefaction technology. The engineering aspects have been concerned with determining the degree of sulfur removal and the distribution of non-carbon elements in the final fuel. Analytical efforts have not stressed identification of the spectrum of complex organics present in the final product stream. The past rationale has been to develop a hydrogenation process which efficiently removes contaminants (sulfur, nitrogen, etc.), is conservative relative to hydrogen demand, and yields maximum product. In short, the perspective has been to develop clean fuels which are environmentally acceptable within the context of the common air pollutants. The data required to assess health impacts of the technology and product stream itself have not had a high priority.

Again, the available data may be limited in usefulness by the small scale of the pilot plant facilities, which have been routinely geared to utilize coal at a rate of 10-20 pounds per hour and are only intermittently in production. Further, the design characteristics of the liquefaction reactor(s) have been modified with time, and it is known that such changes will modify the composition, chemical, and physical characteristics of the product stream. It is also evident that product characteristics are influenced by type of catalyst and matrix, and that the chemical composition, physical configuration, and catalyst age all contribute to the quality of the product stream. Further, once processed, the product changes in terms of its physical properties, generally becoming more viscous. This suggests that chemical shifts in the quantity and type of poly-condensed aromatics might be taking place; but this is speculation at present.

An important aspect of the technology is the use of heavy, high-boiling fractions which resemble coke-oven tars as a vehicle for initial slurry preparation. It is expected that the final product will have some of the characteristics of these tars and that the processing and handling of these materials present hazards inherent in the technology, especially from an occupational standpoint. Table 7 and Table 9 present data generated by GC-mass spectrometric techniques, giving clear indications of the complexity of these product streams. Moreover, the commercialization of lique-

Table 9

Mass Spectrometric Analyses of the Benzene-Soluble Tar (volume-percent)

Structural type (includes alkyl derivatives)	Run HP-1 No. 92, Illinois[a] No. 6 coal	Run HPL No. 94 lignite	Run HPM #111 Montana sub-bituminous coal	Run HP-118 No. 118[a] Pittsburgh seam coal
Benzenes	2.1	4.1	3.9	1.9
Indenes	[b]8.6	1.5	2.6	[b]6.1
Indans	1.9	3.5	4.9	2.1
Naphthalenes	11.6	19.0	15.3	16.5
Fluorenes	9.6	7.2	9.7	10.7
Acenaphthenes	13.5	12.0	11.1	15.8
3-ring aromatics	13.8	10.5	9.0	14.8
Phenylnaphthalenes	9.8	3.5	6.4	7.6
4-ring pericondensed	7.2	3.5	4.9	7.6
4-ring catacondensed	4.0	1.4	3.0 .	4.1
Phenols	2.8	13.7	5.5	3.0
Naphthols	(b)	9.7	9.6	(b)
Indanols	.9	1.7	1.5	.7
Acenaphthenols	-	2.5	4.6	2.0
Phenanthrols	2.7	-	.9	-
Dibenzofurans	6.3	5.2	5.6	4.7
Dibenzothiophenes	3.5	1.0	1.5	2.4
Benzonaphthothiophenes	1.7	-	-	-
N-heterocyclics[c]	(10.8)	(3.8)	(5.3)	(8.8)
Average molecular weight	212	173	230	202

Source: Forney et al. (1974).

[a]Spectra indicate traces of 5-ring aromatics.

[b]Includes any naphthol present (not resolved in these spectra).

[c]Data on N-free basis since isotope corrections were estimated.

faction will result in the continuous recycling of a portion of the final product in the preparation of slurry. This point is stressed by the indication from Table 9 that the quantitative mix, especially phenolic and N-heterocyclics, is affected by the type of coal being processed. In short, chemical characterization of the complex products from liquefaction is as dynamic as the technology itself, and present data is insufficient for meaningful long-term assessment and risk prediction.

This is at best a cursory analysis of the chemical residues and contaminants available as a result of coal conversion and may have no resemblance to the final product. One is struck, however, by the fact that the gasifier gas contains a variety of toxic agents, including some substances which are included in the recently issued list of "Suspected Carcinogens" (HEW 1975), and which can affect a variety of human organs and systems when inhaled in toxic quantities. Thus development should be approached with caution.

Similarly, it also appears that the benzene-soluble tar produced during the gasification stage of SYNTHANE production contains a number of substances which may be carcinogenic. Examinations of the "Suspected Carcinogens" list reveals a number of compounds which have been identified in the tar from the SYNTHANE gasifier. These include benzene, naphthalenes, fluorenes, acenapthene, phenols, naphtols, as well as acenaphols, phenanthrols, and benzonaphthothiophenes.

Several coal tar constituents have carcinogenic properties. As early as 1775 scrotal cancer in London chimney sweeps was attributed to exposure to coal tars (NIOSH 1973). Increases in lung cancer mortality rates have been described in Japanese workers in gas-producing plants, and also in English workers in similar processes.

At this time there appears to be inadequate information to assess accurately the carcinogenic activity of benzene-soluble tars from the SYNTHANE process. The problem is aggravated by the complex nature of the tars. Some of the products may be co-carcinogens, or tumor-promoting agents.

While the carcinogenic potential of these tars is perhaps the most obvious health problem with the SYNTHANE process, it should not obscure the other toxic activities of the tar constituents (e.g., benzene), or of the other wastes and products.

A mass spectrometric analysis of product water from the SYNTHANE gasifier lists a number of compounds in the suspected carcinogen list, namely pyridine, pheonol, cresol, dihydroxybenzene, indole, and acetophenone compounds. A number of related compounds are also present in the list.

Although data on coal liquefaction are less adequate than comparable data for the SYNTHANE process, a brief analysis is possible. In the initial or catalytic hydrogenation phase, powdered coal and product oil are present, and the product oil which is returned to this phase of the cycle probably contains organic carcinogens, trace metals, and organo-metallic compounds, as well as vapors which may contain toxic or carcinogenic substances.

The second, or separation phase for at least one methodology, produces a solid, liquid, and gas effluent. The gaseous effluent contains hydrogen sulfide and ammonia, among other potentially hazardous substances. Oil and water scrubbing of the gas to remove salable by-products should reduce the hazard from the gaseous effluent. Data are not available on the composition of the tarry solid residues, but there is no reason to believe that these tars would have less carcinogenic potential than tars from other coal conversion processes. Pyrolysis might be a useful way to reduce the hazard from a portion of the tars, but the question of effluents to the community must also be considered in addition to the occupational hazards.

In the remaining phases leading to production of a synthetic crude oil, it appears that vapors, carcinogenic compounds, and trace metals may be present. It has been demonstrated that the product oil from pilot activities contains benzo(a)pyrene, benzo(a)anthracene, and phenanthrene, and must be considered to have carcinogenic potential. In addition, there is a wide variety of aromatic compounds, phenols, cresols, and other hazardous substances present in the product oil produced to date.

The above is not meant to be an environmental scare story. It is meant to illustrate the potential problems that exist as a major new industry begins to develop.

It is clear from past experience that recognition of a problem early in development at worst permits society to avoid the problem if it appears to be too costly or too intractable of solution. Ideally, such recognition offers the possibility of designing a cost-effective solution into the development. In either case, understanding the problem in its broadest sense—as in the case of present fossil energy usage—will permit society to address the available options, clarified by existing knowledge.

UNCERTAINTY IN THE AVAILABLE DATA BASE

As indicated in the previous sections, potential environmental problems associated with current and extended usage of fossil resources should be considered and weighed in assessing available options. This requirement demands an adequate, manipulatable, environmental impact data base. It was suggested that the available information base is not sufficient to allow more than limited assessment. To illustrate the inadequacy of these data, consider a matrix that attempts to describe the potential environmental impacts that could result from activities associated with the use of fossil energy. This matrix, taken from a recent report to ERDA (Greenfield et al. 1976), is presented in Table 10 and is as can be visualized to date. In actual fact, the impacts presented in Table 10 should not be assumed to cover all possibilities. They are at best a simplified description of the varied types of impacts that must be examined in assessing the total environmental problem associated with a given process. No attempt has been made to weigh the importance of any class against any other. At this time, such a weighing would have no basis in fact.

Of greater importance for our purposes is the evaluation presented in Table 11, whose format basically repeats the matrix in Table 10 with one exception. Table 11 includes columns for "data base" and "analytical ability" relating to the information necessary for a useful assessment of the impact. Analytical ability

Table 10

Potential Environmental Impacts Due to Use of Fossil Energy

Activity	Ecological		Health			Welfare	
	Water	Terrestrial	Occupational	General Public	Direct	Indirect	
EXTRACTION							
Strip Mining	Need for water, effects on aquifers, leachate, sedimentation, drainage destruction, acid and toxic run-off effects on aquatic ecologic systems.	Erosion, need for reclamation, waste disposal, spoil piles, slurry piles, hauling roads and right of ways, effects on terrestrial biomes.	Effects of dust and airborne toxic materials on workers.	Effects on drinking water and food chain.	Noise, aesthetic destruction of pristine areas.	Rapid growth and development to support mining operations and attendant industries.	
Underground Mining	Acid mine drainage, water from coal cleaning and preparation, effects on aquatic ecological systems, effects on aquifers.	Subsidence, hauling roads	Effects of dust and airborne toxic materials, adequate ventilation and safety measures.	Effects on drinking water and food chain		Noise	
Waste Collection for fuel	Positive impact of removal of waste material from potential of producing otherwise detrimental effects						

Table 10 con't

Activity	Ecological		Health		Welfare	
	Water	Terrestrial	Occupational	General Public	Direct	Indirect
TRANSPORT (INITIAL)						
Rail		Spillage and subsequent leaching: need for additional right of way.			Noise and aesthetic effects from increased rail traffic.	Increased growth to support building and operational activity.
Truck		Spillage and subsequent leaching.			Noise and aesthetic effects from increased truck traffic.	
Slurry Pipe	Need for water, disposal of carrying water with entrained and leached materials.	Spillage and need for right-of-way.	Treatment and disposal of carrying water.	Toxic materials carried into drinking water and food chains.	Aesthetic impacts along pipeline right-of-ways.	Temporary increased growth to support construction.
STOCKPILING OF MATERIALS (COAL AND WASTE MATERIALS)	Runoff and leachate from stockpile into ground and surface waters, effects on aquatic ecosystems.	Effects of runoff and leachate on terrestrial biomes.	Impacts of air and water borne toxic materials and dust on stockpile workers.	Fugitive toxic airborne materials and dust carried beyond stockpiles water-borne toxics into drinking water and food chain.	Noise, odors and aesthetic effects.	

Table 10 con't

Activity	Ecological		Health			Welfare
	Water	Terrestrial	Occupational	General Public	Direct	Indirect
FINAL CLEANING AND PRETREATMENT	Waste water from final coal preparation and pretreatment. Waste water effects on aquatic organisms.	Waste pile disposal from coal preparation and pretreatment. Waste water effects on terrestrial biomes.	Emission of chemical derivatives resulting from high temperature, high pressure pretreatment of coal. Effects of dusts from final coal preparation.	Emissions from coal pretreatment plant either airborne or from waste water into drinking water or food chain.	Noise aesthetic effects, odors.	
COAL LIQUEFACTION AND GASIFICATION PROCESSES	Large water quantities produced (20-30 gal/ton of coal) containing unknown amounts of potential toxic materials. Potential impact on aquatic systems and water supplies. Leachate from solid residues in disposal dumps. Scrub waters from purification systems, water needs for industries and supporting activity	Airborne materials as well as unused chars, tars, ash and other solid waste residues requiring ultimate disposal with potential impact on terrestrial biomes. Residues can contain significant quantities of toxic substances, trace metals, etc. General siting and development impacts for industry and support.	Unquantified occupational hazards due to high pressure system and the process production of potentially carcinogenic and toxic materials containing phenols, polynuclear aromatics, etc. Materials both air borne and liquid in form of tar, etc.	Potential hazards due to exposure of general public to material generated in plant and escaping to environment. Water borne materials into drinking water or food chain.	Noise, odors, aesthetic (general siting problems).	Impact of energy availability on growth and development to support new technology or resulting industry.
IN SITU COAL GASIFICATION, IN SITU SHALE OIL AND GAS PROCESSING	Product and clean up water, potential carrying of various toxic elements such as phenols, etc. into water bodies and resulting impact on aquatic systems. Migration of liquids containing toxics into underground water supplies. Need for water for process and support functions.	Disposal of waste materials extracted and their impact on terrestrial biomes. Effects of waste gases on terrestrial biome system. Siting problem with attendant terrestrial biome disturbance. Combustion of fuel on surface to provide hot gases or liquids, resulting in air pollution impacts.	Unquantified impact of residues from clean-up and fugitive products on workers.	As per occupational hazard, release of materials to general environments. Impact on air and water pollution as indicated with man as receptor, impact through food chain.	Noise, odors, aesthetic effects.	Increased growth and development associated with building of sites and supporting activity.

Table 10 con't

Activity	Ecological		Health		Welfare	
	Water	Terrestrial	Occupational	General Public	Direct	Indirect
UNDER-GROUND BED PREPARATION						
In situ coal and Shale (including drilling and fracturing)	Possible disturbance of aquifer.					
Modified **In Situ** Shale Processing (partial excavation)	Possible disturbance aquifer.	Possible subsidence.	Potential problems to workers underground during retorting - potential carcinogens emitted, dust, etc. during mining activities.			
FRACTURING UNDER-GROUND FORMATION FOR OIL AND GAS STIMULATION	Possible damage to aquifers.					
STIMULATION OF OIL AND GAS FUEL						
Injection of Solvent	Migration of solvents to aquifers and surface waters.	Solvent spilled on ground affecting terrestrial biomes. Impact of solvent vapors on vegetation.	Impact of fugitive solvents, liquids and vapors on work.	Escape of spilled or fugitive solvents so as to affect public. Solvents in drinking waters.	Odors in water and air.	

Table 10 con't

Activity	Ecological		Health			Welfare
	Water	Terrestrial	Occupational	General Public	Direct	Indirect
Injection of Water	Contaminated water migration underground. Impact of separated contaminated water on aquatic systems.	Impact of contaminated water on terrestrial biomes.		Contaminated waste water impact on drinking water and food chain.	Odors in water and air.	
Injection of Industrial Waste	Contamination of aquifer.	Effect of contamination on terrestrial biome.	Impact of industrial waste of undetermined content on workers.	Impact of industrial waste that escape into environment		
Extraction and Separation	Contaminated, separated injection water, solvents, or industrial wastes on surface waters and their ecosystems.	Contaminated separated injection water solvents or industrial wastes on terrestrial biomes.	Potential danger to worker during separation, clean-up and disposal stages.	Similar to occupational depending on escape to general environment.		
DIRECT COMBUSTION OF COAL						
Fluid Bed (press or atmospheric)		Ash. disposal impact on terrestrial biomes.	Release of fugitive particulates, vapors, and/or tars in the working area. Waste gases containing unknown pollutants.	As in occupational, release to general atmosphere.		Increased growth through improved availability of coal options.
New Stack Gas Cleaners (Citrate-coal ash) Waste Disposal	Leaching of ash contaminants into surface or ground water, impact on aquatic systems.	Sludge and ash disposal, impact on terrestrial biomes.	Contaminated residues as source of pollutant impact on workers.	As in occupational plus impact on drinking waters and food chain.		

Table 10 con't

Activity	Ecological		Health		Welfare	
	Water	Terrestrial	Occupational	General Public	Direct	Indirect
PRODUCT TRANSPORT AND DISTRIBUTION						
Gas and Liquid Pipelines	Spills (oil) into water systems, leaching into aquifer.	Spills on land. Damage to terrestrial biomes. Impact of right-of-way.	Contact and respiratory damage to pipeline operators due to pollutants in products (phenols, aromatics, etc.)	Same as occupational when escape to general environment. Effects on drinking water and food chain.	Siting problems for pipelines and transfer points-aesthetics, odors, etc.	Increased growth and development associated with operation of pipelines and transfer points.
Slurry Pipe	Spills into water system, leaching into aquifers.	Spills on land, damage to terrestrial biomes. Impact of right-of-way.	See above	See above	See above	See above
Truck Tanker	See above	See above		See above	See above	See above
Tanker	Spills in water bodies, impacts on aquatic ecosystem.		Contact and respiratory damage to tanker and transfer point operators due to pollutants in products, (phenols, aeromatics, etc.).	See above	Siting problems for tanker transfer points.	See above
Refining and/or Petrochemical	Effluent stream to the water, of pollutants unique to the discussed process. Damage to aquatic ecosystem and penetration into water supplies.	Effluent stream (air, water, land) of pollutants unique to the discussed process, damage to terrestrial biomes.	Unquantified impact on refinery and/or petrochemical industry workers in handling materials from new processes with unique characteristics.	Same as occupational when escapes to general environment.		
END USE	Depends on the method, product used and its unique character reflecting its origin, e.g. a fuel oil derived from coal containing a multitude of potential carcinogens and other toxic substances. The determination of these impacts requires the ability to trace the contaminant and its derivatives from origin to end point.					

Table 11

Information and/or Analytical Ability Available for the Determination of Environmental Impact*

| ACTIVITY | ECOLOGICAL | | | | HEALTH | | | | WELFARE | | | |
| | Water | | Terrestrial | | Occupational | | General Public | | Direct | | Indirect | |
	Data Base	Analytical Methods	Data Base	Analytical Methods	Data Base	Analytical Methods	Data Base	Analytical Methods	Data Base	Analytical Methods	Data Base	Analytical Methods
Extraction:												
strip mining	I-B	B	I-B	I-B	I	A	I	I-B	I	I	I	I
underground mining	B	B	B	A	I-B	A	I	I-B	I	I	I	I
waste collection for fuel	A	B	A	B	A	B	B	B	I	I	I	I
Transport (initial)												
rail	A	A	A	A								
truck	A	A	A	A								
slurry pipe	B	B	B	B	I-B	B	I-B	I-B	I	I-B	I	I
Stockpiling of Materials	I	I-B	I	I	I	I	I	I-B	I	I-B	I	I
Final Cleaning & Pretreatment	I	I-B	I	I	I	I-B	I	I-F	I	I	I	I
Coal Liquefaction & Gasification	I	I-B	I	I	I	I-B	I	I-B	I	I	I	I
In situ coal gasification	I	I-B	I	I	I	I-B	I	I-B	I	I	I	I
In situ shale oil & gas	I	I	I	I	I	I-B	I	I-B	I	I	I	I
Underground bed preparation												
(coal & shale)	I	I-B										
Modified In situ shale	I	I-B	I	I	I	B						
Fracturing underground	I	I										
Stimulation of oil & gas field												
Injection												
Solvent	I	I	I	I-B	I	I-B	I	I-B	I	B		
Water	I	B	I	I-B								
Industrial waste	I	I	I	I-B	I	I-B	I	I-B	I	B		
Heat												
Extraction & separation	I	I-B	I	I-B	I	I-B	I	I-B				
Direct combustion of coal			I	I-B	I	I-B	I	I-B				
New stack gas cleaners											I	I
(waste disposal	I	I-B	I	I	I	I-B	I	I-B				
Product Transport & Distribution												
gas & liquid pipeline	I-B	I-B	I-B	I	I	I-B	I	I-B	I	I		
slurry pipe	I-B	I-B	I-B	I	I	I-B	I	I-B	I	I		
truck trailer	I-B	I-B	I-B	I	I	I-B	I	I-B	I	I		
tanker	I-B	I-B			I	I-B	I	I-B	I	I		
Refinery and/or petrochemical	I	I-B	I	I	I	I-B	I	I-B	I	I		
End Use	I	I	I	I	I	I-B	I	I-B	I	I	I	I

Source: Greenfield et al. (1976)

*Refers *not* to the process technology but to the application of analytical techniques sensitive to process residuals that may impact upon health, welfare, or ecological systems.

LEGEND: I - inadequate
B - barely adequate to draw initial conclusions
A - adequate for analytical purposes.

refers to the capability to obtain an adequate data base and perform the needed assessment. This table represents an evaluation of the current ability to provide a visible impact assessment. Admittedly this is a subjective evaluation, but one born from many years' experience in dealing with the total available environmental data base. The evaluation parameters utilized are "I" indicating either a data base that is *inadequate* to permit the assessment, or the lack of the analytical methods needed to utilize this base; "B" represents a *barely adequate* situation with enough capability to make an initial assessment; "A" is the rare situation of *adequate capability.* It is clear that the lowest common denominator determines the adequacy of each element of what we might designate as our "ignorance" matrix.

Even with these caveats, it is interesting to note that our collective experience reveals that the available date base is almost universally inadequate to assess environmental impacts resulting from the use of fossil fuel. This deplorable conclusion is due to the fact that we have spent most of our collective efforts over the past several years in characterizing oil and coals from the standpoint of heat content, flowability, ash content, etc.—i.e., from the standpoint of their fuel characteristics. On the other hand, very little has been accomplished towards characterizing the multitude of compounds contained in the tar, gases, and oils produced from coal and crude as a product, a by-product, or effluent stream. We do not know very much about what happens to these compounds during further refining and end use. What little we do know raises concerns over potential toxic effects of these materials either alone or in combination. Our knowledge about their effects on man or on ecological systems is practically nonexistent. Nor do we have sufficient information to understand how these materials move through the environment and in what form they finally arrive at a target organism. Yet it is precisely this type of information that is required if proper decisions are to be made about the use of these available sources of energy and how they should be constrained to ensure public safety (see Table 12).[5]

This discussion explains the reasons why Table 11 presents such a negative picture of the current state of knowledge. Man's

Table 12

**Anticipated Environmental Concerns
Specific for Coal Liquefaction Plants**

Plant Effluent	Potential Pollutant	Needed Research
Product Oil	Organic Carcinogens	A. Analyze for know carcinogens B. Test oils on animals.
Product Oil	Metal Compounds	A. Analyze for metals. B. Analyze for organo-metallics
Product Oil	Inhalable Vapors	Analyze for health hazards.
Vapor Leak in Slurry Prep. Residue Take-Off	As above	As above
Inorganic Residue Disposal	Leachable Inorganic Compounds	Analyze for soluble metals, sulfur, halides, etc.
Dissolved Gases in Scrub Water	HCN, Se, As, F, etc.	Analyze liquor.

Source: Forney et al. (1974).

information concerning coal and coal products is surprisingly incomplete. It is only in the past few years that interest and analytical methods have been available to produce what little knowledge we have.

THE GLOBAL ENVIRONMENTAL PROBLEM WITH FOSSIL FUELS

Having examined some potential local or regional environmental impacts resulting from the use of fossil energy, we might close with a brief examination of more global aspects of the problem. We shall concentrate here on two issues: the problem of low pH rainfall (acidic precipitation),* and the climatic consequences of increasing the CO_2 content of the atmosphere.

Rainfall Acidity

In the past several years, the monitoring of increased rainfall acidity and its relation to anthropogenic emissions of nitrogen and sulfur oxides has become a topic of considerable interest for potential environmental effects. Knowledge of the problem is limited but maturing, as witnessed by two recent international conferences held in Ohio and Norway (Dockinger and Seliger 1976; Overrein 1976). At present the data base is inadequate to provide the scientific criteria necessary for sound regulatory decisions, and there is much diversity in available expert opinion. Where acidic precipitation occurs, educated estimates of effects range from extensive, irreversible, chronic damage to regional forest and aquatic ecosystems, to negligible and/or reversible acute impacts on an isolated local scale.

Over time, long-term chronic changes in the pH of fresh-water ecosystems can have a considerable impact on the biological communities. A transition to acid-tolerant species (or species adaptation to pH-induced ecosystem changes) occurs, and the damaging effects are generally on the fecundity (impairment to the most sensitive stages in the life cycle) of acid-tolerant organisms. Though marked differences in acid tolerance are evident between species, one notable example of family-specific effects are on the hatching of eggs and larval stages of Salmonidae where survival is impaired below pHs of 4.5-5 (Bua and Snekvik 1972; Krishna 1953). Similarly, the zooplankton, *Daphnia pulex,* has been shown to survive between pHs of 4-10, but reproduction is limited to between 7-8.7 (Davis and Ozburn 1969).

The gradual shift of water pH to acidic conditions (1-2 pH units) is believed to be associated with chronic acid precipitation in the northeast United States and Scandinavia, and has shown similar changes in the trophic levels of some examined lakes of

*I am indebted to my colleague, Dr. Thomas O. Peyton, for the majority of the discussion on the effects of acidic precipitation.

those regions. These trophic changes have been observed as: reduced rates in decomposition, and increase in fungal hyphae for the decomposer community; flora community changes from dominance of macrophytes to filamentous algae and decreased population activity of phytoplankton; diminished specie diversity of benthic invertebrae, such as the loss of snails (less than pH 5.2), decrease in crustacean zooplankton, and impairment of adult insect emergence; and decreases in the fish community or loss of the salmonid populations (Hendrey et al. 1976).

Nutrient and heavy-metal cycling can be altered by aquatic pH changes which can directly affect ecosystem population dynamics. Concern has been expressed for the simultaneous atmospheric input of heavy metals (Peyton et al. 1976; Wright and Gjessing 1976), and the metal's ecological availability and impact as a function of aquatic pH (Peyton 1975). But other than some observations of elevated levels of metals in sediment and the water column, no meaningful conclusions can be drawn about direct damage to the biological communities.

Chronic effects of acid precipitation on forest ecosystems are less defined than those on aquatic systems. Effects analyses have considered the leaching of metallic cations and nutrients from soil (Malmer 1976) which, in some instances, may make them more available. There is, however, no direct proof that rain of the acidity commonly occurring in southern Scandinavia has adversely affected tree growth. Hypothetical exercises on the complex interrelationships of forest ecosystem structures indicate that positive/negative feedback effects can occur from chronic acid rains over long periods of time (Tamm 1976).

Most information on field effects of the acid rain phenomenon (normal pH = 5.6 due to dissolved CO_2) has been acquired in regions where long-range transport and wet-removal of sulfur and nitrogen oxides occur at a significant level. A *multiregional* transport process involves integration of many urban-industrial source plumes transported over many days. Major locations for observed chronic acid precipitation have been detected in the northeastern United States and Scandinavia, as discussed above, and are linked to the long-range transport, multiple source integration, and wet-removal of NO_X and SO_X plumes. In long-range transport, accumulation due to cloud scavenging of NO_X and SO_X, as opposed to direct short-term washout, becomes an important factor (Greenfield 1957).

From available data, there is little doubt that rainfall acidity has increased over the last several decades in several distinct geographic regions. This increase has exposed the ecosystems in those regions to lower pH media. The combustion of fossil fuels increases the atmospheric concentrations of sulfur dioxide, oxides of nitrogen, and CO_2, which are transformed in the atmosphere into sulfates, nitrates, and carbonates. When dissolved in raindrops they will all contribute to a change in pH of the water, depending on the bases available. SO_2 and CO_2 have both natural and anthropogenic origins (primarily fossil fuels). On the other hand, NO, the precursor for nitrate, is predominantly anthropogenic, hence the major sources of nitrates are fossil fuel and fertilizers.

The information currently available does not permit one to determine effective approaches to inhibiting harmful increases in acidic precipitation on a geographic basis. One's natural inclination is to place most of the blame on fossil fuels and to demand a general limitation as an approach to solution. But, as we have seen, this is an irrational and impractical approach; once again man is in the uncomfortable position of not being able to address options and make intelligent decisions. One cannot deny that the use of fossil fuels contributes to acidic precipitation, at least regionally. It is essential that we acquire an understanding that will allow us to use this information intelligently in formulating national energy strategies.

Carbon Dioxide in the Atmosphere

With regard to atmospheric CO_2 and its impact on the global climate, it is extremely difficult even to attempt qualitative description of the appropriate relationships. CO_2 is one of the major radiation-absorbing constituents in the atmosphere. The physical effects of increased concentrations of CO_2 is to decrease the radiative loss to space. Thus, in the absence of counteracting mechanisms, an increase in CO_2 can cause a warming of the global atmosphere. It is estimated that the CO_2 resulting from the combustion of fossil fuels is approximately 10 percent of that produced biologically and emitted from land and ocean surfaces. The increase in anthropogenically produced CO_2 has been exponential since the industrial revolution, reaching almost 5 percent per year during the past thirty years. Examining measurements of CO_2 concentrations in the atmosphere (Erdahl and Keeling 1973) show an increase of 3 percent (313 to 323 ppm) during the period 1959 to 1971. It is generally assumed that this long-term increase represents a global perturbation of the atmospheric CO_2 concentration by man's activities, primarily through increased use of fossil fuels. Our current knowledge does not permit us to fully understand the implications of this change, or to predict the effect of further variations. Machta (1973) estimated that a doubling of the atmospheric CO_2 might produce a rise in the global mean sea-level temperature on the order of 2° C. Our current knowledge of atmospheric dynamics does not permit us to assess the consequence of such a change other than to indicate that it would represent a major disturbance in global heat balance. In terms of projected increases in global CO_2, Kester et al. (Dahlem 1977) have calculated a doubling of current values by approximately the year 2030. In making this calculation, it should be pointed out that one must assume, among other things, that essentially half of the CO_2 emitted into the atmosphere each year through the use of fossil fuels remains (with a half-life of about four to ten years).

At present levels of understanding, we can have little confidence in our ability to calculate changes in atmospheric CO_2 and their consequences. We assume that half the CO_2 emitted by man's activities remains in the atmosphere each year, yet there is reason to believe that a more thorough consideration of biomass changes would significantly alter this value. We calculate global warming, but on the basis of only the assumed change in CO_2 concentration. Yet we know that increases in the particulate loading of the atmosphere could conceivably lower the global temperature. Furthermore, the industrial development which has contributed significantly to the increase in atmospheric CO_2 over the last several decades has also contributed to an observed increase in turbidity (aerosol concentration) during the same period. Finally, at present we do not possess sufficient understanding of atmosphere to permit us to relate a change in mean sea-level temperature to a climatic change.

We are left, then, with the observation that, in his use of fossil energy, man has produced a significant change in at least one part of the global chemical cycle; but we are unable to decide if this change is, or will be, deleterious. There is no question, however, that the change is occurring. It is thus essential that we understand the implications of such changes before they reach a level of potential damage which, in man's lifetime, might be irreversible. In the final analysis, these environmental dangers might be our ultimate limitation on the use of fossil fuel.

V

NORMAN C. RASMUSSEN   DAVID J. ROSE

NUCLEAR POWER: SAFETY AND ENVIRONMENTAL ISSUES

Safety issues: nuclear reactor safety; fuel cycle safety; mining and milling; UF_6 conversion, enrichment, and fuel fabrication; normal reactor operation; fuel reprocessing; radioactive waste; sabotage and diversion. Thermal pollution and the environment. Comparison of nuclear with other energy systems.

INTRODUCTION

The major public policy issues regarding the use of nuclear power for the production of electricity concern either public safety or the environment. Public safety discussions center on reactor safety, radioactive waste disposal, the potential for proliferation of nuclear weapons, and the effectiveness of security against malicious acts such as sabotage. Environmental degradation is also a concern, along with thermal pollution, low-level radioactive release, and the effects of uranium milling and mining. Since these are not all equally important, the following discussion will emphasize the authors' opinions of their relative significance. An exception is the problem of nuclear proliferation, with Albert Carnesale considers at greater length in Chapter II.

This article is divided into three parts. The first section deals with safety, addressing both the power plant itself and other operations in the nuclear fuel cycle. Consideration is then given to environmental issues, and the final pages attempt to place nuclear risks in perspective by making comparisons with other methods of producing electricity. Such comparisons are important, since all energy alternatives available to society entail risk; optimum decisions on future courses of action therefore must be based on a careful balancing of risks against other considerations.

SAFETY ISSUES

Nuclear Reactor Safety

The term "nuclear reactor safety" refers, in this paper, to risks associated with possible accidents in the nuclear power plant. We might begin by reviewing some basic facts which all informed participants in the current debate would accept.

A modern nuclear power plant typically generates electricity at a rate of 1 million kilowatts (kW) (1,000 megawatts). Because the thermodynamic efficiency for conversion of heat to electricity is about 32 percent, the plant generates heat at a rate of about 3.1 million kW. This heat is produced by a chain reaction which causes uranium atoms to fission, a process that produces more than 1 million times more energy per pound of fuel consumed than does the burning of oil. Thus one of the principal advantages of nuclear power is the relatively small quantities of fuel required.

The process also has its disadvantages, since the products of the fission process are a variety of radioactive species. The principal concern in power plant accidents is that system failures may lead to release of a significant fraction of these radioactive fission products. This will happen only if the uranium dioxide fuel (UO_2) melts; if it remains solid, it effectively traps almost all the fission products. The main problem of reactor safety, therefore, is to assure that the probability of fuel melting is acceptably low, since all would agree it cannot be made zero.

Contrary to what some believe, the primary concern is not that the chain reaction will get out of control and cause the reactor to explode like a bomb. Such an event is impossible with the low enrichment fuel used in today's water reactors. In fact, today's reactors are designed so that inherently they tend to shut themselves down when the chain reaction runs at too fast a rate.

The principal problem is removing the heat generated by radioactive fission products, even after the chain reaction stops. Though the rate of heat generation declines with time after shutdown, without cooling it is sufficient to melt the fuel for many weeks after shutdown. The quantity of heat can readily been seen from Figure 1, which gives this heat decline in relation to time following shutdown. Thus a major problem of reactor safety is to provide a highly reliable cooling system which will remove decay heat under both normal conditions and a variety of abnormal conditions resulting from failures in the plant.

The Reactor Safety Controversy

Most of the current controversy about reactor safety centers on establishing an acceptable level of risk, and on whether current design and operating practices actually achieve the low risk claimed. Both are difficult questions. Defining an acceptable risk, or how safe is safe enough, are perennial queries with which society has struggled. Where acceptable risk levels have been defined, generally they have been so on the basis that the risk in question is significantly less than other similar risks currently being accepted. Despite numerous attempts, there is no widely accepted quantitative definition of an acceptable risk level for nuclear power plants. The Nuclear Regulatory Commission approves applications for licensees when their detailed investigation finds that the plant presents "no undue risk to the public health and safety." Not surprisingly, utility applicants, federal regulators, and private groups and individuals concerned with

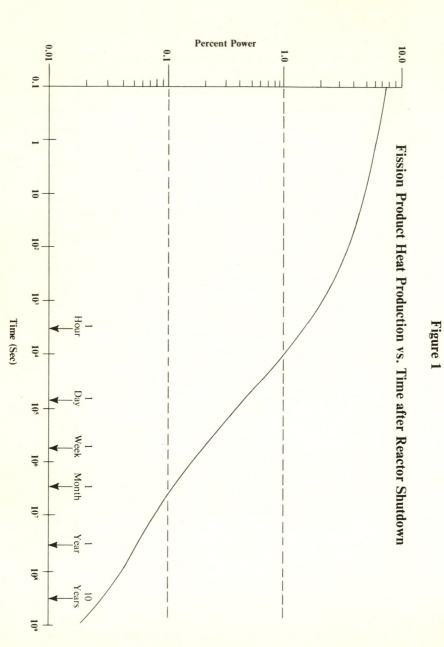

Figure 1

Fission Product Heat Production vs. Time after Reactor Shutdown

Source: AEC (1975: App. IX, 13)

nuclear power tend to have quite different interpretations of what "no undue risk" should mean.

Several approaches deal with the question of what safety level is being achieved in today's plants. The most obvious is to estimate it from the experience to date with power reactors. Since no power plant reactors have had their core melt or even seriously overheat, this approach can only provide an upper bound. If we consider water reactors of the type being built and operated today in the United States and a number of foreign countries, the total operating experience has been about three hundred plant years. This would indicate that the probability of melting the fuel is probably less than 1 in 200 (5×10^{-3}) per reactor year. The design intent, i.e., that the number should be very much smaller than this, cannot be verified from such limited experience.

In 1972 the Atomic Energy Commission undertook the Reactor Safety Study under the direction of one of the authors (NCR). The goal of the study was to quantify the risks from reactor accidents using recently developed reliability analysis methods. The study involved some seventy-five scientists and engineers and was completed in draft form in 1974. The final report (AEC 1975) included many corrections and changes in the draft report as a result of extensive comments received from all sides of the controversy. Based on a detailed system-by-system analysis of a typical boiling water reactor (BWR) and a typical pressurized water reactor (PWR), the study concluded that the probability of core melting in these reactors was 1 in 20,000 (5×10^{-5}) per reactor year. An uncertainty of plus or minus a factor of 5 was assigned to this probability. This value is a factor of 100 smaller than the upper bound estimate based upon experience noted earlier.

To determine the consequences of these core melt accidents, a considerable amount of the study effort was devoted to developing a calculational model. Six specific consequences were calculated: three short-term effects: (1) early fatalities, (2) early injuries, (3) property damage; and three latent health effects: (1) (1) cancer fatalities, (2) thyroid illness, and (3) genetic effects. The model gave the probability vs. magnitude of the various consequences. The curve for early fatalities is shown in Figure 2. The

Figure 2

Probability Magnitude of Early Fatalities for 100 Reactors, Compared to Other Man-Made Causes

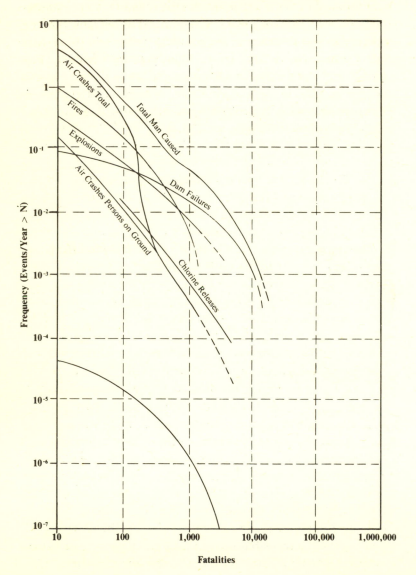

Source: AEC (1975:119)

early fatalities refer to persons who would receive radiation dose levels large enough that they would be expected to die within a relatively short time. For comparison, similar curves for early fatalities for some other risks are also presented. Similar curves were produced for the latent health effects and they are summarized in tabular form in Table 1. The numbers in the tables are the expected annual increases of these health effects for a thirty-year period from ten to forty years following the accident. For comparison, the normal incidence rate of these diseases in the exposed population is also given. Thyroid illness refers to growths on the thyroid gland which require medical treatment but from which the patient can expect to recover.

Table 1
Probability versus Magnitude of Latent Health Effects for Reactor Accidents

	Consequences		
Chance per Year	Latent Cancer Fatalities[b] (per year)	Thyroid Nodules[b] (per year)	Genetic Effects[c] (per year)
One in 20,000[a]	1.0	1.0	1.0
One in 1,000,000	170	1400	25
One in 10,000,000	460	3500	50
One in 100,000,000	860	5000	100
One in 1,000,000,000	1500	8000	170
Normal incidence	17000	8000	8000

Source: AEC (1975)

(a) This is the predicted chance per reactor year.

(b) This rate will occure approximately in the 10 to 40 year period following a potential accident.

(c) This rate would apply to the first generation born after the accident ($\approx$10 years). Subsequent generations would experience effects at a lower rate.

By appropriate mathematical procedures, these curves can be integrated to obtain the average annual rate of these effects for a nuclear industry of 100 reactors (the number expected in the U.S. by the early 1980s). These results are given in Table 2. The societal risk is the average annual rate in the entire U.S. population. For comparison, the normal occurrence rate of these health effects is also given. The uncertainties on all the numbers given are about ± 5 on probability and about ± 3 on consequence magnitude.

Table 2

Comparison of Average Annual Societal Risk from 100 Nuclear Plants to Casualty Rates from All Causes in the United States

	Nuclear*	All Causes
Early Fatalities	3×10^{-3}	110,000
Early Illness	2×10^{-1}	
Latent Cancers	2	365,000
Thyroid Nodules	20	160,000
Genetic Effects	2	160,000
Property Damage		$ 50-100 \times 10^{9}$

Source: AEC (1975)

*To obtain risk per gigawatt-year, divide these numbers by 100.

This study provides several important insights that are sometimes forgotten in the nuclear debate. The first is that nuclear accidents, as all other accidents, can be expected to have a wide range of consequences. In addition, as would be expected, small accidents are much more likely than large ones. There is a tendency in discussion on nuclear safety to talk about the worst possible accident, forgetting about its low probability of occurrence, and further to assume that all nuclear accidents would be of this type. Curves generated by this study show that this is not correct. For example, the melting of the reactor core is the ultimate plant failure, and many believe any such event would be a disastrous accident; however, only one in one hundred of such events would be expected to produce one or more early fatalities. This conclusion depends only on the relative probabilities calculated in the Reactor Safety Study, not the absolute probabilities. Thus, even if the absolute probabilities should turn out to be wrong, the chance of seeing a large accident before seeing small ones is very small. As noted earlier, to date no power reactor has had a core melting accident.

There have been many comments on the Reactor Safety Study ranging from highly complimentary to highly critical. However, as was pointed out in the recent Ford Foundation study (1977), even if one assumes a very conservative upper bound for reactor accident probabilities based upon experience, the risks seem relatively small when compared to other activities in which society engages. For example, that report states: "we have concluded that, even when the possibility of reactor accidents is included, the adverse health effects of nuclear power are less than or within the range of health effects from coal." Even though the nuclear accident risks seem quite low, this low risk has been achieved by careful attention to safety issues. In view of the fact that nuclear accidents can be potentially large, and since we expect the number of reactors to increase, it seems reasonable to continue a strong and aggressive program in nuclear reactor safety. We agree with the above-cited report that reactor safety issues do not seem to present a large enough risk to warrant any drastic action such as a moratorium on nuclear plants proposed by some.

Fuel Cycle Safety

As with reactors, the nuclear fuel supply has both occupational and public risks; but here consensus consigns the heavier burden to the workers.

The fuel cycle has a rich spectrum of activities. Uranium ore is mined but, being typically sandstone containing 0.2 percent uranium, it must be milled to separate the useful bit. Then the

uranium "yellow cake" (U_3O_8) is converted to uranium hexa-
fluoride, so that its 0.711 percent uranium-235 content can be
enriched in gaseous diffusion plants (and soon in ultracentrifuges
and maybe even by lasers) to about 3 percent, suitable for use in
present pressurized water or boiling water reactors. The enriched
uranium is then converted to uranium dioxide (UO_2), fired into
ceramic pellets, and loaded into zirconium alloy fuel tubes about
1.2 cm diameter by 3.4 hm long. As many as 40,000 of these
"pins," arranged in bundles, fuel the reactor; about one-third of
them are removed from the middle of the reactor core each year.
At present, the U.S. does not reprocess the spent fuel, but rather
stores it in water pools. The process is well known and has been
carried out here and abroad. Finally (it is planned) the radioactive
wastes will be stored away, probably by interment in geologic
formations.

All these things must be done with acceptable safety. Tables 3
and 4 give very recent estimates of these risks, expressed as
fatalities per GWe-year (NAS 1977). (GWe = 1 million kW.)

Mining and Milling

These two activities are best discussed together. All mining is
hazardous. Both tables show that the risks associated with uranium mining dominate all others (with some caveats and possible
exceptions to be noted below). Even the radiation risk (from
radon, produced by decay of the small amount of radium that in
turn comes from thorium-230 in the ore) exceeds all other occupational radiation risks connected with nuclear power, and the
public risk from radon also dominates Table 4.

In regard to milling, the occupational risk again arises from
radon released as the ore is crushed, but the work environment is
better. The public risk has been a matter of some debate. The
table shows 0.059 deaths/GWe-year for no fuel recycle, but that
assumes timely burial of the mine tailings. They still contain
thorium-230, which has an 80,000 year half-life, so radon production continues. The total (say, 100 Ci/GWe-year for a lightly covered tailings pile) augments the natural background radon level

Table 3

Estimated Impact of 1 GWe year from Nuclear Fuel Cycle upon Fuel Cycle Employees

Fuel Cycle Operation	Fatalities to Employees (number/GWe year)								
	No Recycle			Uranium Recycle			U and Pu Recycle		
	From Radiation	From Accidents	Total	From Radiation	From Accidents	Total	From Radiation	From Accidents	Total
Mining	0.082	0.378	0.46	0.073	0.336	0.41	0.065	0.30	0.37
Milling	0.029	0.014	0.043	0.025	0.012	0.037	0.023	0.011	0.034
UF_6 Conversion	8.1×10^{-3}	3×10^{-4}	1.1×10^{-3}	8.1×10^{-4}	3×10^{-4}	1.1×10^{-3}	7×10^{-4}	2.6×10^{-4}	9.6×10^{-4}
UF_6 Enrichment	1.1×10^{-4}	2.2×10^{-3}	3.3×10^{-3}	1.1×10^{-3}	2.2×10^{-3}	3.3×10^{-3}	9.6×10^{-4}	1.9×10^{-3}	2.9×10^{-3}
Fuel Frabrication	0.021	8×10^{-4}	0.022	0.021	8×10^{-4}	0.022	0.020	8×10^{-4}	0.021
Fuel Reprocessing	—	—	—	0.004	2×10^{-4}	0.0042	0.005	2×10^{-4}	0.005
Transportation	1×10^{-4}	0.02	0.02	1×10^{-4}	0.04	0.04	3×10^{-4}	0.04	0.04
Fuel Storage	0.003	1×10^{-4}	0.0031	3×10^{-4}	1×10^{-4}	4×10^{-4}	3×10^{-4}	1×10^{-4}	4×10^{-4}
Total	0.14	0.42	0.56	0.13	0.40	0.53	0.12	0.36	0.49

Source: NAS

Table 4

Impact on U.S. Population from Normal Emissions (per GWe year) from Nuclear Fuel Cycle Facilities[a]

Fuel Cycle Step	Radiation Induced Fatalities (Number/GWe year)		
	No Recycle	Uranium Recycle	U and Pu Recycle
Mining	0.29	0.26	0.23
Milling[b]	0.059	0.053	0.046
UF_6 Conversion	0.0023	0.0023	0.0020
UF_6 Enrichment	2×10^{-5}	1×10^{-4}	9×10^{-5}
Fuel Fabrication	2.4×10^{-4}	2.5×10^{-4}	2.7×10^{-4}
Fuel Reprocessing		(See text)	
Transportation	3.5×10^{-5}	3.7×10^{-5}	5.2×10^{-5}
Waste Management		(See text)	

Source: NAS 19

[a] Does not include continuing impact of long-lived nuclides distributed in the environment.

[b] Does not include continuing release of ^{222}Rn from tailings pile left after mill operation ceases.

only slightly, and it in turn contributes little to the total public dose of natural radiation. However, if the cancer and genetic incidence is proportional to radiation level down to these background levels (a conservative and conventional assumption), the total deaths from one GWe-year would be several hundred (spread over 100,000 years). The annual incidence is small but, like many environmental effects, adverse effects tend to build up bit by bit (from many operations, not just nuclear). It seems better to bury or cover the wastes adequately—the cost is small. Then the risk drops to a negligible level.

Note that the uranium and plutonium recycle in reactors reduces the risks because less ore is mined. A breeder reactor needs only about one-hundredth as much uranium mined per unit of energy output, so these fuel cycle risks would virtually disappear.

UF$_6$ Conversion, Enrichment, and Fuel Fabrication

The risks from these operations are very small, except to fuel fabrication workers who inhale insoluble radioactive dusts. Their general work environment could be further improved to reduce this hazard to low levels also.

Normal Reactor Operation

There are some releases of radioactivity during normal reactor operation. These releases are now required to be "as low as practicable," which, with modern technology, has been interpreted to mean that the maximum dose permitted at the boundary of the power plant site may not exceed 5 mrem/year (mrem = millirem, the measure of radiation dose to human beings). To put this number in perspective, the average dose to U.S. citizens from natural sources (terrestrial radioactivity, cosmic rays, etc.) is about 100 mrem/year. Medical X-ray doses add about another 50 mrem.

The actual operating records show that most power reactors, in fact, are able to achieve release levels well below the 5 mrem limit. The program of reducing release levels has been so successful that it is no longer a major issue.

Fuel Reprocessing

Most of the actuarial fatalities are expected to come from release of krypton (^{85}Kr), tritium (^{3}H), and radiocarbon (^{14}C), with small additions from radio-iodines and other elements. The first three tend to come off as gases when the fuel is chopped up and dissolved; present plans have them vented to the atmosphere after holdup to allow the most active ones to decay (e.g., iodine-131). Estimates based on operation of U.S. weapons production facilities (which are different from commercial plants) and experience abroad put the occupational hazard very low. The gaseous effluents are dispersed over much of the earth, and estimated fatalities are 0.2-0.3/GWe-year from the small rise in background radiation. It seems likely to us that, in the future, krypton, tritium, and radiocarbon will be required to be caught and sequestered.

Following are other risks that are probably small, but not yet quantified: (1) If plutonium is recycled, then other elements formed from it (neptunium-237, americium-241, curium, etc.) also build up in the fuel fabrication stage as the plutonium, etc., cycles round and round. (2) Also regarding recycle of high burn-up fuel, some small portions of the oxide fuel become extremely resistant to dissolving in the (usual) nitric acid; these materials then either contaminate the supposedly cleaned-out fuel pin hulls, or require dissolving by fluorides, which complicates the whole chemical process. (3) If thorium cycles are adopted, as some have proposed, several changes must be considered. First, the so-called Thorex process separates thorium and uranium-233 (which is the fissionable isotope that was bred) much less completely from the fission product wastes than the well-known Purex process separates uranium and plutonium from the wastes. Thus, a thorium cycle reprocessing plant will be bigger and more complicated. Second, the heavy-element wastes are different. Neptunium, plutonium, americium, etc., are almost totally absent (provided the fuel was not "diluted" with natural uranium-238 to foil putative weapon-makers), but new troublesome and toxic species appear, for example thorium-228.

Radioactive Waste

This is probably the most disputed technical issue involving the fuel cycle. Can the wastes be disposed of safely?

Most generally, the waste consists of three main kinds: (1) high-level waste from the fuel, containing fission products plus heavy radioactive elements formed from uranium (neptunium, plutonium, americium, curium); (2) wastes contaminated with low levels of these heavy elements, mainly plutonium arising from fuel reprocessing and fabrication (the so-called TRU wastes); and (3) general low-level wastes, such as protective clothing, wash water, etc. The last category contains relatively little total radioactive material, despite its bulk. Therefore, we concentrate on the other two.

Figure 3, taken from Dance (1975), shows the relative risk of wastes from a light water reactor. The risk index is the volume of water required to dilute the waste to specific radiation concentration guidelines ("RCG") appropriate to general release. A 1 GWe reactor produces about 2 m³/year of waste in the highly insoluble glassified form envisaged here by Dance and others. Thus at the start, 1 GWe-year of wastes would require about 10¹³ m³ (10,000 cubic kilometers) of water to dilute it to innocuous levels. Hence the need for safe storage.

The hazards arise principally from fission products and plutonium. Thus curve A with 99.5 percent of uranium removed (i.e. nearly all the original fuel material) closely represents the case of unreprocessed fuel. Successive removal of plutonium (B), most of the other heavy elements (C), and finally the longest-lived fission products (D), show how in principle the wastes could be made less noxious after long times. The fission products alone resemble curve C, and the heavy elements contribute about 0.1 percent of the risk initially. They become relatively important later because of their long half-lives, when the fission products decay away.

Nothing can be done to decrease the hazard index until a few hundred years have passed, at which time the main culprits, strontium-90 and cesium-137, with half-lives of about thirty years, have decayed (to about one-millionth of this original activity at 600 years). It has been proposed to separate the wastes during reprocessing well enough to approach curve C, then recycle the heavy elements through the reactor where they eventually fission into short-lived fission products. However, this extra separation complicates the fuel cycle and might create enough radioactive side-streams to vitiate the benefit. Thus present ideas about fuel reprocessing aim toward curve B, where about 0.5 percent of the Pu and the other heavy elements pass into the high-level waste.

Comparing the total toxicity of the waste to the toxicity of the ore from which it came is instructive. The 2 m³ of waste come from about 3000 m³ of 0.2 percent ore, a volume 1,500 times larger. Thus comparing curve B with the "ore" curve, we see that the total risks are equal after about 10,000 years, and thereafter the wastes are in principle less toxic than the original ore. This point has been made by Cohen (1976), and serves only as a crude guide, because all differences in where the ore and the waste are

Figure 3

Relative Risk from Nuclear Wastes*

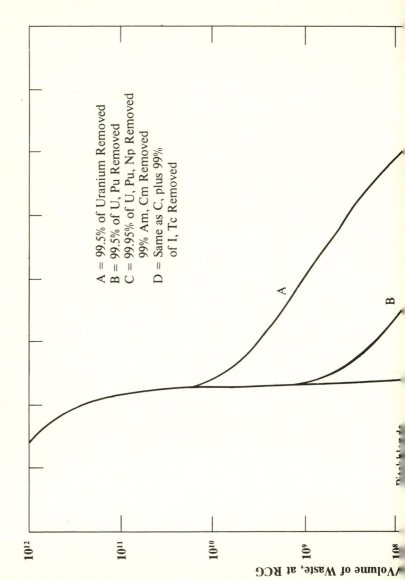

A = 99.5% of Uranium Removed
B = 99.5% of U, Pu Removed
C = 99.95% of U, Pu, Np Removed
    99% Am, Cm Removed
D = Same as C, plus 99%
    of I, Tc Removed

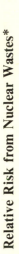

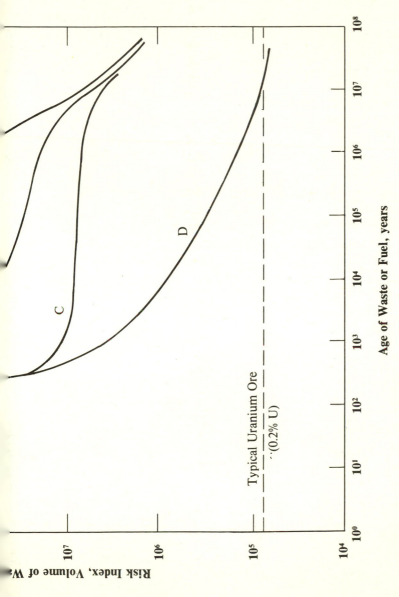

Age of Waste or Fuel, years

Risk Index, Volume of Wa

Typical Uranium Ore
(0.2% U)

[SEE V-19A for note and source]

located geographically, and what may happen to them as a result, have been ignored.

We see that the problem reduces to one of arranging very sure storage for the first several hundred years, and relatively safe storage until some 10,000-100,000 years have passed, depending on the nature of the waste and social decisions about it. These requirements can be met by storing wastes in many thick salt deposits, granite structures, or perhaps under some of the oceanic tectonic plates. For example, consider the disposal in thick salt beds, chosen for having been stable for 100 million years. Several hundred feet below the surface, the wastes will remain secure for many centuries. After that, in the unlikely event that water penetrates, the volume needed to dissolve the salt exceeds the required dilution of the wastes.

We thus arrive at a peculiar position: nearly all serious students of the problem, be they pro- or anti-nuclear, agree that the waste disposal problem is technologically tractable, even without fuel processing; but the public opposition remains severe.

Three explanations come to mind. First, the public identifies the commercial wastes with the radioactive wastes from weapons production decades ago. That chemically different debris was stored in carbon steel tanks, and has precipitated a sludge into the tank bottoms which cannot now be removed except at great expense; meanwhile, the tanks slowly corrode. The problem is peculiar to those weapons wastes residing at Richland, Washington, and Savannah River, South Carolina—as well as at the Nuclear Fuel Services, West Valley, New York, plant which unfortunately adopted the same liquid storage scheme. The second explanation is that the Atomic Energy Commission since 1974, and its successor the Energy Research and Development Administration, let the problem go too long and worked on it lackadaisically. Thus one can ask "Will they really do it?" Third, the level of toxicity comes as a shock to the public—which, however, does not realize that other materials with greater toxic potential move about the nation's travel routes every day.

Sabotage and Diversion

We have left the international weapons proliferation problem to Dr. Carnesale, and here consider only efforts by sub-national groups. Even though both activities might aim toward the same thing, the nature of the risks and the protection against them are very different. For proliferation, the national government aids the effort, and for sabotage, etc., the government opposes it.

Some terrorist activities pose only imaginary threats. For example, consider buried nuclear waste. What would the terrorists do after drilling 200 meters into the earth, in plain sight of all, to reach a radioactive slug that can only be approached remotely or moved in a heavy shielded cask? Used fuel is also self-protecting and must be carried in similar casks. Contrary to some impressions, it is very hard to disperse.

Nevertheless, several real problems exist. If time permits, terrorists can cause a reactor accident comparable to the most severe ones listed under reactor safety; whether they could rig all the circumstances of loss of secondary containment, weather inversion, and wind direction necessary to accomplish the maximum public event is doubtful. Yet the probability exists, especially of lesser events; hence the increase in security during the past several years.

The question arises whether this increased security leads to a *de facto* police state. It is easy to show that the total number of guards needed in a developed nuclear economy to foil anything short of a military assault is small compared to (say) the present number of bank guards in the U.S., and no one thinks of them as bringing about a police state. Still, the worry persists, and for this social concern we must seek a social answer. We suggest the following.

Civilization and elements in it may be described as ranging from totally permissive at one end, to totally authoritarian at the other, as in Figure 4. All societies permit elements within them that cover a considerable range along the scale. We might imagine the U.S. to occupy the range shown, averaging a little to the left of center.

Now, what about a person or group that uses the permissivity the commit acts that could only be prevented by strongly authori-

Figure 4

Conceptual Social Range from Totally Permissive
to Totally Authoritarian Regimes*

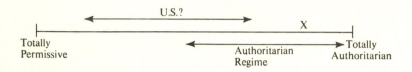

*For discussion, see text.

ι..tive methods? That is, can the U.S. society stretch far enough to the right, to point X let us say, where terrorists will know that punishment is swift, sure, and painful, without moving its center of gravity? The debate has little to do with numbers, but elasticity of view and ethical basis inherent in the society itself. In passing, we note that authoritarian regimes have no troubles of this sort. If the bank guard lets the robber escape, our present society figures to catch him later, or perhaps write off the loss. But that cannot be done with extreme nuclear terrorists. This same dilemma appears in other terrorist activities—airplane hijackers, Olympic Games assassins, etc. We do not know the final answer, which only time will tell, and meanwhile we support the increased security measures because their presence helps prevent the test.

Diversion of material usable for making nuclear weapons by sub-national groups is possible only at certain stages in the nuclear fuel cycle. If there is no fuel reprocessing, a potential diverter must build a modest fuel reprocessing facility, then steal spent fuel, all of which surely could not escape notice.

Every fuel cycle that involves reprocessing the fuel has some vulnerability. If fuel were to be reprocessed for its plutonium (for recycle as mixed uranium-plutonium oxides), the chemical separation stage of plutonium and uranium is the most sensitive point.

This loophole can be partly closed by co-precipitating plutonium and uranium together in ratios to permit use in power reactors but to be useless for bombs. However, the process could be undone chemically; thus some diversion hazard persists.

Some fuel reprocessing cycles are more self-protecting. The thorium-232/uranium-233 (U-233) fuel cycle is not diversion-proof because weapons-grade U-233 can be obtained by chemical separation. Adding U-238 to isotopically dilute the U-233 will positively end that route to weapons material, but now the combined fuel produces plutonium. To be sure, only about 15 percent as much plutonium is produced this way as in the common U-235/U-238 cycle used today; but even so, there is plenty for bombs.

The best security comes by co-locating the fuel reprocessing and fuel fabrication operations. Only one such facility needs protection for each fifty nuclear reactors (more or less) and transshipment of weapons-usable material in any readily usable form is eliminated. Irradiation of new fuel before shipment would make it almost as self-protecting during shipment as spent fuel, and facilities at reactors could be built to receive it in this condition. We think that these arrangements, plus shipment in vehicles with special communications and some internal self-protecting mechanisms, will be sufficient. In particular, we consider little is to be gained and much lost by locating many reactors in nuclear parks. Local thermal pollution becomes serious, social benefits obtainable from the waste heat disappear, transmission path becomes longer, and the whole assembly becomes a delicious military target.

THERMAL POLLUTION AND THE ENVIRONMENT

A 1 GWe nuclear plant operating at its usual overall thermal efficiency of 32 percent produces 2.1 GW of waste heat, almost all of which appears in the water that cools the condensers at the end of the steam cycle. By comparison, a new 1 GWe coal-burning plant with overall thermal efficiency of 37 percent (it was 39-40 percent before stack gas scrubbers and reheat) produces about 1.4 GW of waste heat at the condenser coolers, and 0.3 GW up to the stack to the atmosphere directly. All this excess heat eventually ends up in the atmosphere, to be radiated away from the Earth. But in terms of warm waste water, the nuclear plant produces 50 percent more than a fossil fuel plant. Also, roughly speaking, the 1 GWe plant produces not only enough electricity for a city of 600,000 (using average capacity factors) but enough waste heat to warm its buildings in winter. Scandinavian countries and the USSR use waste heat this way. The U.S. currently does almost nothing in this area, yet this use offers an attractive opportunity for conserving resources.

Over how large an area does the sun deposit 2 GW of energy, considering day, night, seasons and the Earth's reflectivity? It is about twelve square kilometers, at average U.S. latitude. Thus, the thermal load is locally substantial, but globally very small (area = 500 million km^2). A large nuclear park with thirty power plants would augment the natural insolation by 10 percent over an area of 3,600 km^2; the change would be noticeable.

The main problem with nuclear waste heat is disposing of it properly, especially inland and in dry areas. Wet cooling towers need only about 5 percent as much water input as does a once-through system, but they evaporate it all. In addition, natural draft towers are 100 meters or more high, and some consider them less elegant than other large artificial objects, such as urban buildings or La Tour Eiffel. Despite their size, they add less than 5 percent to the total plant cost.

Burning fossil fuels adds another truly global thermal load not much noted until very recently. About half the carbon dioxide is absorbed quickly into the biosphere and top ocean layers; but the other half depends on transport to the deep ocean, which takes about 1,000 years. Meanwhile, this CO_2 traps infrared radiation (i.e., heat) as does a greenhouse; and so the sun itself in effect amplifies the heat from fossil fuel combustion by a factor of 50 to 100. Climatologists calculate the largest temperature increases at high latitudes, which would substantially change the polar ice caps and the ocean level, and affect agriculturally productive zones.

COMPARISON OF NUCLEAR WITH OTHER ENERGY SYSTEMS

Our problem is not the comparison, but the restraints of brevity. Relative thermal effects have already been mentioned. In this respect, properly arranged solar power would be superior to any other system. Beyond this, we consider these features worth attention, especially since the main choice is between nuclear power and coal.

1. Energy conservation far beyond what has been implemented or yet seriously discussed would be better and cheaper than more energy, either by coal or nuclear power. But the coming shortage of oil and gas will force us to conservation, and to coal and/or nuclear power besides. Thus the comparison remains important.

2. Derivative or related materials can be used to make nuclear weapons. Some perceive the connection to be close, in that an established nuclear power industry makes it easier, therefore more likely, to slide into the weapons business. Others see the connection as frail, because easier ways exist for nations bent on making weapons to do so; and besides, lack of energy can itself lead to international destabilization. Dr. Carnesale discusses these matters further.

3. The technology is more demanding, in the sense that the necessarily high standards make maintenance and repairs more exacting and expensive. Thus arises the need for a higher quality engineering staff that has hitherto been the norm in electric utilities.

4. In the long term, burning much of the Earth's fossil fuels in the next few generations will probably cause more harm. When the fuels are gone, any civilization so dependent on them will suffer agonies of withdrawal, and the climatological effects of CO_2 will remind it of its past profligacy for a long time.

5. The general health and environmental impacts of a normally functioning nuclear system are much more benign than those of coal, and that is probably true even for a "clean-coal" economy. Every substantial analysis shows this (Hamilton 1974; Rose et al. 1976; Lave and Siskin 1977). The admittedly poor data indicate that the risk, again measured in fatalities/GWe-year, from burning coal without emission control probably lies in the range of 20-200; that is a high price to pay. If the data could be trusted, removing the sulfur and particulate emissions to 1975 standards would lower the mortality rate by a factor of about five, but we have little idea about the effects of nitrogen oxides, trace metals not scrubbed out, etc. The EPA "CHESS" data on these health and environmental effects (summarized in NAS 1975) have been attacked as inadequate, a valid complaint but also a condemnation of our selective unconcern. Repair will be hard; even if underground coal gasification produced a billion tons of burnable product, it might leave behind a million tons of carcinogens to leach out later.

This unflattering view of coal should not be read as any cause for complacency about nuclear power; rather, it points out that we know a great deal more about the effects of ionizing radiation and what goes on in the interior of a nuclear fuel pellet than we do about the effects of chemical effluents in our environment and what goes on during oxidation of a piece of coal.

VI

ROBERT S. PINDYCK

PRICES AND SHORTAGES: EVALUATING POLICY OPTIONS FOR THE NATURAL GAS INDUSTRY *

FPC regulation and natural gas shortages. Projecting prices and shortages under FPC regulation, the Carter plan, and phased deregulation—1977-1985. Calculating the costs of shortages: lost consumer surpluses, lost GNP, and induced expenditures for oil and coal.

prices and shortages: policy options for the natural gas industry*

Natural gas is an important and growing source of energy in the United States. Beginning in 1971, demand for natural gas began to exceed its supply, and since that time natural gas shortages have been steadily growing. In the severe winter of 1976-1977 the shortage reached 23 percent of "firm" requirements, and apart

*The author would like to thank Joseph Langsam, Kevin Lloyd, and Roy Henrickson for their excellent research assistance.

from the direct cost, this resulted in additional unemployment of about one million people during January and more than $4 billion of lost GNP.

The direct cause of the shortage has been a long history of price regulation by the Federal Power Commission (FPC). If present policy is continued, shortages can only grow worse as demand continues to increase and supplies to dwindle. The costs of the policy—in lost consumer surplus, induced expenditures on oil and coal, and lost GNP—are enormous, and they are growing. To mitigate the problem, President Carter has proposed in his National Energy Plan to increase new contract wellhead prices of "new" gas and tax industrial consumers of gas. We find that the Carter proposals will help to reduce projected shortages, but they will not eliminate them; significant shortages will continue in comparison with a program of phased price deregulation. Although the Carter plan is clearly preferable to present policy, over the next nine years (1977-1985), conservatively estimated, the net cost of the Carter plan will still equal $25 billion in relation to phased deregulation. If present policies continue, the net cost will rise to a staggering $126 billion.

These conclusions are based on a detailed econometric model of the natural gas industry developed and used at MIT to project the effects through 1985 of three alternative natural gas policies: a continuation of current FPC national area rates, President Carter's proposed plan, and a plan of phased deregulation in which new contract prices would be raised in steps toward their free market level. The results suggest the urgency of fundamental reform of natural gas pricing policies.

INTRODUCTION

Natural gas has become an increasingly important source of energy in the United States over the last thirty years. Between 1945 and 1970 natural gas production and consumption increased by 450 percent, from 4 trillion cubic feet (Tcf) per year to 22 Tcf per year, and as a share of total energy consumption, natural gas rose from 12 percent to about 33 percent. Natural gas became the major fuel for home heating; for the U.S. as a whole, it now accounts for over 40 percent of residential energy consumption, and in some regions of the country the fraction is much greater. Because gas prices have been maintained at low levels, this fuel has increasingly become the choice of electric utilities and large industrial consumers. This, of course, is not surprising; gas has been clean, convenient, and most of all, cheap.

Between 1970 and the present, the demand for natural gas has continued to grow at an average annual rate of 5.3 percent. Production, however, ceased growing in 1970, and began declining in 1972. The result has been a growing shortage which began in 1971 when some industrial consumers found their non-interruptable ("firm") contracts being interrupted.[1] By 1973 it was no longer possible to have gas lines installed in new homes built in many regions of the country, and a larger number of industrial consumers found their supplies curtailed. The Federal Power Commission and the Federal Energy Administration (FEA) predicted serious shortages for the winter of 1975-1976, and the Congress considered proposals for allocating natural gas in case these shortages occurred. That winter was mild, so the actual shortage was only about 2.5 Tcf (10 percent of total demand), but the following winter was severe, and large shortages materialized. By the FPC's own reckoning, curtailments nationwide were 23 percent of "firm" requirements, and the shortage was particularly severe in several states. Aside from the direct cost of unfulfilled demand, the shortage resulted in additional unemployment of about one million people during the month of January, and over $4 billion of lost GNP.

The direct cause of this shortage has been price regulation by the Federal Power Commission. By maintaining an artificially low price, the FPC made natural gas the choice fuel (for those consumers who could obtain it), so that demand grew rapidly. At the same time, low prices depressed supplies. This occurred for two reasons. First, the incentive was removed for the exploration and discovery of new natural gas reserves, and as a result total U.S. reserves of gas fell by about a third between 1967 and 1976. This dwindling reserve base made it impossible for producers to satisfy the demand for new long-term contracts. Second, low prices removed the incentive to produce gas out of existing higher cost reserves, so that production fell even with respect to a particular level of reserves. This situation of rapid growth in demand combined with dwindling supplies can only grow worse if recent policies of price regulation are continued.

How did we manage to institute this system of price controls, given that it has resulted in shortages? The FPC was originally authorized by the Natural Gas Act of 1938 to regulate the transport charges of the interstate pipeline companies (which do have considerable monopoly power in several regional consumption markets). But the scope of the act was unclear, and as prices paid by gas consumers began increasing, pressure was brought on the FPC to extend controls to wellhead prices. The FPC refused to extend its jurisdiction until 1954, when the Supreme Court, in the Phillips Decision, ordered it to regulate the prices of gas sold to the interstate pipelines.[2]

The FPC first attempted to regulate wellhead prices following the practices of state public utility commissions, i.e., by choosing an allowed rate of return on capital, and then determining the price that would equate revenues with the sum of operating costs, depreciation, and the allowed rate of return applied to undepreciated capital. However, this approach resulted in wellhead prices nearly doubling between 1954 and 1959, and in the FPC becoming bogged down in a backlog of cases. As a result, the FPC turned to areawide price ceilings that were based on regional average accounting costs. The result was that wellhead prices were essentially frozen after 1960, since these price ceilings forced producers to limit exploratory effort to low cost drilling projects—which in turn maintained low price ceilings (MacAvoy and Pindyck 1975a: 14-16). The average new contract price was 18.2 cents per thousand cubic feet (mcf) in 1961, and only rose to 19.8 cents per mcf in 1969; and the average wholesale price paid by utilities only rose from 32 cents per mcf to about 33.2 cents. On the other hand, wholesale oil and coal prices increased 15 percent and 22 percent respectively during this period.

After shortages began occurring in 1971, the FPC ended its price freeze, and in a series of rate decisions allowed new contract prices to rise.[3] By 1972 average new contract prices had increased to 33.6 cents per mcf, although with considerable regional variation. In July 1975 the FPC announced a uniform "national area rate" of 42 cents per mcf; this rate was raised by the FPC to 51 cents in November 1975, and cost-justified price increases were to be allowed in future years. In fact new contract prices averaged about 55 cents in 1974 and 60 cents in 1975, because of allowances by the FPC. While these prices are about three times those prevailing in 1969, they are still grossly below the true value of natural gas. In terms of barrels of oil-equivalent, the world price of energy in 1975 was about $12 per barrel, but 60 cent gas is equivalent (in thermal content) to oil at $3.50 per barrel. Thus the price increases that occurred up to and including 1975 were not sufficient to bring the price of natural gas anywhere near its free market level.

In order to avert extreme shortages, the wellhead price of gas had to be increased significantly. Congress failed to pass legislation to deregulate natural gas prices, but instead considered various emergency allocation schemes to deal with the shortages that they recognized were inevitable.[4] Fortunately the FPC took a step in the right direction in June 1976 when it announced, in Opinion 770, that the national area rate for new contracts would be nearly tripled to $1.42 per mcf, with future price increases of 4 cents per annum. This decision was immediately challenged in the courts, leaving the effective price of natural gas in doubt for about a year. However, on 16 June 1977 the U.S. Court of Appeals for the District of Columbia unanimously upheld the FPC decision.[5] Thus the new contract price in 1977 will average about $1.46 per mcf.

Unfortunately the new FPC area rates still do not go far enough in bringing natural gas prices up to free market levels. Natural gas at $1.46, for example, is equivalent to oil at about $8.50 per barrel, again well below the world market price. Also, 4 cents per annum price increases will result in natural gas prices *falling* in real terms (unless the aggregate rate of inflation drops below 3 percent, which is unlikely). As a result, we will continue to be threatened by natural gas shortages. There is thus a pressing need to revise our natural gas policy.

It is important to recognize that any natural gas policy involves a trade-off between two evils—higher prices to consumers, and growing shortages. Evaluating any particular policy thus requires estimating the magnitudes and effects of higher prices, and the magnitudes and effects of shortages, that are likely to result. In the next two sections we will use a detailed econometric model of the natural gas industry developed at MIT to project the effects on prices and on shortages through 1985 of three alternative natural gas policies: a continuation of current FPC national area rates, President Carter's plan to increase new contract wellhead prices of "new" gas and tax industrial consumers of gas, and a plan of phased deregulation in which new contract prices would be raised in steps towards their free market level. In the fourth section we evaluate these three policies by estmating and comparing the costs of higher prices and the costs of shortages for each. This will provide us with a basis for determining a preferred policy.

WHAT IS AT STAKE—HIGHER PRICES

It is not surprising that this country's natural gas policy (and for that matter, its entire energy policy) has been dominated by a desire to hold down prices. Policymakers are not ignorant of the simple economics of supply and demand (although they may have underestimated the impact of price effects). Rather, there has been a strong political incentive to prevent consumer prices from rising, and to prevent producing companies from receiving large profits from price increases. In effect, a major goal of our natural gas policy has been distributional in nature; politicians are reluctant to pass legislation that would redistribute income from gas consumers to gas producers. With this in mind, let us consider what might happen to natural gas prices under alternative policies. Three such policies must be considered, since these have provided the basis for most recent public debate over natural gas regulation.

Continuation of FPC National Area Rates

The first is simply a continuation of current FPC national area rates (which assumes that the FPC does not by itself change this pricing policy). New contract prices would increase by 4 cents per year from the 1977 level of $1.46. As old contracts expired, average wellhead prices for gas sold on interstate markets would rise but would remain well below new contract prices for several years, only reaching about 87 cents per mcf in 1980. Average wholesale prices (i.e., prices charged by the pipelines to public utilities and large "mainline" industrial consumers) would depend on the particular distribution of gas through the pipeline network and the cost of transmission, which in turn would depend on changing patterns of regional demand. Although we cannot know what these prices will be with certainty, we can predict their likely values using our econometric model of the natural gas industry. We can expect these prices to average about 98 cents in 1978, and $1.16 in 1980. Similarly, based on projected demands and projected interstate supplies, we can project that intrastate wellhead prices would reach $2.00 in 1978 and $2.40 in 1980. To project retail prices, we assume that the 1976 average retail to wholesale markup remains constant in real terms on an mcf basis; we then extrapolate the markup assuming a 6.5 percent rate of inflation.[6] Based on these markups, we estimate that in 1980 average residential retail price would reach $2.83, while the average industrial retail price will reach $1.92. (There will be, however, considerable regional variation in these prices).

The Carter Plan

A second alternative policy is that laid out in President Carter's National Energy Plan (1977). The main aspects of that plan which deal with natural gas are as follows:

> a. The new contract price for "new" gas would be set equal to the BTU equivalent of the average refiner acquisition price of all domestic crude oil, while new contract prices of "old" gas would continue to be limited to existing FPC na-

tional area rates.[7] Based on projections of crude oil prices under the Carter plan, we would expect the price of "new" gas to begin at $1.75 per mcf and rise to $2.40 in 1980 and $3.10 in 1985.[8] We would also expect "new" gas to account for only about 25 percent of all new contracts in 1978, but nearly 100 percent of all new contracts by 1981. As a result, the *average* new contract price ("new" and "old" gas) on interstate sales would be about $1.58 in 1978, and $2.00 in 1980.

b. New contract prices for intrastate gas would also be regulated. All new contracts of intrastate gas (both "old" and "new" gas) would be tied to the price of "new" interstate gas, i.e., would increase from $1.75 initially to around $2.40 in 1980. Average wellhead prices of intrastate gas would thus be below their free market levels, but only for a few years, and not by very much (since the price of "new" gas will rise as the average refiner acquisition price of domestic crude oil rises over the next five years).

c. Pricing policy would discourage the use of gas by industry and electric utilities. The wellhead cost of higher-priced ("new") gas would be allocated to residential rather than industrial users. In addition, beginning in 1979 a tax would be levied on industrial users of gas which would be keyed to the difference between the price of gas and the BTU equivalent price of oil. This tax would increase so that on an mcf basis, the effective industrial price of gas would be $1.05 below the BTU equivalent price of oil in 1979, and equal to the BTU equivalent price of oil in 1985 and beyond.[9] Based on projections of oil prices, we estimate that this tax would increase from about 25 cents per mcf in 1979 to about $1.00 per mcf in 1985. Based on our projections[10] of average wellhead prices and average wholesale prices under the Carter plan, we estimate that the average retail industrial price of gas (including the tax) would be about $2.39 in 1980 and $4.07 in 1985. Despite the tax and allocation of higher-priced gas to industrial users, residential retail prices would still be higher because of the relatively high cost of retail distribution to residential consumers: $2.93 in 1980 and $4.31 in 1985.[11]

The third alternative policy is designed to increase the new contract price of all gas towards its free market level over the next five years. This would provide a greater incentive to producers to increase supplies of gas, by exploring for new discoveries (thus increasing reserves of "new" gas), by exploring near and extending existing reservoirs (thus increasing reserves of "old" gas), and by increasing production from higher-cost reserves (that would otherwise be uneconomical). Our policy would raise the new contract price in steps, to $2.00 in 1978, $2.40 in 1979, $2.55 in 1980, $2.70 in 1981, with further increases of about 20 cents per year (to keep pace with general inflation). As a result of this policy, average interstate wellhead prices would rise to 80 cents in 1978, $1.30 in 1980, and $2.21 in 1985, while new contract *intrastate* wellhead prices would rise to $2.55 in 1980, and $3.50 in 1985. Using our econometric model, we project average wholesale prices to be $1.06 in 1978, $1.53 in 1980, and $2.32 in 1985. Finally, average residential retail prices would be $2.53 in 1978, $3.20 in 1980, and $4.61 in 1985, while industrial retail prices would be $1.73, $2.29, and $3.36 in the respective years.

These price projections, together with recent actual prices, are summarized in Table 1. Because there is so much regional variation in retail prices, the table also shows projections of residential and industrial retail prices for different regions of the country.

Observe that although the different policies would have very different implications for new contract prices (particularly in later years), in terms of percentage differences the impact on retail prices is much smaller. For example, in 1985 new contract interstate prices under "Phased Deregulation" would be about double those under "FPC Area Rates." Average residential retail prices, however, would only be about 22 percent higher. The reason is that the largest component of the residential retail price is the cost of local transmission and distribution, and this cost would not change as wellhead and wholesale prices increased. The percentage increase in industrial retail prices would be larger; by 1985

Table 1

A U.S. Average Prices*

	Interstate New Contract			Average Interstate Wellhead			Intrastate New Contract			Average Wholesale			Average Retail: Residential			Average Retail: Industrial**		
	(a)	(b)	(c)	(a)	(b)	(c)	(a)	(b)	(c)	(a)	(b)	(c)	(a)	(b)	(c)	(a)	(b)	(c)
1965	0.19			0.17			-			0.30			1.01			0.35		
1970	0.22			0.18			-			0.33			1.06			0.38		
1975	0.60			0.32			1.25			0.52			1.57			0.75		
1976	1.00			0.50			1.75			0.73			1.98			1.29		
1978	1.50	1.58	2.00	0.69	0.70	0.80	2.00	1.80	2.00	0.98	0.98	1.06	2.45	2.45	2.53	1.65	1.65	1.73
1979	1.54	1.85	2.40	0.78	0.86	1.04	2.20	2.15	2.40	1.08	1.12	1.29	2.65	2.69	2.86	1.79	2.09	2.00
1980	1.58	2.20	2.55	0.87	1.01	1.30	2.40	2.40	2.55	1.16	1.26	1.53	2.83	2.93	3.20	1.92	2.39	2.29
1982	1.66	2.65	2.90	1.02	1.36	1.70	2.60	2.65	2.90	1.30	1.56	1.90	3.19	3.45	3.79	2.16	3.05	2.76
1985	1.78	3.10	3.50	1.25	1.93	2.21	3.00	3.10	3.50	1.49	2.02	2.32	3.78	4.31	4.61	2.53	4.07	3.36

B. Regional Retail Prices

	Residential Retail				Industrial Retail			
	1976	1980			1976	1980		
		(a)	(b)	(c)		(a)	(b)	(c)
New England	3.70	5.10	5.20	5.47	2.58	3.62	4.09	3.99
Middle Atlantic	2.63	3.69	3.79	4.06	1.71	2.47	3.94	2.84
East No. Central	1.87	2.68	2.78	3.05	1.40	2.06	2.54	2.44
West No. Central	1.53	2.24	2.34	2.61	0.91	1.42	1.89	1.79
South Atlantic	2.23	3.16	3.26	3.53	1.25	1.87	2.34	2.24
East So. Central	1.60	2.33	2.43	2.70	1.02	1.56	2.03	1.93
West So. Central	1.71	2.47	2.57	2.84	1.29	1.92	2.39	2.29
Mountain	1.58	2.30	2.40	2.67	0.95	1.47	1.94	1.84
Pacific	1.76	2.54	2.64	2.91	1.46	2.14	2.61	2.51

* : In current $/mcf
** : Includes tax under Carter Plan

(a) FPC area rates (b) Carter Plan (c) Phased Deregulation

"Phased Deregulation" would result in prices 33 percent higher than under continued FPC area rates, while the "Carter Plan" would result in prices 61 percent higher (largely because of the tax on industrial use of gas). Finally, note that there has been, and is likely to continue to be, considerable regional variation in retail prices. Part of this variation is due to the differences in interstate transmission costs, and part is due to differences in local distribution costs.

There is no doubt that our three alternative policies imply significant differences in retail prices of gas to residential and industrial consumers. The relevant question, however, is what is the total cost to consumers of a higher-price policy, and how does it compare to the cost of shortages resulting from a lower-price policy? We will answer this question in the fourth section, after first projecting the shortages that are likely to result under the alternative policies.

WHAT IS AT STAKE—SHORTAGES

Our vehicle for predicting shortages under alternative policies is the MIT econometric model of the natural gas industry. This model explains in detail the simultaneous behavior and interaction of natural gas and oil exploration and reserve accumulation, natural gas production out of reserves, natural gas distribution, and finally, natural gas demand. It is therefore ideally suited for forecasting the effects of alternative price policies. The model is described in detail elsewhere, but we summarize its overall structure in the Appendix.[12]

The three policies of interest to us were described in the last section in the context of their implications for wellhead, wholesale, and retail prices. We review them here, with reference to their simulation using the econometric model:

> 1. *FPC area rates.* New contract prices of gas are increased by 4 cents per year from $1.46 in 1977. Intrastate prices range from $2.00 in 1978 to $2.40 in 1980, and remain constant in real terms thereafter.

2. *Carter Plan.* "New" gas prices, which rise from $1.75 to $2.40 in 1980, are the relevant new contract prices for determining exploratory drilling and new discoveries, while "old" gas prices, the same as those in (1) above, are the relevant new contract prices for determining extensions and revisions of gas reserves. Average new contract prices (which determine average wellhead and average wholesale prices) are calculated by assuming that the fraction of "new" gas in new contracts rises from 25 percent in 1978 to 100 percent in 1981. Intrastate prices begin at $1.80 in 1978, but reach $2.40 by 1980. Finally, a tax is added to the wholesale price of gas facing industrial consumers. This tax ranges from 25 cents per mcf in 1979 to $1.00 in 1985.

3. *"Phased Deregulation."* In this policy a set of new contract prices is chosen that results in shortfalls dropping to 3 Tcf. *Such a shortfall would actually represent market clearing,* since it is expected that we would import, at roughly the same prices, 1.5 Tcf of natural gas from Canada and Mexico, and about 2 Tcf of LNG at $4 to $5 from Algeria and Indonesia under (unfortunately) long-term contracts that we are currently entering into. Thus our policy represents a gradual adjustment to free market prices. New contract prices are increased to $2.00 in 1978, $2.40 in 1979, $2.55 in 1980, $2.70 in 1981, and by 20 cents per year thereafter. Intrastate new contract prices are assumed to equal those for interstate gas from 1978 onwards.

The econometric model contains a number of exogenous variables for which assumptions must be made in order to generate forecasts. With the exception of oil prices, our assumptions about these variables are the same for all three policies. The exogenous determinants of the reserves and production of gas include the field price of crude oil in the producing regions, average drilling costs, interest rates, the amount of offshore acreage leased by the Bureau of Land Management each year, and the number of drilling rigs operating offshore. We assume that crude oil prices increase in nominal terms by $1.00 per year from a base of $8.00

in 1977. (In simulating the Carter plan we add the tax to the wholesale price of refined oil products used in the industrial sector.) We assume that average drilling costs increase in nominal terms by 10 percent annually, that interest rates remain constant at 10 percent, that 2 million acres of offshore lands are leased annually, and that five additional drilling rigs are installed each year in offshore Louisiana. Determinants of demand include state-by-state personal income, value added in manufacturing, new capital expenditures in manufacturing, population, and prices of alternative fuels. We assume that income, value added, and capital expenditures all grow in real terms at a rate of 6 percent in 1976, 5 percent in 1977, 4 percent in 1978 and 1979, and 3.5 percent thereafter. Prices of coal and electricity are projected to rise in real terms by 6 percent per year. Finally, we assume that 1 Tcf of gas will be imported from Canada each year, and we include this Canadian gas in our supply forecasts.

The results of our forecasts are shown in Tables 2, 3, and 4, and in Figures 1, 2, 3, and 4. Note that in all the forecasts, about 3 Tcf of predicted excess demand will in fact be filled by imported gas and LNG. Observe that under a continuation of FPC area rates, production of gas will fall off steadily, demand for gas will rise rapidly, and excess demand will exceed 11 Tcf by 1980 and 20 Tcf by 1985. Part of this excess demand (probably about half) will take the form of curtailments, while the remainder will take the form of residential consumers unable to install new gas lines in homes, and industrial consumers unable to contract for gas deliveries. The first component of excess demand (curtailments) will result (as it did during the winter of 1976-1977) in unemployment and lost GNP, and, as excess demand grows, cutoffs in residential deliveries. The second component of excess demand (consumers unable to contract for purchases) will result in increased demand for oil and gas, as consumers are forced to look for alternative fuels. This in turn will drive up the prices of those fuels, or, if those prices are regulated, result in greater imports of oil.

The Carter plan would help considerably in reducing excess demand. It would have its effect largely by reducing the demand

Table 2

Forecast of FPC Area Rates

Year	Exploratory Wells Drilled	New discoveries of gas (Tcf)	Additions to gas reserves (Tcf)	Onshore Production (Tcf)	Offshore Production (Tcf)***	Total gas Production (Tcf)*	Residential Commercial Demand (Tcf)	Industrial Demand (Tcf)	Total demand for gas** (Tcf)	Excess Demand
1976	6282	9.3	10.8	19.4	4.2	24.6	9.2	19.8	30.5	5.9
1977	6045	12.0	16.7	18.5	4.6	24.1	9.4	20.4	31.3	7.2
1978	5896	11.4	15.4	17.3	5.3	23.6	9.6	20.9	31.9	8.3
1979	5524	10.6	13.2	16.0	6.1	23.2	10.2	21.4	33.0	9.8
1980	4860	10.3	11.4	14.3	7.1	22.4	10.6	22.0	33.9	11.5
1981	4317	10.3	11.1	12.2	8.1	21.3	10.9	22.8	35.0	13.6
1982	3957	10.3	11.2	10.3	9.0	20.3	11.4	23.8	36.3	15.9
1983	3646	10.4	12.0	8.5	9.9	19.4	11.8	25.0	37.8	18.4
1984	3385	10.5	12.6	7.1	10.6	18.7	12.3	26.4	39.6	21.0
1985	3136	10.6	13.6	5.9	11.3	18.1	12.9	28.0	41.8	23.7

*Includes 1 Tcf of Canadian imports, as well as gas production used to satisfy lease and plant fuel demand. (For this reason the 1976 figure is higher than most published figures.)

**Includes lease and plant fuel demand (i.e. use of gas as energy source for extraction and pressurization at field site).

***Includes only the Gulf Coast, and assumes no gas supplied from the Atlantic or Pacific coasts.

Table 3

Forecast of Carter Plan

Year	Exploratory Wells Drilled	New discoveries of gas (Tcf)	Additions to gas reserves (Tcf)	Onshore Production (Tcf)	Offshore Production (Tcf)***	Total gas Production (Tcf)*	Residential Commercial Demand (Tcf)	Industrial Demand (Tcf)	Total demand for gas** (Tcf)	Excess Demand
1976	6282	9.3	10.8	19.4	4.2	24.6	9.2	19.8	30.5	5.9
1977	5967	10.4	14.3	18.4	4.6	24.0	9.4	20.4	31.3	7.3
1978	5651	10.0	12.9	17.0	5.5	23.5	9.6	20.9	31.9	8.4
1979	5201	12.3	14.0	15.6	6.5	23.1	10.2	20.1	31.6	8.6
1980	4640	13.3	15.0	13.4	7.6	22.1	10.5	19.3	31.0	9.0
1981	4380	13.8	15.8	11.5	8.7	21.2	10.8	18.4	30.4	9.1
1982	4110	14.1	16.3	9.8	9.9	20.8	11.0	17.5	29.7	8.9
1983	3820	14.4	17.4	8.4	11.1	20.5	11.2	16.7	29.0	8.5
1984	3538	14.8	18.2	7.1	12.3	20.4	11.5	15.8	28.3	7.9
1985	3276	15.2	19.3	6.0	13.3	20.4	11.7	15.0	27.7	7.3

*Includes 1 Tcf of Canadian imports, as well as gas production used to satisfy lease and plant fuel demand. (For this reason the 1976 figure is higher than most published figures.)

**Includes lease and plant fuel demand (i.e. use of gas as energy source for extraction and pressurization at field site).

***Includes only the Gulf Coast, and assumes no gas supplied from the Atlantic or Pacific coasts.

Table 4

Forecast of Phased Deregulation

Year	Exploratory Wells Drilled	New discoveries of gas (Tcf)	Additions to gas reserves (Tcf)	Onshore Production (Tcf)	Offshore Production (Tcf)***	Total gas Production (Tcf)*	Residential Commercial Demand (Tcf)	Industrial Demand (Tcf)	Total demand for gas** (Tcf)	Excess Demand
1976	6282	9.3	10.8	19.4	4.2	24.6	9.2	19.8	30.5	5.9
1977	6120	14.0	19.0	18.5	4.8	24.4	9.4	20.2	31.1	6.8
1978	6424	18.8	24.9	17.6	5.7	24.3	9.5	20.4	31.4	7.0
1979	7066	22.8	31.1	17.2	6.7	24.9	10.1	20.1	31.6	6.7
1980	7275	19.9	29.5	17.2	7.8	26.1	10.2	19.4	31.2	5.1
1981	6671	17.6	24.1	17.0	9.1	27.1	10.3	18.7	30.6	3.5
1982	5557	16.5	19.0	15.7	10.4	27.1	10.3	18.1	29.9	2.9
1983	4784	16.4	16.5	13.6	11.7	26.3	10.3	17.5	29.3	3.0
1984	4263	16.6	15.5	11.3	12.8	25.2	10.4	17.1	28.8	3.6
1985	3912	16.9	15.9	9.0	14.0	24.0	10.5	16.7	28.5	4.4

*Includes 1 Tcf of Canadian imports, as well as production used to satisfy lease and plant fuel demand.

**Includes lease and fuel plant demand.

***Includes only the Gulf Coast.

Figure 1

Total Demand for Gas

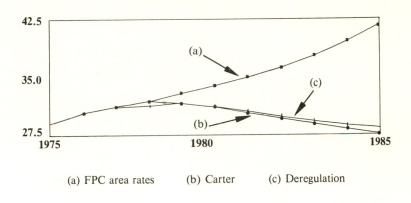

(a) FPC area rates   (b) Carter   (c) Deregulation

Figure 2

Supply of Gas

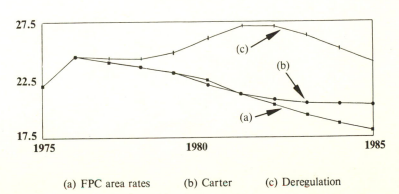

(a) FPC area rates   (b) Carter   (c) Deregulation

Figure 3

Excess Demand for Gas

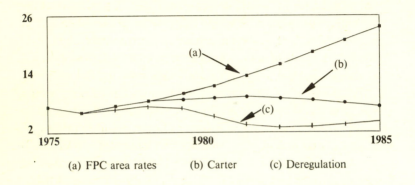

(a) FPC area rates   (b) Carter   (c) Deregulation

Figure 4

Reserves of Natural Gas

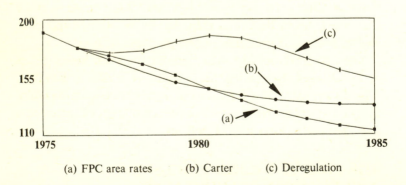

(a) FPC area rates   (b) Carter   (c) Deregulation

for natural gas. Since industrial consumers account for the majority of total gas demands, and since they have a higher elasticity of demand, the imposition of a tax on those consumers would cause a major shift to alternative fuels, as well as some decrease in total energy consumption. Under the Carter plan, total demand for gas would decrease by about 10 percent over the next nine years, whereas it would increase by about 30 percent if current FPC area rates are maintained. Unfortunately, the Carter plan would result in some increase in new discoveries; it would not succeed in bringing forth significant new supplies of gas.[13] Wellhead prices would rise only slowly, and producers would have little incentive to do additional exploratory drilling, or to extend existing pools and reservoirs. The net result would be an increase in excess demand to a peak of 9 Tcf by 1980, and then a slow decrease to about 7 Tcf in 1985. While this scenario is far preferable to the first, it would still result in significant shortages.

Excess demand can be reduced to about 3 Tcf per year if new contract wellhead prices are increased in steps according to our "Phased Deregulation" scenario. This would result first in additional exploratory and development well drilling so that new discoveries and reserve extensions would be larger, and second in additional production out of any given level of proved reserves. Total production of gas would be about 4 or 5 Tcf higher than under the Carter plan, while total demand for gas would be about the same as under the Carter plan. But by increasing supplies as well as decreasing demands, shortages could be averted.

These forecasts set forth the trade-off between higher prices and shortages. Evaluating the alternative policies, however, requires estimating the dollar cost of higher prices and the dollar cost of a shortage. We now turn to the calculation of these costs, and their use in assessing the policies.

THE COST OF HIGHER PRICES
AND THE COST OF SHORTAGES

We begin by estimating the cost of higher prices. The cost is just the resulting increase in expenditures for those consumers able to obtain gas at the lower price.* Since the highest price would result from our policy of "Phased Deregulation," we calculate the cost of higher prices for this policy relative to continued FPC area rates, and relative to the "Carter Plan." These costs are calculated for the residential/commerical and industrial sectors for each of nine regions and for each year over the period 1977-1985, based on projected gas production and retail prices under each alternative policy. By summing these costs across regions and over the nine-year horizon, we can compare policies in terms of the relative cost to the U.S. of higher prices.

The costs of higher prices are presented in Tables 5 and 6. Each number in Table 5 represents, for consumers in a particular region and in a particular year, the cost of higher prices resulting from a policy of "Phased Deregulation" replacing a policy of "FPC Area Rates." (Table 6 represents the same costs for "Phased Deregulation" replacing the "Carter Plan.") Thus we see, for example, that a shift to "Phased Deregulation" will cost consumers in New England an additional $108 million in 1980 and an additional $143 million in 1985. For the U.S. as a whole, the corresponding costs would be $6.45 billion in 1980 and $8.52 billion in 1985, of which a little more than half would be incurred by industrial consumers.

Summing over all nine years in Table 5, we see that the total cost to U.S. consumers from higher prices resulting from "Phased Deregulation" (as opposed to FPC area rates) would be $54.34 billion.[14] Similarly, by summing over the nine years in Table 6, we see that "Phased Deregulation" would cost consumers an additional $0.35 billion in higher prices as compared to the Carter plan. The reason for this small cost, however, is that industrial consumers actually pay much more (in later years) under the Carter plan because of the tax. The tax revenues themselves add up to $46.03 billion over the nine years. Since these tax revenues

---

*Note that this is *not* the change in consumer surplus resulting from a price increase. The net loss in consumer surplus resulting from a price increase would be *smaller* than this increased expenditure because of the gain in surplus to those consumers now able to obtain gas who were unable to do so before. We measure this second component of consumer surplus, however, when we evaluate the cost of a shortage.

Table 5

Cost of Higher Prices: Phased
Deregulation Relative to FPC Area Rates*

Year Region	1977	1978	1979	1980	1981	1982	1983	1984	1985
New England	.012	.027	.068	.108	.133	.141	.138	.143	.143
Middle Atlantic	.072	.176	.425	.679	.836	.879	.869	.893	.899
East No. Central	.177	.433	1.049	1.675	2.062	2.171	2.144	2.204	2.218
West No. Central	.076	.183	.444	.708	.871	.918	.905	.931	.937
South Atlantic	.054	.131	.319	.510	.627	.660	.652	.670	.674
East So. Central	.037	.091	.220	.352	.432	.456	.450	.463	.466
West So. Central	.130	.317	.768	1.227	1.509	1.589	1.569	1.613	1.622
Mountain	.042	.105	.252	.404	.496	.523	.516	.531	.533
Pacific	.082	.198	.486	.776	.954	1.005	.991	1.020	1.026
U.S. Total	.678	1.664	4.034	6.452	7.929	8.347	8.239	8.475	8.524
Residential/ Commercial	.317	.778	1.886	3.012	3.707	3.902	3.852	3.962	3.985
Industrial	.361	.886	2.148	3.431	4.222	4.445	4.387	4.513	4.539

*All numbers are in billions of 1976 dollars.

are available for public consumption (and in fact may be in part rebated to taxpayers), they could be subtracted from the cost of higher prices under the Carter plan—or, equivalently, added to the cost of "Phased Deregulation." Assuming a full public benefit from these taxes, and adding them in, we find that the total cost of "Phased Deregulation" relative to the Carter plan is $46.38 billion.

These costs must now be compared to the costs of shortages resulting from lower price policies. There are three components to the cost of a shortage:

1. Some consumers are unable to obtain gas. There is thus a direct loss of consumer surplus, measured as the value to these consumers of the gas they otherwise would have purchased.

Table 6

Cost of Higher Prices: Phased
Deregulation Relative to the Carter Plan*

Year Region	1977	1978	1979	1980	1981	1982	1983	1984	1985
New England	.012	.027	.036	.053	.056	.053	.030	.022	.013
Middle Atlantic	.071	.175	.174	.264	.264	.246	.081	.021	(.044)
East No. Central	.175	.432	.319	.507	.476	.437	(.026)	(.194)	(.371)
West No. Central	.075	.182	.087	.137	.108	.093	(.131)	(.213)	(.297)
South Atlantic	.053	.131	.038	.075	.051	.040	(.131)	(.193)	(.257)
East So. Central	.037	.090	.015	.038	.016	.010	(.113)	(.158)	(.203)
West S. Central	.128	.315	(.097)	(.069)	(.187)	(.198)	(.703)	(.888)	(1.072)
Mountain	.042	.103	.032	.062	.043	.036	(.098)	(.147)	(.197)
Pacific	.082	.200	.110	.184	.159	.143	(.091)	(.175)	(.264)
U.S. Total	.676	1.658	.705	1.253	.986	.862	(1.179)	(1.922)	(2.691)
Residential/ Commercial	.316	.775	1.520	2.168	2.387	2.266	1.912	1.786	1.623
Industrial	.360	.823	(.815)	(.915)	(1.401)	(1.404)	(3.091)	(3.708)	(4.314)
Tax Revenue under Carter Plan	0	0	3.088	4.413	5.671	6.756	7.748	8.713	9.638

*All numbers are in billions of 1976 dollars. Numbers in parentheses indicate *lower* retail prices under "Phased Deregulation."

2. The shortage of natural gas results in increased demand for other fuels (oil and coal), raising the prices of those fuels to all consumers.[15]

3. Curtailments of gas result in unemployment and thus lost GNP.

We estimate each of these components of the cost of shortages, again comparing FPC area rates and the Carter plan to "Phased Deregulation."

Loss of Consumer Surplus

We begin with the direct loss of consumer surplus. The value of gas for consumers unable to obtain it is measured by the shaded area in Figure 5. P_0 and Q_0 correspond to the free market price at which there is no shortage, while P_1 is the regulated price at which only Q_1 is produced. The demand function itself is needed to compute this lost surplus, since it determines the value of the quantity difference $Q_0 - Q_1$. We use aggregate residential and aggregate industrial demand functions obtained from our econometric model of the natural gas industry, based on a five-year adjustment period. The calculated surplus losses corresponding to lower price policies are shown in Table 7. Note that the total consumer surplus "benefit" is about $11.8 billion when "Phased Deregulation" is compared to FPC area rates, and $8.6 billion when it is compared to the Carter plan.

Figure 5

Lost Consumer Surplus from a Shortage

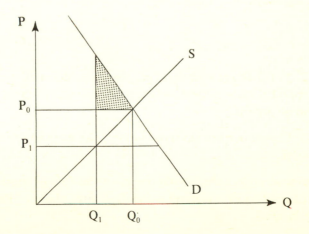

Table 7

Consumer Surplus Losses from Shortages*

		1977	1978	1979	1980	1981	1982	1983	1984	1985	TOTAL
FPC Area Rates Relative to Phased Deregulation	Residential/Commercial	.002	.013	.080	.382	.932	1.296	1.381	1.284	1.110	6.480
	Industrial	.002	.010	.064	.311	.768	1.073	1.145	1.066	.922	5.361
	Total	.004	.023	.144	.693	1.700	2.369	2.526	2.350	2.032	11.841
Carter Plan Relative to Phased Deregulation	Residential/Commercial	.004	.017	.090	.446	.965	1.113	.975	.700	.413	4.723
	Industrial	.003	.013	.072	.363	.795	.921	.809	.581	.343	3.900
	Total	.007	.030	.162	.809	1.760	2.034	1.784	1.281	.756	8.623

*All numbers are in billions of 1976 dollars.

Increased Demand for Oil and Coal

Next we measure the cost of shortage-induced expenditures on oil and coal. To obtain a conservative estimate of this cost, we assume that only half of the excess demand for natural gas is satisfied (on a BTU equivalent basis) by oil and coal. Further, we assume that at 1976 prices, the long-run price elasticities for oil and coal demand and supply are -0.5 and 0.4 respectively.[16] The induced expenditure on oil and gas is given by the shaded area in Figure 6, where S_{OC} and D_{OC} are the aggregate supply and demand curves for both oil and coal, and X is the additional demand for oil and coal (i.e., one-half of the BTU shortage of natural gas). Note that the increased expenditure on oil and coal comes about for two reasons: a larger quantity is consumed, and the shift in demand causes the price to rise.

Figure 6

Shortage-Induced Expenditure on Oil and Coal

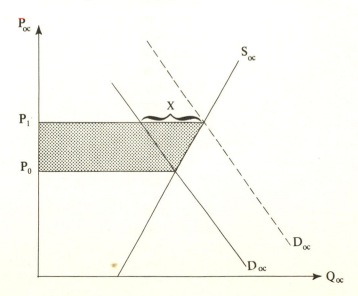

The calculated increases in oil and coal expenditures are shown in Table 8. Note that these increased expenditures are quite large, and in the case of "Phased Deregulation" relative to FPC area rates, the expenditure by itself outweighs the cost of higher prices.

Lost GNP

Finally we measure the lost GNP that would result from shortages. To do this, we begin with an estimate prepared by the American Gas Association (AGA) of the added unemployment resulting from natural gas shortages during the winter of 1976-1977 (AGA 1977; these estimates are quite close to those issued by private economic forecasting firms). The AGA found the following unemployment to be directly attributable to the shortage:

Date	Number Unemployed
Jan. 11	0
26	240,000
27	650,000
28	840,000
Feb. 4	1,212,000
8	870,600
12	532,000
18	218,000
26	92,500
Mar. 4	65,400
14	10,000

We convert this unemployment into an *average increase in the unemployment rate on an annual basis,* which we find to be 0.093 percent. We attribute this increase in the unemployment rate to the year 1976, for which we have estimated the natural gas shortage to be 5.9 Tcf. We now assume that changes in the size of the gas shortage (as measured by our econometric model) will result in *proportional* changes in the induced increase in the unemployment rate, so that our projections of future shortages under alternative regulatory policies can be used to project induced unemployment.[17] Next, we obtain the cost of this unem-

Table 8

Shortage–Induced Expenditures on Oil and Coal*

	1977	1978	1979	1980	1981	1982	1983	1984	1985	TOTAL
FPC Area Rates Relative to Phased Deregulation	0.378	1.232	2.946	6.084	9.610	12.414	14.785	16.816	18.786	83.051
Carter Plan Relative to Phased Deregulation	0.472	1.327	1.801	3.688	5.279	5.646	5.172	4.044	2.728	30.157

*All numbers are in billions of 1976 dollars.

ployment in terms of lost GNP by using Okun's Law, which says that a 1 percent increase in the unemployment rate corresponds to approximately a 3 percent loss of "potential GNP."[18] Finally, we assume that potential GNP grows in real terms by 3.5 percent annually from its 1976 value of $1692.4 billion.

Our alternative policies are compared in terms of relative shortage-induced unemployment and corresponding lost GNP in Table 9. By summing the lost GNP over the nine years 1977-1985, we obtain the third component of the cost of shortages.

The cost of higher prices and the costs of shortages are summarized in Table 10. Observe that in comparing "Phased Deregulation" to continued FPC area rates or to the Carter plan, the cost of shortages resulting from the lower price policy outweighs the cost of higher prices. "Phased Deregulation" is clearly a far superior policy to continued FPC area rates; over the nine-year period the cost of higher prices totals about $54 billion, while the cost of shortages is over $180 billion. By taxing industrial use of gas and providing a somewhat higher price for "new" gas, the Carter plan will significantly ameliorate shortages; the shortages still resulting would be more costly than the higher prices of "Phased Deregulation." We find "Phased Deregulation" to have a total benefit over the Carter plan of about $26 billion over the nine-year period, and this is a highly conservative estimate, since we have taken the entire tax revenue under the Carter plan and attributed it to consumers as a benefit. (Had we included the tax revenue as a cost, the total benefit of "Phased Deregulation" would be $72 billion.) There is thus a significant gain to be had by letting natural gas prices rise towards free market levels, and thereby eliminating shortages.

REVISING OUR NATURAL GAS POLICY

A regulation-induced shortage only makes sense from the point of view of total public welfare if the gain to consumers from lower prices exceeds the losses created by the shortage. We have seen that in the case of natural gas, continued regulation-induced shortages cannot be justified, since the cost of these shortages

Table 9

Shortage–Induced Unemployment and Lost GNP

		1977	1978	1979	1980	1981	1982	1983	1984	1985	Total
FPC Area Rates Relative to Phased Deregulation	Increase in average unemployment rate over year	.0063	.0205	.0490	.1011	.1280	.2054	.2433	.2749	.3049	—
	Lost GNP*	0.33	1.11	2.76	5.89	7.72	12.82	15.72	18.38	21.10	85.86
Carter Plan Relative to Phased Deregulation	Increase in average unemployment rate over year	.0078	.0221	.0300	.0616	.0885	.0948	.0869	.0995	.0458	—
	Lost GNP*	0.41	1.20	1.69	3.59	5.34	5.92	5.61	6.65	3.17	33.58

*Measured in billions of 1976 dollars.

Table 10

Cost Comparisons of Alternative Policies*

	Cost of higher prices	Costs of Shortages			Total Cost (Benefit)
		Lost consumer surplus	Induced Ex-penditure on oil and coal	Lost GNP	
"Phased Deregulation" vs. "FPC Area Rates"	54.34	(11.84)	(83.05)	(85.86)	(126.41)
"Phased Deregulation" vs. "Carter Plan"	46.38**	(8.62)	(30.16)	(33.58)	(25.98)

*All costs summed over 1977-1985, and measured in billions of 1976 dollars.

**This figure assumes that these tax revenues produce a full public benefit.

would far outweigh the gain that some consumers would receive by being able to pay lower prices.

We have, of course, ignored the question of *which* consumers would end up paying higher prices under deregulation. There is no doubt that even a moderate increase in the residential price of natural gas would result in an unacceptable increase in the living expenses of some low-income consumers. But the use of energy policy is the wrong way to achieve equity in income distribution and living standards. Distributional goals can be better attained through the use of tax and transfer policy. For example, expanding our existing food stamp program—by increasing stamp allotments and allowing the stamps to be applied to heating bills (or that portion of rent allocated to fuels)—would be an effective way of buffering low-income groups from the effects of higher energy prices (Hall and Pindyck 1977).

We have already incurred unnecessarily higher costs from the regulation-induced shortage of natural gas. Hopefully, our energy policy in the future will be guided by a better understanding of the trade-off between the cost of higher prices and the costs of the shortages, distortions, and growing foreign dependence that result from policies that attempt to maintain low prices.

APPENDIX

Overview of the Econometric Model of the Natural Gas Industry

Our model of the natural gas industry simultaneously describes gas supplies and demands in both the market for reserve additions (gas producers selling new reserves to pipelines at the wellhead price) and the market for wholesale deliveries (pipelines selling gas on long-term contracts to retail utilities and industrial consumers). The model is highly disaggregated on a regional basis, and describes in detail the spatial structure of the industry; reserve additions are contracted for in regional field markets and gas production is delivered by pipelines to regional wholesale markets, and these regional markets are interconnected by the pipeline network. A block diagram of the model is shown in Figure A-1 that ignores—for simplicity—the regional interconnections between production districts and regional wholesale markets (MacAvoy and Pindyck 1975a; Pindyck 1977).

Equations for new discoveries of gas and oil are specified and estimated that account for shifts in directionality (gas vs. oil) and for shifts between drilling on the extensive (high-risk) and intensive (low-risk) margins in response to price changes. New discoveries begin with the drilling of exploratory wells, of which some will succeed in discovering gas, some will succeed in discovering oil (with or without associated gas), and some will be unsuccessful. An equation predicting the number of exploratory wells drilled is specified based on the assumption that producers

Figure A-1

Simplified Block Diagram of the Econometric Model

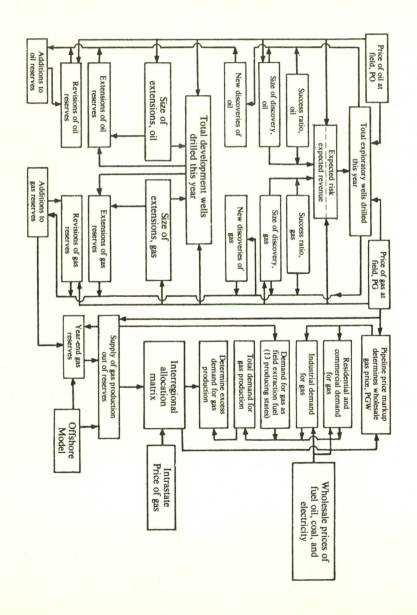

respond rationally to economic incentives as they form portfolios of drilling ventures that may be extensive or intensive, or may favor gas or oil. Economic incentives enter the equation through expected gas and oil revenue (the product of expected prices, success ratios, and sizes of finds), expected risk (an estimate of the variance of expected revenue), average drilling costs, and the interest rate (reflecting capital costs). Two equations then describe the fraction of wells drilled that will succeed in finding gas, and the fraction that will succeed in finding oil. Finally, two equations determine the size of discovery per successful well for gas and oil respectively, and include the effects of price changes and resource depletion. All of these equations were estimated for a set of twenty FPC production districts. Thus new discoveries for gas and oil can be determined on a regional basis as the product of number of wells, success ratio, and size of find per successful well. This level of detail is needed given that oil and natural gas are joint products that must be treated symmetrically.[19]

The model also contains a detailed description of reserve extensions and revisions. An equation is estimated that determines the total number of *development* wells drilled in any year. (Development wells are drilled in preparation of producing gas or oil from a newly discovered field, and it is these wells, rather than exploratory wells, that lead to extensions and revisions of reserves.) The number of development wells drilled depends on prices and on direct drilling costs, capital costs, and existing reserve levels. Two equations then determine sizes of finds for gas extensions and oil extensions. Explanatory variables in these equations include price (which explain directionality), drilling costs (which could induce operators to change drilling patterns and thereby alter the size distribution of the resulting extensions), and an index that describes the process of geological depletion. Extensions of gas and oil are thus determined as the product of development wells and sizes fo finds of extensions. Revisions on the other hand do not depend on well drilling, but instead are functions of price, prior reserve and production levels, and changes in production.

Year-end reserves of gas in any year are equal to reserves in the previous year plus additions to reserves (the sum of discoveries, extensions, and revisions) minus production of gas. Production out of reserves depends on the size of the reserve base and on prices that buyers are willing to pay for increased deliveries. In our model production supply is based on marginal cost pricing, i.e. the marginal cost of developing existing reserves determines a particular level of annual flow, and as the reserve-production ratio becomes smaller, marginal costs rise sharply. Also, there are critical reserve-production ratios below which marginal costs rise extremely sharply. These critical levels could not be estimated econometrically since they have not yet been reached (at least on an aggregate level), but in the model we use engineering estimates to introduce them explicitly. Thus, given some level of year-end reserves in any one production district, the level of gas production in that district will increase with price, but only insofar as the reserve-production ratio stays above a minimum level.

The discovery and production of offshore natural gas is particularly important in policy evaluation, since as both gas and oil prices increase and as more offshore acreage is leased by the federal government, offshore fields will probably provide an increasing share of gas production. The model therefore contains a complete offshore "sub-model" that relates reserves and production of gas off the coast of Louisiana to such policy variables as the new contract field price and the amount of acreage leased annually, and to exogenous variables such as interest rates, the price of oil, and the number of drilling rigs operating offshore. The sub-model operates through three interacting blocks of equations that determine total acreage, producing acreage, and reserves additions and production.

The wholesale demand for natural gas is a function of the wholesale price, as well as prices of alternative fuels and "market size" variables such as population, income, and investment. Average wholesale prices for gas are computed in the model for each consumption region in the country through a series of pipeline price markup equations, which are based on operating costs, capital costs, and regulated rates of profit for the pipeline companies. Finally, the distribution of natural gas is determined from a regional input-output table connecting production districts with consuming regions.

VII

JAMES L. SWEENEY

ENERGY REGULATION—
SOLUTION OR PROBLEM?

Price regulations. Muti-tier price controls. Petroleum price regulation: allocation, the entitlements program. Natural gas pricing. Electricity. Quantity controls: oil import quotas, gasoline rationing, gasoline taxes. Direct regulation of energy-using appliances: new cars, residential and commercial buildings. Summary and conclusions.

Regulations pervade the energy system in the United States and, if current proposals are enacted, will become even more pervasive. Price controls govern markets for natural gas, oil and electricity —for all major energy carriers but coal. The Carter plan promises to broaden these controls. Restrictions controlling or allocating aggregate quantities abound. Natural gas and oil face federally managed allocations; oil import quotas, gasoline rationing, and gasoline refining limitations have recently been proposed; and direct regulations governing energy-using devices are extensive and growing, with more proposed under the Carter plan. Efficiency standards for new cars and new buildings exist; and proposals have been made for restrictions banning use of oil and gas in electric utilities and in new industrial boilers, or for requiring insulation retrofit of existing dwelling units.

Each existing regulation has reduced flexibility in the energy system; each has reduced the ability of the economic system to respond to changing conditions and to variations in individual circumstances. Price regulations reduce the ability of the energy system to signal changes of costs to the various participants and thereby eliminate many of the incentives to increase supply and reduce demand when circumstances require. A combination of quantity controls and price controls creates shortages. The insulation retrofit regulations reduce the ability of people in different circumstances to respond appropriately to their own individual conditions.

The existence of one set of regulations has motivated additional regulations. Oil and gas price regulation have made it necessary to allocate oil and gas to the various classes of users. And the low, regulated energy prices lead to overuse of fuels and thus motivate direct controls on use.

This paper describes some existing and frequently recommended regulations governing the energy system. We shall consider three major types of regulation—price controls, quantity controls, and controls on energy-using equipment. In doing so, we hope to show that widespread energy regulation significantly reduces flexibility and promotes widespread inefficiency and waste. And the problems caused by regulation tend to stir demands for still more regulation.

PRICE REGULATIONS

The most common forms of regulation are controls on prices facing consumers, producers, or both. Examples are price controls on crude oil, refined petroleum products, natural gas, and electricity. Among the major sources of energy, only coal is not subject to price regulation. Crude oil is controlled under a multitier pricing system which sets different prices for domestically produced oil, depending on time of initial development and on production rates from given fields. Natural gas trading in inter-state markets is subject to price regulation, while natural gas trading in intrastate markets currently is not. With the Carter plan all natural gas would become subject to price regulations under a multi-tier pricing system. Electric utilities face price regulations administered by state public utility commissions. The state commissions set prices to allow utilities to earn an authorized rate of return on invested capital. Most coal production and virtually all geothermal and nuclear energy are used to generate electricity, an energy carrier facing price regulation. Under the Carter plan 91 percent of the United States domestically supplied energy faces price regulation, including fuels used to generate electricity. Ignoring electricity, 67 percent of the domestic energy supply would face price regulation under the Carter plan. Price regulation alone is a pervasive characteristic of the U.S. energy system.

Price controls are normally established to keep consumer prices below market levels, or to reduce profits accruing to the energy supplier. As a rule, price controls will satisfy these objectives, although there is even disagreement about how effective they really are in reducing energy prices facing consumers. To the extent that petroleum product prices are set on the world market, U.S. crude oil price control would fail to reduce refined product prices facing consumers, but would simply shift refining activities toward the more costly domestic refineries (Phelps and Smith 1977).

For natural gas, the pipeline transportation costs must be shared among all users. Price regulations that reduce the quantity of natural gas shipped in pipelines will thereby increase the shipping cost per unit of gas. Natural gas wellhead price controls therefore could increase consumer prices if increases in the wellhead price of natural gas increased its supply sufficiently. In this case the increase in average pipeline costs could cause an overall increase in the consumer price. However, energy price regulation can be expected to succeed in reducing the price obtained by the producer, and in reducing at least the money price to consumers.

Energy price regulations produce undesirable consequences. The normal effect of regulating prices below market-clearing levels is to increase demand, reduce supply, increase imports, and reduce demand for substitutes. Thus oil price controls tend to increase demand for petroleum, decrease oil exploration and production, and increase imports of crude oil and refined products. Moreover, the reduced price for oil decreases the demand for oil substitutes, particularly coal. The natural gas price regulation increases demand, decreases supply, and thereby increases demand for imports. However, opportunities to import natural gas—either in the form of Canadian natural gas or liquefied natural gas (LNG)—are limited. Natural gas price regulation has thus created shortages.

Shortages created by price controls force consumers to find alternatives—generally, more costly or less desirable fuels. For example, one effect of natural gas shortages has been to force many newly constructed buildings to use electricity for space heating—at greatly increased cost. Thus where shortages result, price controls reduce the money price to consumers who have access, but increase the cost for consumers without it.

Under a normal, unregulated market, impending shortages or scarcities translate into price signals for producers to increase supply, and for consumers to reduce consumption. Both influences thus tend to compensate for growing scarcity. Price controls, on the other hand, eliminate this signaling and incentive function. In distorting this sophisticated information system, they thereby reduce significantly the flexibility of the energy system to harness the cooperation of thousands of suppliers and millions of consumers to assist in solving the energy problem. This reduced flexibility increases the need for new regulations to deal with the problems created in part by price controls.

Multi-tier Price Controls

An added indirect effect occurs when price regulations allow different prices for the same fuel, such as currently for oil and, under the Carter plan, for natural gas controls. The problem arises from competition among purchasers for access to lower-priced over higher-priced fuel. Such competition can artificially increase the price of any uncontrolled commodity purchased from the same source selling the price-controlled commodity.

For example, a firm that produces both old oil, controlled at $5.17 per barrel, and stripper oil, which is uncontrolled and has a normal market price of $14.00, could sell access to each barrel of old ($5.17) oil by selling stripper oil for $20.83 per barrel. In such a case, the refiner whose only alternative is $14.00 imported oil would save $1.00 per barrel on the oil he purchases in comparison to imported oil, and the producer would make $6.00 per barrel more than he would if he sold the two types of oil separately.

Phelps and Smith (1977), in their discussion of the Phase IV mandatory price controls, cite one rumor of a refiner alleged to have paid $50,000 for one barrel of new oil in order to gain access to a larger quantity of price-controlled old oil! When there are several different prices for one commodity, there is an incentive artificially to raise the price of the decontrolled portion in order to secure access to the controlled. To eliminate artifical pricing normally requires new regulations—which, for oil, has meant an allocation and entitlements program, to be considered presently. Other more subtle transactions are also available when all units of a commodity are controlled, but at different prices.

There is also an incentive on the supplier to spend resources to change his product from a low-priced to a higher-priced category. For example, if natural gas found within 2.5 miles of producing wells will have a lower price than natural gas found at a greater distance—as proposed by President Carter—firms will have an incentive to search for natural gas at the greater distance, even though it may be more likely they will find gas inside the 2.5 mile area. This distorted incentive of a multi-tier pricing system is very costly to the economy.

An additional important incentive occurs when exemptions to the regulations are granted to small producers. For example, stripper wells—wells producing no more than 10 barrels per day—are exempted from crude oil price controls. This creates a "notch effect" whereby revenues decrease discontinuously when the threshold quantity is passed and the exemption no longer applies. The notch effect provides a strong incentive against increasing supply above the threshold. Thus an oil well producing at 10 barrels per day, and exempt from controls, will generate revenues of $140 per day (10x$14), while one producing at 11 barrels per day will face controls and generate revenues of only $57 per day (11x$5.18). Even producing at 25 barells per day generates less revenue than producing at 10 barrels. A strong incentive against increasing production above 10 barrels per day is thereby established. This distortion is also very costly to the economy.

This discussion shows that the problems associated with price regulations thus mandate establishment of new regulations, which in turn can be expected to create still more problems. In the case of incentives to spend resources to change a fuel from a lower- to a higher-priced category, it is difficult to imagine any regulations that would eliminate the real social losses produced by a multi-tier pricing system.

The remainder of this section will consider the specific regulations governing oil, natural gas, and electricity.

Petroleum Price Regulation

The price of domestic crude oil has been controlled since 1973— first under the Phase IV mandatory price controls, and currently under the Energy Policy and Conservation Act (EPCA). Four related regulatory mechanisms are currently in effect: price ceilings on domestically produced oil, an allocation of different classes of oil to refiners, an entitlements program, and refined products price controls. The first, second, and fourth provisions above were needed to control prices throughout the energy system effectively, while the third addressed problems created by the others.

Under the provisions of EPCA, in February 1976 the average price of domestically produced crude oil (excluding stripper wells) was required to average no more than $7.66 per barrel. EPCA allows prices to increase by a maximum of 10 percent per year until June 1979, at which point, unless it is extended, the act is scheduled to expire. At that time the average domestic price of oil could not exceed $10.52, which compares with the February 1977 wellhead price of uncontrolled (stripper) oil of $13.32 and the refiner acquisition cost of imported crude oil of $14.50.

Under current regulations a multi-tier pricing system exists for crude oil. Domestic oil production is divided into three categories or tiers: The lower tier, the upper tier, and stripper oil. Lower-tier oil—old oil—comes from fields producing in 1972. All oil from such fields up to the quantity produced in 1972 or 1975 (whichever is less) is deemed to be old oil, and its price is controlled at an amount equal to its price in May 1973 plus $1.35 per barrel. This price currently averages $5.18 per barrel. Under current regulations, these lower-tier prices will be allowed to increase with the overall inflation rate.

Stripper oil is produced from a property whose average production does not exceed 10 barrels per day. The stripper oil price is not controlled. Upper-tier oil—new oil—is all domestic production other than stripper oil or old oil, and its price is set to satisfy the average price controls mandated by EPCA. In February 1977 the price was controlled at $11.39 per barrel.

Under current law, then, oil of a given type can have one of four different prices: the lower-tier price, the upper-tier price, stripper price, or the imported price, although the last two prices tend to be roughly equivalent. The price paid for oil under current regulations depends less on its quality than on its development rate. And under the Carter plan this regulatory tangle would be thickened by the addition of a fifth category of oil—new-new oil—with a separate controlled price.

Allocation. As noted earlier, the price regulations could not be effective without mandating access to the low-priced old oil. Otherwise, those holding old oil could sell access to it by increasing the price of imported or stripper oil up to the difference between the controlled price of old oil and its market value. Under the 1973 Emergency Petroleum Allocation Act (EPAA), property rights to old oil were established by allocation. Refiners purchasing old oil in December 1973 were given the right to continue purchasing it at the controlled price. The allocation program thus reduced circumvention of the price controls.

Entitlements Program. The crude oil controls and allocation program created problems of equity among the refiners, for refiners with access to old oil would have lower production costs and thus would earn more profit than refiners lacking access. To combat this regulation-induced problem, an entitlements program was established to roughly equalize the price of crude oil obtained by each refiner. The entitlements program provides that for every barrel of crude oil refined, a refinery receives a fraction of an entitlement to purchase old oil, the fraction being equal to the national total domestic refinery purchases of old oil divided by the national total quantity of oil domestically refined. Refiners are required to have entitlements for the quantity of old oil they refine. Firms with more entitlements than needed can sell them to firms having insufficient quantities. The price of an entitlement is set by the Federal Energy Administration (FEA) to equal the difference between the average price of uncontrolled oil and the average price of old oil. Under this program, a refinery pays an effective price of oil equal (including the value of entitlements) roughly to the average price of all oil refined in the United States.

The following example will illustrate how the entitlements program works under a two-tier pricing system (the current three-tier system is analogous but slightly more complex). Let's assume that old oil comprises 25 percent of all oil used in the United States and sells for $5.60 delivered to the refinery, while new oil and imported oil sells for $14.00 delivered. The average price of oil used in the United States thus would be $11.90. Under the entitlements program, refiners would be given 25 percent of an entitlement for every barrel of oil they refined; the entitlement would be worth $8.40—the difference between $14.00 and $5.60. A refiner using only imported oil would get one entitlement worth $8.40 for every 4 barrels of imported oil he refined, for a value of $2.10-worth of entitlements per barrel of oil. Thus the net cost for importing oil would be $11.90 (the difference between $14.00 and $2.10), the average cost of oil. Similarly, a refiner who used only old oil would get 25 percent of an entitlement for each barrel of oil refined, and would have to buy 75 percent of an entitlement at a cost of $6.30 for each barrel; the net cost would be the sum of

$6.30 plus $5.60, to reach the same total of $11.90. The net cost of purchasing the crude oil thus would be the same no matter what fraction of old oil the refiner were allocated.

Several complications exist. The price of an entitlement actually equals the difference between the average prices of uncontrolled oil and of old oil minus 21¢ per barrel, which is the fee imposed upon imported oil. Therefore, refiners importing oil or using stripper oil will pay slightly more than refiners using old oil. A second complication is caused by the current three-tier pricing system, under which entitlements are distributed according to an average of receipts of low-tier oil and upper-tier oil. But the fundamental principle is the same even though the program's administration is rather complex.

Finally, a price ceiling has been established for refined products, based on prices in May 1973—with ceiling prices allowed to increase with costs. Cost increases must be allocated to refined products in proportion to output, except for gasoline. A refiner may choose to allocate to gasoline as much of the cost increases as he likes, which correspondingly reduces the cost allocable to other refined products. As a result, price controls on gasoline are effectively less rigid than the price controls on other products. Recently, however, the price controls for several fuels, including residual fuel and middle distillate, have been eliminated, and gasoline price controls are scheduled for elimination.

The combination of regulatory programs has the effect of taxing most domestic crude oil and subsidizing imports, with a March 1977 subsidy of $2.38 per barrel. The tax on domestic oil tends to discourage production from U.S. sources, reduces exploration, discourages secondary and tertiary recovery, and discourages stripper wells from being increased in production above 10 barrels per day. The subsidy to imports encourages imports of foreign oil, which directly conflicts with the policy goal of reducing imports and especially reducing dependence on OPEC. Moreover, keeping the average price of oil low encourages wasteful consumption of petroleum products. This under the current system consumers are using oil for activities in which it is worth only $11.90 per barrel, while the additional oil used in that consumption costs the economy $14.50 per barrel as an import. At the same time, the system discourages domestic firms from producing oil that could be obtained at prices above the low controlled price and below the $11.90 price at which additional barrels of oil for consumption are valued.

In addition, the system is extremely difficult to regulate. The Carter administration seems to be having great difficulty defining new-new oil. The definition proposed by the administration would exclude the majority of promising exploration sites, leaving only less promising sites more than 2.5 miles from currently producing wells. Even if a satisfactory definition can be found, enforcing compliance is extremely difficult. An FEA task force (MacAvoy 1977) has estimated that reporting and compliance costs under the current regulations (which are far less complicated than those proposed by Carter) amount to about $500 million per year, with an additional cost of $47 million per year—borne by taxpayers—to maintain FEA's regulatory program. Carter's more complex regulations would result in proportionately greater costs.

President Carter has proposed permanent continuation of controls in a multi-tier system. The controls would be coupled with taxes on the various categories of domestic oil to bring the price of oil to the consumer up to the world oil price. This proposal would eliminate the price advantage enjoyed by consumers and therefore would eliminate much of the uneconomic overuse of oil caused by the artificially low prices. At the same time, however, the proposal would not change the prices faced by suppliers and therefore would do nothing to increase supplies to economically efficient levels. Oil company and oil lease profits would remain unchanged from the current system, and the taxes collected would either be rebated to the population or used to fund government programs.

Among possible alternatives, one would be to decontrol crude oil prices over a limited time, say, three years. To accomplish this, crude oil pricing regulations could be altered to redefine the maximum allowable prices of upper-tier oil and to define a schedule phasing out the quantity of oil from each property considered to be old oil. For example, Congress could allow the upper-tier oil price to increase by 10 percent per year above the inflation rate. If an alternative rate were chosen, it should be less than the before-tax interest rate facing firms, to avoid problems of withholding inventories of oil from the market.

Under such a rule, if the world price of oil increased at just the rate of inflation, the upper-tier oil price would reach the world oil price by 1980. If the world oil price were to increase more rapidly than general inflation, then the upper-tier price would reach the world price at a later date. Once this occurred, all controls on upper-tier oil could be eliminated.

Lower-tier oil prices could be increased at just the rate of inflation. However, from a given field the quantity of oil considered to be ''old'' can be reduced monthly: at a given time the quantity of old oil from a particular property could be set as a base. The quantity of oil considered as old oil from that property can be decreased by 3 percent of the base level each month. At the end of thirty-four months, by definition, all old oil will have disappeared and all oil will be considered ''new.''

Under such a plan, if the world oil price increased at just the rate of general inflation, the average per barrel price of domestically produced oil would increase about $1.50 per year, and the average price by $0.75 per year above the inflation rate. This decontrol plan would thus increase the per-gallon price of petroleum products by less than $0.02 per year—a rate small enough to avoid negative impacts on the domestic economy. At the same time, the plan would provide consumers and producers with information about oil prices expected over the next three or four years. The expectation of continuing increases would encourage producers and consumers of petroleum to take that into account in making investment decisions. Finally, this plan would not require a permanent bureaucracy, but would rely on self-policing market forces.

Natural Gas Pricing

In light of Robert Pindyck's extensive discussion in Chapter VI, I will consider natural gas regulation here only briefly.

Under current law, the Federal Power Commission (FPC) exercises federal regulatory jurisdiction over natural gas transmitted or sold in interstate commerce. Natural gas marketed in intrastate commerce is free from federal regulation. The FPC sets the maximum price that can be charged for natural gas at the wellhead and regulates the price of gas delivered to local natural gas distribution companies. Natural gas distributors are regulated by state public utility commissions or by local governments.

The price for new natural gas contracts in the interstate market has been controlled at $1.42 per mcf since August 1976, when it was increased from a price of $0.52 per mcf.[1] This contrasts with average prices for new interstate contracts in Louisiana of $2.19, in Oklahoma of $1.69, and in Texas of $1.97 per mcf.

The price differential between the interstate and the intrastate markets sustains a strong incentive for new natural gas finds to be dedicated to the intrastate rather than the interstate market. The magnitude of this incentive can be illustrated by comparing the average annual reserve additions of natural gas in the interstate market to the additions in the intrastate market over two time periods. In the period 1964-1969, when price controls in the interstate market were not particularly severe, 68 percent of annual reserve additions went to the interstate market and 32 percent to the intrastate market. These figures closely correspond to the rate of deliveries of natural gas to the two classes of pipelines: in 1974, 65 percent of natural gas was delivered to interstate pipelines while 35 percent was delivered to intrastate pipelines. In the period 1970-1975 the price of natural gas in the intrastate market grew rapidly while prices in interstate markets were not allowed to increase as rapidly. During this period 95 percent of the average annual reserve additions were dedicated to the intrastate market while only 5 percent were dedicated to the interstate market (FEA 1976). Thus the current natural gas price controls imply that a differential access to new natural gas is afforded to the intrastate market over the interstate market. Under current controls, new natural gas contracts have been virtually unavailable to interstate markets except for natural gas found on the outer continental shelf (OCS), which by law must be dedicated to the interstate market.

The second significant impact of the natural gas price regulations has been reduced supply. Regulations in the interstate market have led to price decreases in the intrastate market also, and therefore to an aggregate supply reduction through a reduction in exploratory and production activities. An even more pronounced effect has occurred on the OCS, where all finds must face the lowest price.

A third effect has been the increase in the demand for natural gas. Since it is a clean, desirable fuel, and is priced lower than petroleum,[2] there has been an incentive for consumers to favor natural gas above all other fuels wherever it can be used.

In summary, natural gas price controls have reduced supply, increased demand, and have led to the creation of shortages, and these shortages have been concentrated in the regulated interstate market. For more extensive discussion of shortages projected under continued FPC regulation, the Carter plan, and phased deregulation—and of their effects—see Chapter VI.

Electricity Pricing

Electric utilities probably comprise the most highly regulated component of the energy supply system. This regulation has been predominantly at the state level through state regulatory commissions, which normally have the power to establish authorized rates of return, determine the base upon which the rate can be applied, set the electricity price structure, license plant expansion, establish safety and liability standards, and prescribe accounting and reporting standards. This section will focus only on price regulation.

Electric utility rate structures are established to allow a rate of return on invested capital corresponding to the utilities' estimated cost of capital. Electricity prices therefore tend to reflect the average cost of generating electricity, rather than the added cost of producing additional quantities (i.e., the marginal cost). This can lead to underpricing, particularly in a time of rapid inflation when the historical cost of capital equipment may be significantly less than replacement cost.

The rate-of-return regulatory system also leads to prices which are too low whenever the utility has developed low-cost sources of electricity which are not available for further development. This phenomenon is particularly important in the Pacific Northwest, where a large portion of electricity is generated using hydropower with a very low average cost. Since most potential sites for hydropower have been fully developed, new generating capacity tends to require nuclear, coal, or other fossil-fuel fired plants, with significantly higher costs. Consumers face a low price of electricity and are thus encouraged to expand consumption. The expansion, however, requires development of new, high-cost facilities which impose large costs on the electric system. Since the additional costs are larger than the value of the additional electricity consumed, this overuse of electricity leads to deadweight losses in the overall economy.

The magnitude of the problem may be seen by comparing some electricity average prices to the costs of increased electricity generation. In 1975 the average price of electricity sold to ultimate customers in the United States was 2.7¢ per Kwh.[3] In New England this price averaged 4.1¢, while in Oregon and Idaho the price averaged 1.3¢ per Kwh, and in Washington, 0.9¢. The computer runs supporting the FEA's *National Energy Outlook* (1976) showed a marginal cost of new electricity generation ranging between 3.0¢ and 3.7¢ per Kwh, with an average of about 3.5¢. Thus for the nation as a whole the additional (i.e., marginal) cost of electricity generation was roughly 30 percent higher than the average price being charged. In the Pacific Northwest the cost of additional electricity in 1975 was 3.5 to 4.0 times as great as the prices being charged. These differences between price and marginal cost create strong incentives to overuse electricity, especially in locations like the Pacific Northwest.

Although complete deregulation of electric utilities is probably not justified because of their monopoly position in most service areas, the situation could be improved if regulatory commissions began moving towards marginal cost pricing by establishing rates corresponding to the costs of generating additional quantities of electricity rather than to the average cost. In most cases such a move would lead to large profits earned by the electric utililties, but these profits could be captured by a highly progressive tax. For example, all profits above the allowable rate of return could be taxed at a rate of, say, 90 percent. Revenues could be distributed to the public by reduced property or income taxes, new governmental programs, low rates for a "lifeline" quantity of electricity for low-income families, or a combination of these measures.

Marginal cost pricing, coupled with a highly progressive tax on earnings above the allowable rate of return, would provide an incentive to the electric utilities to cut costs, for the cost-cutting activities would allow after-tax profits to increase. The major administrative obstacle to this approach results from the fact that marginal costs are much harder to estimate than are average costs. Under such a plan, electric utilities would have a strong incentive to overestimate the cost of new generating capacity to allow increases in the rates which can be charged, and rate hearings would become more complex. However, economic efficiency would increase with decreased growth of electricity consumption. Price signals would again become compatible with costs, and the self-interest of electricity consumers would be harnessed to reduce the rate of electricity growth.

QUANTITY CONTROLS

A second broad class of regulations attempts to control the aggregate quantity of energy produced, imported, or consumed, or to allocate these various quantities among different classes of energy consumers. Supplies of natural gas and supplies of old oil both face mandatory allocation systems. Until 1973 the Mandatory Oil Import Program set limits on the quantity of crude oil and products that could be imported into the United States. During the oil embargo, provisions of the 1973 Emergency Petroleum Allocation Act allocated crude oil and petroleum products to various users. Gasoline rationing has often been proposed, and administration spokesmen have recently threatened to impose upper limits on the production of gasoline if the 10 percent reduction goal in gasoline consumption is not met.

It is useful conceptually to separate programs which rigidly allocate fixed quantities of energy products to consumers (allocation programs) from programs which restrict aggregate quantities but allow flexibility as to allocation among potential users (aggregate quantity control programs).

Allocation programs generally have been established in response to shortages. Natural gas allocation has become necessary because of the shortages caused by price regulations. Refined petroleum product allocations were initiated during the oil embargo to distribute shortages as equally as possible. The current crude oil allocation program has been made necessary by the multi-tier pricing system, which creates a shortage-like situation for old oil.

Allocation systems normally require massive efforts to enforce compliance, and what flexibility there is can come only by complex judicial proceedings. They require federal centralization of decision making, along with extensive collection and processing of information. The cost to firms of compliance and reporting can be extremely high. Nevertheless, without allocation, shortages caused by regulation would be virtually impossible to manage. As energy shortages have been caused by government programs, therefore, allocation programs have become unavoidable.

Aggregate quantity controls restrict the quantity of a product which can be produced, imported, or consumed, but without rigidly allocating it. Petroleum import quotas and gasoline rationing are good examples. Aggregate quantity controls require a complementary mechanism for allocating rights to import or consume. Ration coupons which can be freely traded on a "white market" provide one such mechanism. Governmentally distributed (allocated, sold at a fixed price, or auctioned) rights to import crude oil would be another. Whatever their allocation mechanism, the rights will have a value and thus will command a market price.

Controlling aggregate quantities will normally increase some aspect of the commodity price. In the case of oil-import quotas, the market price of crude oil will rise. For gasoline rationing, the market price of the ration coupon will increase to equate the total demand for gasoline to the aggregate quantity allowed under the scheme.

In general, quantity restrictions will produce effects very similar to those under an excise tax; both will increase the price of the commodity and decrease the quantity consumed. In the case of a tax, the price is determined, and the quantities then adjust to the policy-determined price. The specific change in quantities depends on how the markets respond to price increases—or the "elasticity of demand." Aggregate quantity controls, on the other hand, determine the quantity allowable; the price adjusts depending on market conditions, especially on elasticity of demand. Thus one principal difference between excise tax programs and the aggregate quantity restrictions concerns which variable—prices or quantity—is controlled accurately and which is allowed to adjust to market forces. A second principal difference, of course, is in ease of administration.

The above comments apply only to aggregate quantity restrictions when prices are not controlled. However, when *both* aggregate quantity and prices are controlled, shortages will result and must be managed. If the price of gasoline ration coupons were controlled along with the price of gasoline, black markets would develop. Limitation of the aggregate quantities of gasoline available, without coupon rationing, would lead to long lines at the gasoline pumps, such as those that formed in early 1974. Crude oil import quotas coupled with petroleum price controls would lead to shortages such as experienced during the oil embargo, and would require additional strict regulations to reduce the disruption associated with the shortages.

The remainder of this section discusses two of the more important aggregate quantity controls—oil import quotas and gasoline rationing.

Oil Import Quotas

One frequently suggested mechanism for reducing the oil imports is a quota on crude oil imports and/or refined petroleum products. Such a program has been in effect in the past. In 1959 President Eisenhower established the Mandatory Oil Import Program (MOIP) which set quotas on petroleum, and MOIP remained in effect until 1973 when the quotas were removed. It is now suggested that the U.S. return to such a program to deal with the problems of growing imports.

An import quota could be effective in reducing crude oil imports, although of course complex additional regulations would be necessary to make implementation feasible. Several classes of regulation are possible. One approach would be for the U.S. government to act as the sole petroleum-buying agent. Under this plan all foreign producers would submit sealed bids to fill the quotas. A second possibility would be for the U.S. to auction off import rights to firms, who would then be allowed to import oil in amounts equal to the number of rights possessed.

Under MOIP, imports of crude oil were reduced and the U.S. price of oil was increased above the world price. Such a price effect would also occur in the future if crude oil quotas were reestablished, unless domestic crude oil price controls were continued. The price increase would increase supply and reduce demand just enough to reduce imports to the quota levels. The extent of price increases would depend on the severity of the import restrictions and on the degree of demand and supply responsiveness to price (the elasticities of demand and supply, respectively). If the elasticities were low, then domestic prices would increase greatly, while high elasticities would produce only small price increases.

An import quota with marketable import rights sold by the government is equivalent to a tariff on imported oil. The quota might be imposed to reduce the imports by a given quantity, say, 1 million barrels per day; if so, the domestic price of oil would rise by some amount, say, $2.00. On the other hand, the same results would occur from a $2.00 tariff on all imported oil; the domestic price would rise until it equaled the new import price including the tariff. The result would be to increase supply and reduce demand so as to reduce imports by 1 million barrels per day—precisely the amount reduced under the quota system. Although the mechanisms of implementing the two alternatives are quite different, a tariff and an import quota have equivalent effects.[4]

Note that if the elasticities of demand and of supply are small, then a large tariff would be needed to reduce imports by a given amount, just as a large price increase would result from the given quota. Thus arguments about precise supply and demand elasticities are not relevant in judging which of the two instruments is more desirable.

Oil import quotas might tend to influence world petroleum prices. One motivation for the OPEC nations to moderate price increases is that such increases reduce demand for OPEC oil, and this reduction falls disproportionately on one or two of the major OPEC producers. Thus the more responsive is the demand for OPEC oil to OPEC prices, the greater will be the incentive for OPEC to moderate price increases. On the other hand, a U.S. import quota makes U.S. demand for OPEC Oil independent of OPEC prices, and thus reduces the degree which OPEC price increases will reduce demand for oil. For this reason an inflexible import quota could encourage further rises in OPEC-administered oil prices. This would not be true of an import tariff.

Gasoline Rationing

Proposals have been offered time and again for gasoline rationing to reduce the consumption of energy in transportation. Under recent proposals, gasoline rationing would be implemented with ration coupons which would be freely traded on a "white market." Members of the population would be allocated gasoline ration coupons under some rule. For example, the ration coupons could be distributed in equal amounts to all licensed drivers, or to all individuals of driving age, or equally on a per capita basis, or equally within a state, with different states obtaining rations in proportion to the historic gasoline consumption. Under rationing, consumers would be required to transfer to the gasoline retailer (along with the monetary cost of the gasoline) a number of coupons equal to the number of gallons of gasoline purchased. The gasoline retailer would be required to turn over to a governmental facility a number of coupons sufficient to cover his retail sales of gasoline. Thus the quantity of gasoline sold would equal the aggregate amount of gasoline coupons distributed to the public.

Under a rationing system, individuals could buy as much gasoline as they desired, as long as they had sufficient ration tickets. If people wanted or needed to consume more gasoline than could be covered by their allotment of tickets, they could buy additional coupons at the market price from those who desired to consume less than their allotment. There would thus be no absolute limit on the gasoline used by any one individual. Gasoline consumption would simply have a price equal to the monetary prices of gasoline plus the coupon.

The ration coupon price would be set by market forces so as to equate the demand for gasoline to the aggregate quantity of gasoline rationed. If the elasticity of demand is low—that is, if consumption changes only slightly in response to increased prices —then the ration coupon price would be very high; if the elasticity is high, the coupon price would be low.

A gasoline rationing system would influence the distribution of wealth, depending on how much gasoline individuals used and on the initial scheme of allocation. The wealth of those who use exactly as much gasoline as their initial allotment will be unaffected by the program. Those who use more gasoline than their allotment will be hurt, while those who use less will get a windfall.

A gasoline rationing system would produce effects virtually identical to those under a gasoline tax system, with tax revenues rebated to the public. For concreteness, let's assume that the ration coupons are equally distributed to all people of driving age.[5] Assume that each driving-age adult is given a monthly allotment of 50 ration coupons, each good for one gallon of gasoline, and that the equilibrium market price for coupons is $0.40 per coupon. If the gasoline price were $0.65 per gallon, then the total price facing each consumer would be $1.05 per gallon of gasoline purchased. The 50 coupons distributed to each adult would have a total value of $20.00. A person using only 40 gallons of gasoline in a month would gain $4.00 a month, while a person using 60 gallons of gasoline would lose $4.00.

Consider now an equivalent gasoline tax system in which the government imposes a tax of $0.40 per gallon of gasoline. In this case, each consumer would face a gasoline price of $1.05 per gallon. Since consumers face the same total price under this tax system as they would under the rationing system, total demand for gasoline would be the same, as would total consumption. The government would collect tax revenues of $0.40 times the number of gallons of gasoline sold, which would yield revenues just sufficient to distribute tax rebates of $20.00 per month to each driving-age adult. Under such a tax system, people who consume 60 gallons of gasoline per month would lose $4.00 a month, while those using 40 gallons would gain $4.00.

Thus a gasoline rationing system would be identical to a gasoline tax system in several respects. Consumption of gasoline, prices facing consumers, and distribution of wealth would all be identical under the two systems. Conceptually, for every gasoline rationing system there is an equivalent gasoline tax system, and vice versa.

There are differences between the systems, however. The first relates to uncertainty of outcomes. With a tax system, while one would have confidence in the gasoline price facing consumers, total consumption of gasoline would be uncertain because of uncertainty about the economic forces and parameters which influence consumption. With a gasoline rationing system, on the other hand, the quantity of gasoline consumed would be known with a high degree of confidence, but the coupon prices would be uncertain. Price uncertainty would allow individuals to make more intelligent decisions about the type of automobile to purchase, the location of their home vis-a-vis job location, and vacation and travel options. In normal circumstances, price certainty is more important than certainty about the quantity consumed, although in emergency circumstances such as an oil embargo, the quantity certainty of gasoline rationing may be preferable to the price certainty of a tax system.

A second major difference between the two types of plans is in administrative feasibility. A gasoline tax system could be easily implemented through existing mechanisms. The rebate could be accomplished through the income tax and withholding system. In contrast, a rationing plan would require a new system for printing, distributing, and collecting ration coupons—as well as new enforcement mechanisms such as to insure against forgery, and against incorrect allotment of coupons. The administrative problems of rationing could be overwhelming compared with a gasoline tax program.

DIRECT REGULATION OF ENERGY-USING APPLIANCES

The third broad class of energy regulations impose restrictions on energy-using appliances or on their use. Many such regulations are described in terms of "conservation," or as a "coal conversion program," or "environmental protection program." Such regulations normally specify the types of energy-using equipment that are allowable for certain activities and/or specify use limits.

Some of the more important of these regulations include efficiency standards for newly purchased cars, for new commercial and residential buildings, and for appliances, restrictions requiring "best available technology" for coal-fired electric power generation, restrictions against the use of oil and natural gas in electric utilities or in new industrial boilers, the national 55 mph speed limit, and proposed regulations for the insulation retrofit of existing dwelling units.

Among the many goals for such direct regulations, predominant are those to reduce consumption of energy, or to shift demand for energy away from oil and gas to coal and nuclear power. But such restrictions normally have indirect effects as well.

New-car efficiency standards may increase transportation costs for large families, many of whom may find that large station wagons provide the most efficient transportation. Mandatory insulation of existing homes can be extremely costly—often more costly than the value of the energy it would save (which tends to explain why insulation has not already been installed). As a requirement of resale, mandatory insulation of existing dwelling units would reduce mobility, would inhibit families from shifting residence location as job locations change, and would tend to keep families in homes no longer suited to their current circumstances. Thus new-car efficiency standards and existing home-insulation retrofit requirements reduce flexibility for the population to respond to changing circumstances or diversity of situation.

Appliance efficiency standards also limit flexibility. For example, the appropriate trade-off between new purchase price and energy efficiency for an air conditioner depends on the intensity of use. In many parts of California, where air conditioners are used only infrequently, purchase price might be the dominant consideration, while in many parts of the southeast the expected intensive use of air conditioning would make energy efficiency dominant. National efficiency standards for appliances thus would penalize people who use appliances infrequently.

Prohibiting the use of oil and gas in electric utilities may impose excessive costs in the southwestern section of the United States, where electric utilities were constructed to burn natural gas. This contrasts to utilities in the northeast, where generating plants were initially constructed to burn coal but were converted to oil and gas because of government environmental regulations.

The diversity of proposals here makes it impossible to generalize, other than to note that strict regulations often greatly reduce the flexibility of individuals to respond to the particular circumstances facing them; the result is almost inevitably inefficient and wasteful. The remainder of the section will consider two existing regulations: the efficiency standards for new cars, and those for residential and commercial buildings.

New-Car Efficiency Standards

To reduce the growth rate of gasoline consumption, the Energy Policy and Conservation Act (EPCA) mandated new-car average minimum efficiency standards under which the mean efficiency of all cars sold by each manufacturer must meet or exceed 20 miles per gallon by 1980 and 27.5 miles per gallon in 1985. A civil penalty (not deductible for tax purposes) is imposed on manufacturers failing to meet the standard, and the penalty structure is strong enough to ensure that the manufacturers will comply rather than pay the penalty (see Sweeney 1978).

Under EPCA regulations, manufacturers have an incentive to add price differentials to individual models according to their efficiency, because the total penalty is based on the average efficiency, increasing with every inefficient car and decreasing for every efficient one. Therefore, prices for efficient cars will be reduced, and they will be increased for inefficient ones. By motivating consumers to buy fewer inefficient cars and more of the efficient, average efficiency will increase and the civil penalty will decline. This scheme allows flexibility in permitting cars of different efficiency, while imposing implicit prices on consumers purchasing inefficient cars.

In light of the strong congressional desire to force consumers to buy more efficient cars, the new-car efficiency standard and penalty has been well designed to allow individual choice.[6]

On the negative side, new-car efficiency standards do increase transportation costs for large families who rely on large automobiles such as station wagons. The same penalty would be imposed on a family buying a station wagon to transport five children as would be imposed on the buyer of a large luxury car for commuting alone to work. Thus the standard does not account for different automobile uses. For example, a car getting 12 mpg and used to transport six people at a time obtains an efficiency of 72 person-miles per gallon of gas. A small car getting 30 mpg, but used typically to transport only one person, has an efficiency of 30 person-miles per gallon of gas, less than half the efficiency of the former car. Yet under the efficiency standard the former would be subject to a large penalty on purchase, and the latter would receive a subsidy. Regulations such as efficiency standards on new cars simply cannot deal adequately with such a diversity of uses. However, a gasoline tax can. A gasoline tax of 30.0¢ per gallon would impose a penalty cost of 0.4¢ per person-mile on the 12 mpg car used to transport six people, and would impose a penalty of 1.0¢ per person-mile on the 30 mpg car used to transport only one person. Therefore, a gasoline tax would be more equitable and more efficient in taking into account different use patterns as well as efficiency characteristics of the capital equipment, while providing incentives to modify utilization patterns. The EPCA average efficiency regulations do not do this.

Residential and Commercial Building Efficiency Regulations

EPCA also provides for the development and implementation of performance standards for new residential and commercial buildings—standards "designed to achieve the maximum practicable improvements in energy efficiency and increases in the uses of non-depletable sources of energy" (EPCA 1975). Under this law, the Secretary of Housing and Urban Development is required to develop and publish building energy efficiency standards which account for climatic variations among different regions of the country. Once performance standards are approved, federal financial assistance could be allowed for construction of new commercial or residential buildings only when the appropriate state or local bodies are implementing building restrictions that meet the standards.

This law will be extremely far reaching. The term "commercial building" is defined by EPCA to include all buildings that are not residential, including any building developed for industrial or public purposes. EPCA defines the term "federal financial assistance" to include loans made by any financial institution subject to federal regulation through bodies such as the Federal Deposit Insurance Corporation, the Home Loan Bank Board, and so on. Virtually all new construction financed through conventional financial institutions thus would be regulated for energy efficiency.

Such regulation is very different from the more flexible new-car efficiency standard which applies, not to individual cars, but only to the average. The new residential and commercial buildings regulations, on the other hand, apply to each individual building and therefore, unless designed to permit maximum flexibility, are unlikely to allow for differing circumstances. While the law specifies that performance standards must account for differences in climate, the standards need not account for other differences.

One among the many trade-offs in constructing a new building is that between capital cost and subsequent operating cost. Many features such as insulation can be designed into new buildings to reduce energy consumption and hence operating costs. But such design features require increased capital investment. The most efficient level of insulation or other design features depends on the trade-off between costs of capital and of operation. Therefore, the concept "maximum practicable improvements in energy efficiency" should suggest a construction designed to minimize the discounted stream of cost over the building lifetime. rather than to minimize energy consumption.

Other issues related to flexibility are important in designing such standards. Intended use of a building can be a significant issue in choosing appropriate energy performance standards. The insulation desired for a summer vacation home is typically much less than for a year-round home in the same place. It may be appropriate for air-conditioned buildings to be better insulated than those relying upon the circulation of outside air for summer cooling. Different styles of architecture may require different costs to obtain the same energy performance. It may be far less costly to obtain a given energy efficiency in a compact colonial-style home than in a ranch-style home with an inner patio. The standard thus should account for the wide variety of architectural styles. Unfortunately, unless the standards are flexible, they may do more than regulate energy efficiency; they may also end up regulating life styles, architectural styles, and other legitimate differences in individual choices.

Recent congressional proposals also seek to mandate insulation retrofit for existing dwelling units. One proposal would exclude federally regulated financial institutions from financing the resale of any home unless it were "adequately" insulated. As noted earlier, such a law could never account for differences in individual preferences. The cost of insulation retrofit and its desirability differ with the type of initial construction, the financial circumstances of the homeowner, the age of the dwelling unit, as well as differences in intended use and in climate. For many homes, insulation retrofit is simply not economically justified; therefore it would be inefficient to require it.

There are other potential undesirable side effects of mandating insulation retrofit. It has been noted that mandatory insulation on resale would tend to reduce the mobility of the population. Among other results, in discouraging people from moving closer to their jobs, the net effect could increase the average length of a commute trip, thereby increasing both family cost and gasoline consumption.

Building efficiency standards have been justified on several grounds. The most important is the so-called "first-cost bias," which asserts that purchasers of new dwelling units are more concerned with the initial purchase price than with the discounted stream of lifetime housing costs. This is alleged to occur for several reasons. First, consumers may not have adequate information about future heating costs. Second, banks may disregard future operating costs in judging allowable mortgages. Third, since people typically live in a given housing unit only a limited number of years—a number which is small in comparison to the lifetime of the house—they may not take into account more than a few years' worth of operating costs. And, finally, there is the argument that the new building standards are required because natural gas, oil, and electricity are all underpriced. The consumer therefore will put too little value on energy savings in choosing appropriate energy efficiency characteristics. Each of these arguments suggests appropriate actions other than the imposition of energy efficiency standards.

The first argument, that consumers have insufficient information, might have been correct in earlier years, but it is unlikely to be valid in a situation of higher energy costs, an enhanced energy consciousness amongst architects and builders, and an extensive information campaign conducted by elements of both the private and the public sector. But if it is still felt that insufficient information is available, agencies such as the Department of Commerce and the new Department of Energy could increase publicity campaigns.

If the second argument were true, that banks create a first-cost bias through their loan practice, then this practice could be modified through an information program directed at banks. A person facing lower home operating costs could afford correspondingly higher mortgage payments, leaving unchanged the risk of default. Information made available through such organizations as the Home Loan Bank Board, the Federal Deposit Insurance Corporation, and so on, should be sufficient to eliminate any first-cost bias in bank behavior, if any.

The limited length of typical home occupancy by an individual family will not lead people to underinsulate. Currently home buyers are considering heating costs, electricity bills, insulation adequacy, and so on, in purchasing homes. Thus the higher the energy efficiency of a home and the lower the operating cost, the greater the market value of the home when it is ultimately sold. A person who builds a home with a lower operating cost will experience lower costs during occupancy and a higher sale price when he moves. The higher price will capture both the next owner's reduced operating costs and the increased market value he expects to enjoy when he himself decides to move. The benefits of future operating cost savings thus accrue to families, even though they intend to live in the house only a limited period of time.

Finally, it is true that distorted information does result from other energy regulations, and that fact may create a need for building energy efficiency standards. Regulations that maintain low energy prices encourage underinsulation. But this is an argument to eliminate the price controls which have created the problem, rather than to impose another set of regulations to compensate.

SUMMARY AND CONCLUSIONS

The energy system in the United States today is dominated by controls on supply, conversion, and consumption. Prices are controlled at artificially low levels in most energy markets, and these artificially low prices have reduced supplies of domestically produced energy and increased demands. The result has been growing shortages of natural gas and growing imports of foreign oil.

Price regulations have exacerbated our energy problems and have helped create an environment in which additional regulations are proposed and implemented. In transportation, efficiency standards have been legislated for new cars, and gasoline rationing and mandatory restrictions have been proposed. In the residential sector, energy efficiency standards for newly constructed dwelling units are being developed; regulations requiring insulation retrofit of existing units have been proposed; and efficiency standards for energy-using appliances have been mandated. In the commercial sector, similar regulations are in effect. In the industrial sector, regulations have been proposed to prohibit oil and gas from new boilers, and voluntary programs of energy efficiency improvement have been instituted along with threats that these ''voluntary'' programs could be mandated. And in the electric utility sector, regulations have been proposed to prohibit electric utility use of oil and natural gas and to force conversion to coal. This move comes just seven years after federally imposed environmental regulations forced many electric utilities to convert from coal to oil or gas. However, current environmental regulations still make the use of coal difficult in electric utilities and in industrial boilers.

The present system of regulation thus creates demands for new regulations, as yesterday's ''solutions'' have become today's problems. Each regulation reduces individual flexibility to make personal choices based on particular circumstances. Under current proposals the controls would be expanded further.

What could be done to untie this Gordian knot?

The first step would be gradually to deregulate natural gas prices. All newly discovered gas and all new contracts should be deregulated, although existing contracts should be enforced. Under the system of long-term natural gas contracts, consumers would face a natural gas price rising slowly towards a free market price over the next ten to fifteen years, but there would be no price discontinuity. Natural gas suppliers, on the other hand, would immediately face a market-determined price for all marginal supplies; and after a relatively short transition period, shortages could be eliminated and exploration and new development stimulated.

The second step would be to decontrol crude oil prices over a period of three to five years. This could be accomplished by allowing the upper-tier price to increase at the rate of 10 percent per year faster than the rate of inflation until the world price is reached. At the same time, the quantities of oil considered to be "old oil" should be gradually reduced to zero over the next three years. A gradually increasing proportion of oil therefore would be considered to be "new," and the new oil price would rise towards the world price. The smooth price adjustment implied by this plan would eliminate adverse impacts on the economy and would provide users of oil with the appropriate price information to guide their investments in energy-using equipment.

The resulting increase in the price of domestically produced oil would shift significant wealth toward the owners of oil-bearing lands and oil leases. These so-called "windfall profits" are inventory profits—profits gained as the price of commodities (in this case, oil) held in inventories increases. By estimating reserve holding of the various firms, these inventory profits can be assessed and "windfall-profit taxes" could be imposed, based on the increased value of these reserve holdings. These taxes could be amortized and paid off by the companies to the government over a period of, say, ten years. Tax revenues generated could be rebated to the population.

The strategic petroleum reserve should be expanded above the current legislated minimum level (see Chapter II for Arthur Wright's more extensive discussion of this issue).

The environmental cost of using energy could also be incorporated into energy prices. For example, evidence exists that there is a significant environmental cost associated with the large quantities of CO_2 emmission into the atmosphere. To deal with this, the government could impose emissions charges—equalizing the estimated marginal cost of CO_2 emissions—to internalize environmental costs (see Chapter IV).

The federal government might also expand its information programs, which already include labeling for new appliances and automobiles, to include mandatory information programs on operating costs of new buildings. Labeling should facilitate consumer estimates of the discounted life-cycle cost of appliances, including energy costs and other operating costs, when significant. Ongoing information programs which alert consumers to costs and benefits of energy conservation measures could be continued or expanded. The government should also continue or expand programs making information available about the probable future course of energy supply, demand, and prices, to allow individuals the best available information to guide their decision making.

For electric utilities, state regulatory commissions could begin moving on a experimental basis towards peak-load pricing and long-run marginal cost pricing systems. The experimental beginning is important, because we do not have enough information as yet about the best way to manage such a pricing system.

Lastly, a way must be found to eliminate those regulations which have become unnecessary.

Taken together, these steps could go a long way toward reclaiming the flexibility needed to solve energy problems without sacrificing individual diversity.

VIII

WILLIAM R. MOFFAT

FEDERAL ENERGY PROPRIETORSHIP: LEASING AND ITS CRITICS

Proprietorship and its problems. The pace of leasing: coal; Outer Continental Shelf. Fair value: problem areas; recommended reforms. Environmental acceptability. The role of the states. The political problem. Amendment and reorganization.

INTRODUCTION

Coal, oil, and gas leasing may be byways of overall federal energy policy, but they are important and interesting ones. As owner of energy deposits, the federal government must decide how fast to lease them, try to capture a fair return for their use, pay proper heed to environmental risks, and deal with often fractious states whose interests are different from its own. These tasks are difficult, but at all of them federal performance could be improved.

The most important energy leasing program—offshore oil and gas—labors under a special burden: while it generates sizable benefits to the nation at large, it is a program nearly everyone dislikes. What to do about a productive program that is a pariah is the federal proprietor's biggest single challenge.

PROPRIETORSHIP AND ITS PROBLEMS

The federal government is the largest single owner of domestic energy resources. It owns large quantities of minerals because, at one time or another in its history, it has held title to some 80 percent of the nation's land and to all of the undersea area of the continental shelf beyond state boundaries. Despite disposal through the Homestead Act and other land laws, about one-third of the land area and all of the outer continental shelf (OCS) are still in federal hands (BLM 1973:1). But federal control of minerals is more extensive than the surface measures suggest, because in some cases mineral rights underlying federal lands were retained when the surface was disposed of, thus producing the most intricate energy policy problems. In the near term 20 to 30 percent of domestic oil and gas production is forecast to come from federal deposits (some three-fourths of that from the OCS) (FEA 1976: 64), and about 15 percent of national coal production from federal deposits (mostly in the west) (BLM 1976:1, 7).

These percentages are likely to rise in the future unless policies prevent it, because federally owned oil, gas, and coal comprise a larger portion of undeveloped resources than of current production. The federal OCS is the major domestic prospect for new oil and gas, and more than half of the extensive western coal reserves are federally owned. Should shale oil and geothermal steam become important energy sources in the future, federal proprietorship will be of major significance for them as well.

The broad policies of federal mineral proprietorship have been set by a series of statutes, notably the Mining Law of 1872, the Mineral Leasing Act of 1920, the Outer Continental Shelf Lands Act of 1953, and the Geothermal Steam Act of 1970. These laws set up three generic systems, each with many variants, for transferring federal minerals to private hands: the claim and patent system, noncompetitive leasing, and competitive leasing. Though the claim and patent system is still in use for so-called "hard-rock" minerals, all energy minerals were placed under leasing systems by the 1920 and later acts. Amendments to the Mineral Leasing Act passed in 1976 restrict future coal leasing to the competitive system, and OCS oil and gas have always been leased competitively. Among major energy minerals, only onshore oil and gas in areas not known to be promising may now be leased noncompetitively. Competitive leasing always involves some form of bidding, with award of the lease to the highest bidder. Ideally, competition would force bids up until the government received the full value of the deposit in excess of necessary compensation to the lessee. But approaching this ideal without causing undesirable side effects is a problem still unsolved.

The responsibilities of federal energy proprietorship are carried out by the U.S. Geological Survey (GS) and the Bureau of Land Management (BLM)—both in the Department of Interior. The Conservation Division of GS gathers prelease resource data, advises BLM on tract selection and on acceptance or rejection of bids, and then supervises lessees' operations and collects royalties. The role of BLM centers around choice of tracts to be offered, setting the terms of the leases, preparation of environmental impact statements, and conduct of the lease sale itself. This division of functions between BLM and GS has been basically stable for over half a century, since the Teapot Dome scandal which brought it into being. Now, however, new forces are causing major reexamination of the proprietorship system—not only its organization, but also its basic purposes. These forces include the rise of environmental concern expressed in the National Environmental Policy Act of 1969 (NEPA), and changes in the world energy economy—most dramatically those connected with OPEC, the embargo of 1973, and the sharp rise in energy prices. Together they have made a battleground of proprietorship policy.

I will examine four broad, underlying issues of proprietorship policy: Is the government leasing too slowly or too quickly? Is it getting a fair return? Are the leasing programs environmentally acceptable? What role should state governments play in decisions on leasing from federal lands?

THE PACE OF LEASING

Federal energy resources are nonrenewable: if used up today, they are not available tomorrow; if held for tomorrow, they cannot be enjoyed today. At various times, federal leasing has been criticized for being too fast or too slow. The pacing decision is probably the most important and most difficult the federal proprietor must make.

In principle, one can imagine an all-knowing federal resource owner who could look into the future and calculate the value of each of his deposits for alternate production time periods—a different value depending on whether the deposit were extracted and sold beginning in 1978, 1979, 1980, and so on into the future. Depending on interest rates (a dollar now is worth more than a dollar next year) and on future costs and prices, the worth of the deposit would be high or low depending on the time at which it was produced. The proprietor would then either mine his deposit himself at the time when its value was at its peak, or sell it now, for its peak value less interest, to someone else who would do the same. He would thus maximize his own wealth and also that of the community as a whole, assuming costs, prices, and interest rates were set competitively and that they measured social values. After evaluating the cost of waiting, the resource would be used when its net value was the greatest. Such an outcome would not only serve the goals of conservation; in fact, it embodies the very *definition* of proper conservation, which for energy should not mean saving it forever, but saving it until the best time for use. It also defines successful "speculation." The owner "withholds" the resource from the market until he can realize the greatest value from selling it (and society from consuming it). Thus the most basic task of the federal energy proprietor is to conserve (speculate) so as to supply its energy resources at a rate which will maximize their value to society as a whole. It can do this by leasing rapidly and counting on private lessees to decide when the deposits should be produced, or by leasing more slowly when in its own judgment the time is right; but each method has its set of dangers, one of which has been realized in coal and the other in OCS.

Coal

In recent years, pacing policies in coal have been less than single-minded. Leasing in the 1960s was almost completely permissive: when a company applied for a lease, one normally was issued. While leases under the 1920 Act were "subject to diligent development and continued operation of the mine," "diligence" was not defined or enforced. In effect, the pacing decision was fully in private hands. Indeed, by 1970 some 16 to 18 billion tons of recoverable federal coal were under lease, and prospecting permits were ripening into leases for large additional quantities; but production that year was only 7.4 million tons. Clearly, at this rate leases were being issued long before the time of peak production value; coal was being acquired so rapidly that very little could conceivably have been profitable to produce in the reasonably near future. This situation, combined with environmental criticism of leasing procedures, led the Interior Department to suspend leasing early in 1971, a suspension that continued with minor exceptions until 1976. Almost all existing leases (some 530 of them) and prospecting permits were issued before passage of NEPA, and they had granted rights which in some cases were probably inconsistent with the spirit of the act. Furthermore, most leases had brought little income to the government, even those sold competitively.

Outer Continental Shelf

The proper pace for offer of OCS leases has likewise been the subject of much debate. Through the 1960s the pace of leasing was modest; the area offered was confined to the central and western Gulf of Mexico and the Santa Barbara Channel. Plans to expand leasing to other areas were cancelled when the 1969 Santa Barbara blowout occurred. In 1973 about 1 million acres per year were being leased, all in the Gulf. A decision had been made but not yet implemented to raise the rate to 3 million acres per year. Shortly after the embargo and price rise, the administration announced its intent to raise the rate to 10 million acres and to lease off the east coast, Southern California, and Alaska. This decision aroused heavy opposition, and was soon modified to drop the acreage goal entirely. The new pacing policy was to offer leases six times a year, and at least once in each frontier area by 1980. How, if at all, the Carter administration will modify this pace is not yet clear, though its early decisions have all been to delay, not accelerate it.

On the OCS, basic diligence policy was determined by the OCS Lands Act of 1953 which set a five-year primary lease term, to be extended only if production in commercial quantities was in progress. There have been sharp debates about the details of administering this procedure; the legitimacy of some extensions of the primary term has been questioned; repeated allegations have been made that lessees were withholding oil and gas from the market. The overall policy, however, has been clear: a lessee is to explore and get into production within five years or relinquish his lease. No buildup of idle leases remotely comparable to that in coal has been allowed to develop.

The primary charge that can be made against OCS pacing is that it has been too slow. When OPEC raised the world price of oil in 1973 to $10 per barrel, and since then closer to $14, the question arose whether OCS leasing should be accelerated. The possibility existed of making at least some new discoveries of oil that could be extracted for as little as $2 per barrel in real resource costs, and much more at costs of $5-7 per barrel. The question was and is whether the nation should use its own cheap oil now and import correspondingly less, or save its own oil to use later. The answer, of course, depends on the future of OPEC and the world oil price. If OPEC stayed in existence indefinitely and raised the world price at about the rate of inflation—as it publicly spoke of doing—the correct policy was to lease quickly and substitute our own production for as much imported oil as possible: the nation could save $5 to $10 for each barrel of imports replaced by OCS production, and could thereby reduce the enormous wealth transfer to world oil exporters. Foreign policy arguments, based on the disadvantages of dependence on imports, strengthened the case. Alternatively, if OPEC were expected to collapse and the world oil price to drop again to something like its former levels, the argument for immediate acceleration of domestic output was even stronger—never again would we be able to save so much by using our own oil.

Postponing domestic production would make sense only if one expected OPEC not merely to remain strong, but to raise the price of oil so rapidly in the future that it would pay us to wait (after taking account of inflation and interest). This is extremely unlikely. The strains already visible on OPEC's ability to restrict production, combined with the probable substitution of other fuels in the face of continued price rises, make it extremely implausible.

These considerations prompted the administration to accelerate leasing early in 1974. Unfortunately, the decision has only partially been carried out. Strong opposition immediately arose from environmentalists and from governors of states adjacent to the new areas to be leased. Even more important, the two agencies which administer leasing in Interior—the Bureau of Land Management and the U.S. Geological Survey—never enthusiastically adopted the acceleration policy, and one administrative delay after another prevented reaching the hoped-for rate of leasing. Despite some progress, the fact unfortunately remains that now, four years after the basic decision, most of the outer continental shelf still has not been opened to exploration.

This must count as a fundamental failure of energy policy. Tracts are held unavailable for development even though the time of peak value for production may have arrived. In the case of OCS, the current sacrifice is plain: $5 to $10 for every barrel of oil imported instead of produced at home—a staggering cost. Failing to accelerate leasing could mean giving up as much as 3 million barrels of production per day by 1985; at the $5 figure, this would mean about $5 billion per year in losses to the nation as a whole. Although it is true that saving our own oil now would allow us to produce it later, presumably substituting it then for imports, postponement makes sense only if the gain from later production exceeds the present gain enough to justify waiting—only if the present value of future gain exceeds the gains of immediate production. No such argument has been made to justify the delays; the fact is that we have failed to accelerate leasing even though it is manifestly desirable. The failure has not been complete; one lease sale has been held in each of three new areas—the Gulf of Alaska, the mid-Atlantic, and off Southern California. But this is only a beginning; time after time, more ambitious lease schedules have been published and then canceled in the face of outside pressure or, more frequently, administrative lapse.

Seeking Improvement

Taken as a whole, then, the record of federal pacing has been a poor one: too fast on coal, too slow on OCS. How can we do better? The most effective procedure might be to maintain moderate diligence requirements, to watch the level of bids for new leases, and, if we err, to be on the side of too-rapid, not too-slow, pacing.

If enforced, moderate diligence requirements will prevent serious overleasing. Some companies—those with little or no prospect of mining a deposit within the allotted time—will be discouraged from bidding; companies which do bid, but whose deposits turn out not to be worth producing, will relinquish their leases. The total amount of the deposit under lease at any time therefore should not be grossly out of line with likely future production. Some excess of leases—in fact, a sizeable excess—is desirable, because it gives users of the resource a wider choice of deposits which can be developed on short notice. More leases should therefore be issued than are expected to be produced, and it should be normal to expect many of them to be eventually relinquished with no production at all. In form, the diligence requirements should distort firms' other decisions as little as possible, merely forcing the early choice between production and relinquishment. Any diligence requirement will cause some deposits to be produced before their peak value is reached, but this is a price we pay to prevent the ill effects of overleasing; and the price should not be high if the requirements are carefully designed.

High bids for new leases are the clearest indicator of too-slow pacing. The enormous prices being paid for OCS leases are the best possible evidence of the need to accelerate: individual tracts frequently sell for over $50 million, and have sold for more than $200 million. When bid levels shot up after the embargo, that was a clear signal that pacing needed a change. Evidence on high bids must be interpreted with some subtlety—particularly valuable tracts should command a high price regardless of pace. But when general bid levels are high, the signal deserves observation and response.

Even with moderate diligence requirements to protect against overleasing and surveillance of bid levels to prevent underleasing, choice of proper pace will always be somewhat uncertain. In making the choice, assuming diligence will be enforced, it is essential to recognize that the dangers of overleasing are far less serious than those of underleasing. Value lost through too-slow pacing is lost forever; too-rapid pacing need result in nothing more serious than excess paper work and perhaps a political flap over "speculation." Consider the rather extreme case—much more extreme than it need have been had moderate diligence been enforced—of the 530 federal coal leases, many of them a decade or more old and very few in production. Most of the reserves involved were leased during the middle and late 1960s, when it apparently grew clear to energy firms that coal was likely to become more valuable. At that time (and still) the bulk of these reserves were worthless for immediate production, but there was a change of demand for them in the future. Since Interior was not enforcing diligence requirements, nothing prevented the lease of large quantities. Although this has been widely bemoaned as a policy catastrophe, and it was certainly embarrassing to Interior to be caught ignoring the clear intent of the law's diligence provisions, the real harm that can result is rather limited, and there are some compensating benefits. If Interior now begins enforcing diligence as it has announced (and has been directed by the 1975 amendments), many if not most of the leases will eventually be relinquished: diligence requirements cannot force unprofitable production, and for many of the 530 leases production is unprofitable and will continue to be so for some time. Federal coal production is now in the neighborhood of 30 million tons per year (of a national figure of around 600 million tons) and rising. But even optimistic forecasts place it at no more than 150 million tons by 1985, and it would take only ten to twenty sizable new mines to supply that much increase. Before 1985 most lessees face the time limit on diligence. So nothing is going to happen on many existing federal leases: given the political will to enforce diligence, they will simply be turned in; even lacking the political will, most leases would remain inactive.

On the few leases that are developed, two problems may arise. First, since they date from before NEPA, they may be in areas where we would now prefer, for environmental reasons, that mining not take place. Interior and other agencies have weapons to ameliorate this problem through surface mining regulations, environmental stipulations for mining plans, air and water quality requirements, and, if all else fails, special legislation to void the leases and compensate their owners. If these available regulatory tools are used intelligently, it is difficult to see resultant massive environmental degradation.

The second problem with the few leases which are developed is that payment to the government may be seen as inadequate. When these leases were issued, the Mineral Leasing Act specified a minimum royalty of five cents per ton, and many of the leases carry that rate or little more. The leases issued noncompetitively of course brought no bonus, and even competitive leases usually sold for rather low bonuses in today's terms. This may arouse complaints, but at that time the leases probably were not in fact worth much; at best there was a speculative chance that they would become valuable in the distant future, and as it turns out a few of them will, though most will not. One's sense of economic justice would have to be delicate indeed to be seriously offended at this.

Thus the harm that can come from the overhang of inactive coal leases is hardly overwhelming. Moreover, there is a positive side. By virtue of the large amount of coal under lease, there is a wide choice available for satisfying new coal demand, and to that extent it is less likely that the OCS mistake is being repeated in coal by the government's refusal to make valuable resources available for use. All in all, while the problems of having overleased in the 1960s are real and not to be ignored, it seems clearly out of place to exaggerate them. With enforcement of diligence and intelligent environmental regulation, little serious harm should result.

The risks of an error in pacing are primarily in leasing too slowly. This is the cardinal rule for federal proprietorship; with reasonable diligence requirements and a close eye on the level of bids, serious pacing mistakes should be avoidable.

FAIR VALUE

A major objective of competitive leasing is to capture "fair value" for sale of a resource—that is, to reward lessees with only a sufficient return to justify their investment, and to return any excess to the Treasury. It is almost impossible to say whether energy leasing has in fact accomplished this. What evidence there is (Mead 1968) suggests that OCS lessees are not profiting unduly; but the evidence is both scarce and weak, and there are good, logical reasons for continuing to worry about the problem. At the same time, there is little danger it will be ignored, since the notion that the energy companies are ripping off the Treasury fits so conveniently into the ideology of a vocal section of the public.

One naive version of the rip-off argument should be disposed of immediately. The idea is that the Treasury loses money because "we don't know what we're selling." The "evidence" cited is usually an OCS tract for which the lessee's bid was far less than the value of the actual discovery. In fact, of course, we know *something* about what we're selling, but not *everything;* there is information, but not complete information, prior to bidding. An analogy is the flip of a true coin. We know that in a large number of flips heads will come up about half the time, but we do not "know" whether heads or tails will come up the *next* time: we have information, but it is incomplete. If you could win a dollar each time you correctly guessed whether heads would appear on the next flip, you would presumably be willing to pay somewhere near 50 cents per try to participate in the game (especially if others were bidding against you for the privilege). And if the bid were 50 cents, the proprietor of the game would receive "fair value": neither he nor you would have been cheated in the transaction. But note that if you look back at individual previous coin flips, the amount paid by the bidder was always wrong: he paid 50 cents each time, but the flip was worth either nothing or a dollar—he *always* paid either too much or too little. If you want to argue that the proprietor is being ripped off, all you need to do is cite as evidence one of the flips on which the bidder won. This is exactly the logic of citing individual OCS tracts on which bids were "too low," and the argument deserves exactly the same amount of one's attention. Clearly, it is the average over many tracts that matters, not any single outcome.

Problem Areas

More substantial reasons exist for concern, however, than "we don't know what we're selling." First, pre-bidding information may be unequally available to different firms. The problem here does not lie in normal pre-bidding exploration on a proposed lease, which is done under federal permit only on condition that the information be available to anyone who will pay his share of the costs; rather, the problem lies in the information advantage enjoyed by the lessee of an adjacent or nearby tract who has already drilled there. It is clear from the record of OCS leasing that such a situation "chills" the bidding on a tract; frequently the *only* bidder is the adjacent lessee. And when federal coal leasing resumes in areas of the west where federal and railroad-owned coal lands are intermingled in a checkerboard, the problem will almost certainly exist there too. If there is only one bidder for an energy lease, a major risk exists that the bid will not be close to the full value of the resources.[1]

Second, if firms are averse to the risks involved in making an offer on a lease, they will reduce their bids correspondingly. Where large sums must be committed before the main uncertainties (such as the presence of oil or gas) are resolved, and where the firm is not large enough to bid on a substantial number of tracts so as to improve the accuracy with which it can predict the average outcome, such aversion may well be a problem. Its seriousness should not be exaggerated; large energy companies spread their risks over very many tracts indeed, and even smaller ones do so by forming joint bidding consortiums among themselves or with the majors. But where, for any reason, small firms find it difficult or impossible to submit joint bids, risk aversion may tend to force them out of the auction, reduce the total number of bidders, and again create a danger that bids will be substantially below the expected value of the resource.

Third, the number of bidders may be reduced directly by the formation of too many joint bidding consortiums. Joint bidding has advantages in permitting risk-averse firms to spread their investment over a larger number of tracts; to that extent it increases the number of firms that can participate and enhances competition. On the other hand, competition is reduced if firms join together who might otherwise have bid separately. Interior recently banned joint bidding on the OCS between large firms, but allowed it to continue as long as no more than one large firm was in the consortium. A similar ban for coal has been considered but not yet promulgated (OPA 1976).

Recommended Reforms

It clearly seems wise to enact an appropriate joint bidding ban for coal. Two additional changes would almost surely enhance competition for the leases and raise the level of return to the government, and a third, which is less certainly advisable, is worth experimentation.

First, to reduce the information advantage of lessees of adjacent tracts, results of all drilling on leases should be published no more than six months after a hole is drilled. Until 1975 such results were held confidential for the life of the lease; in that year, Interior reduced the period to two years. The two-year period was an improvement, but not a sufficient one; it left open the chance that results of many exploratory holes would not be available by the time the next lease sale was held in a given area. A six-month period would solve that problem.

Second, on the OCS, to increase everyone's level of pre-bidding information and reduce the risks to bidders, a program of limited government presale exploratory drilling should be undertaken. Authority for exploratory drilling on the OCS already exists, but there has been resistance to it, in part because most discussion has involved not limited but complete government exploration, under which leases would be sold only to tracts containing reserves proven to exist to a high level of certainty by government drilling. Such a policy is correctly regarded as a very bad idea; first, because there is good reason to expect the government to be an inefficient explorer but, even more important, because giving an exploration monopoly to anyone—whether the U.S. Geological Survey or Exxon—would prevent testing of multiple competing exploration hypotheses and almost certainly reduce the number of discoveries. A further fear about government exploration has been that even if the intent were to drill only a few holes prior to each lease sale, wherever holes succeeded in finding hydrocarbons, it would be politically difficult for the government to resist pressure to continue drilling, delineate the discovery, and estimate its volume with high accuracy before selling the lease. If this occurred, any ineffectiveness in government management of the exploration process could be extremely harmful.

Despite these problems, there is a strong case for the government's drilling a limited number of holes before each OCS lease sale in the locations most likely to reveal presence of oil and gas. To avoid pressure to drill more, a statutory limit would be helpful, perhaps in number of holes (say, ten) per million acres offered. To be a net gain to the government, such a program would have to raise bids by more than enough to pay for the government's cost of drilling. A potential lessee would tend to raise his bid only if the government drills holes which he would otherwise have drilled himself at his own expense; and this is the reason for strictly limiting the number of government holes: the first few holes, those most likely to reveal hydrocarbons, may also be those whose locations are most likely to be agreed upon by explorationists. But the more government holes drilled, the more likely it is that spots will be selected which prospective bidders will see as "wasted" in the sense that they would not have drilled there themselves, and would not reduce their estimates of their own costs correspondingly.

Even a "perfect" government drilling program would raise bids by *more* than the cost of the holes only if bidders generally are risk averse, or if enough firms are risk averse to cause the number of bidders to rise in the presence of better information. But one or both of these is apt to be the case. On balance, government presale drilling, if kept strictly limited, seems quite likely to raise the value of the resource and improve the government's overall return.

There is much less certainty about the third policy change, but it does deserve at least careful experimentation. This involves substitution of profit sharing for royalties as a means of transferring surplus value to the government. Most energy leases now contain a fixed royalty payment (typically 16⅔ percent of the value of the oil and gas on the OCS; varying amounts, either cents per ton or a percent of value, in coal); then the bidder who offers the highest immediate cash payment, or bonus, is the winner. Clearly, the more the bidder must pay in bonus, the greater his risk, because the bonus is committed before the outcome of exploration is known. The royalty, on the other hand, is a contingent payment which must be made only if production actually takes place. To the extent that the royalty level is raised (and the bonus bid therefore reduced), there is less risk to the bidder.

The problem with a wholesale increase in royalty rates is that royalties reduce gross revenues to the lessee; the higher they are, the more they will discourage development or encourage abandonment of tracts which would be profitable without the royalty obligation. In principle, converting the royalty into a profit share would avoid this problem; the profit share, if correctly calculated, would reduce only *net* revenues, and any production that would be profitable without the payment would also be profitable with it. Therefore, high profit shares, reducing bonus bids and the risk to bidders, could be used where high royalties could not.

The main uncertainty is administrative feasibility. Unfortunately, the definition of profits for corporate tax purposes could not be used, since its theoretical imprecision would distort the firms' behavior nearly as much as would a royalty. It remains uncertain whether a better definition could be worked out (even limited exposure to the cost accounting problems of the oil and gas business raises doubts), and whether the cost of surveillance of firms' cost and revenue computations could be held to tolerable limits. These uncertainties should be resolved by experiment before general changes are made, but the theoretical advantages of profit sharing seem well worth an experiment.

ENVIRONMENTAL ACCEPTABILITY

The issue of environmental acceptability embodies a conflict of values between those who are willing to balance environmental against economic benefits and those who will tolerate no significant environmental costs regardless of economic benefit. The National Environmental Policy Act, which is imprecise like most statutes, can be read to support either view. A certain line of NEPA court decisions, notably *Calvert Cliffs*[2] and its successors, indicates that courts will accept a balancing test, but devotees of "no significant damage" are unpersuaded. A good example of the conflict is the current dispute over development of the so-called Santa Ynez Unit, an oil field beneath federal waters in the Santa Barbara Channel. The California State Coastal Commission, operating under the California Coastal Act of 1976 which commits it to the no-significant-damage position, is in bitter disagreement with the federal Interior Department which has tended, at least under the Ford administration, to argue the issue on balancing grounds.

The no-significant-damage philosophy tends to encourage a feeling that OCS leasing (which brought the Santa Barbara blowout and other lesser accidents) and western coal leasing (which threatens surface reclamation and like problems) at best should be halted, or at least delayed, or restricted to geographic regions that are environmentally least risky. The balancing philosophy, on the other hand, acknowledges that environmental resources are valuable, but the economic value of OCS oil, gas, and in some cases, coal, makes blanket opposition to leasing an obvious error. The proper procedure, rather, is a tract-by-tract judgment on whether each particular energy deposit is valuable enough to justify the probable environmental costs of extracting it.

The no-significant-damage philosophy led many, for example, to oppose issuing any OCS leases in the Gulf of Alaska, where all sides agreed that the environmental values at stake were probably higher than anywhere else off American shores; but the balancing philosophy led others to favor at least selective leasing there on grounds that the high potential for oil and gas discoveries justified the risks. Similarly, there is a long-standing debate over whether all western federal coal leasing should be banned (or, in another version, all leasing in areas with less than a certain yearly rainfall). But "the west" is a big place, with lots of variation both in environment and in coal deposits. Should there be a regional leasing ban, or should we search out and be willing to lease in any region those individual deposits whose value justifies the environmental risks?

These are very basic differences, hardly resolvable by either logic or evidence. Beliefs about whether environmental values are of an order that makes them fundamentally incommensurable with the value of oil, gas, and coal are simply that—beliefs. By "incommensurable" is meant more than "unquantifiable." The argument that environmental values cannot be measured in dollars may often be true, but it is irrelevant to the present point. The dispute is between those who would balance (judgmentally if not quantifiedly) economic against environmental values, and those who would not take the size of the economic values into account at all.

The dispute is lent emotional fuel by a subtle but important implication of the balancing view: it leads to tract-by-tract decision making in which the focus is on the particulars of individual cases. The balancing view therefore demands more information, tends to be more decentralized, or at least more heavily dependent on knowledgeable staff work, and is thus far less subject to influence by those who, because they are not direct parties to the leasing transaction, cannot devote their careers to mastering the details. It is far easier for an outside group to influence a general debate on whether strip mining should be permitted anywhere in the west, than in a debate over whether the surface mining of each of twenty or thirty specific tracts with varying environmental characteristics in Wyoming and Colorado is individually justified by the value of the coal in each. One could understand if not agree with partisans of no-significant-damage if they felt "balancing" only made the real decisions inaccessible to potential critics. "Balancing" leaves many line officials within the bureaucracy cold as well, because it tends to give a greater role in the decision process to analytic staff people who are often natural enemies of line officialdom.

Nor is it surprising that partisans of no-significant-damage have tended to insist that a concrete, detailed, comprehensive plan should be adopted which specifies in advance how much is going to be leased, where, and why. This was a major argument in the Sierra Club's coal leasing case,[3] and has been a repeated demand for OCS as well. Going through such a planning exercise would provide an opening for outside groups to influence decisions, which is presumably one reason it was proposed and one reason the federal government refused to do it (supported, so far, by the courts).[4] Such planning would, of course, be superfluous to a balancing procedure under which the specific amounts leased, and where, are *results* of the process, not prior decisions to which it must conform. The thoroughgoing balancer would stand ready to lease anywhere, in any amount, if the balance of values for the deposit were favorable.

There is no doubt that balancing is ultimately a better procedure. We elect officials to make difficult choices among competing values, and we must hope that they avoid big sacrifices that achieve only small gains, which is all that balancing means. But balancing cannot be practiced effectively without a consensus on its usefulness. The Interior Department could now do one concrete thing in leasing policy that would both move toward balancing and (presumably) make more environmentalists happy. About 180 applications, involving as many as 10 billion tons of coal, are now pending for noncompetitive coal leases which stem from exploration permits issued before the 1971 leasing moratorium and, in most cases, before passage of NEPA. The law entitles such an applicant to a lease if he shows he has discovered coal "in commercial quantities." For decades Interior interpreted "commercial quantities" in largely physical, geologic terms: that other deposits of a similar physical character were known to have been mined commercially. In 1976 the department changed its policy, and defined commercial quantities to mean "marketable at a profit." In doing so, it rejected arguments that it go one step further and make commercial quantities a true balancing concept by defining it to mean that the economic values outweigh expected environmental costs. There is excellent legal authority for such a broadening in NEPA's section 102,[5] and Interior should now strike a blow for environmental protection so that it can refuse to issue noncompetitive coal leases where the balance against the environment is adverse.

Less pleasing to some environmentalists (and, of more political importance, to some miners' unions), but also in the spirit of balancing, is firm rejection of the notion that coal mining is good in the east but bad in the west, and that federal leasing in the west (which effectively means *all* federal leasing) should be curtailed. This policy involves a serious error, but it still has its advocates, some now with the new administration in the Interior Department. The world is far too complex to be operated on with a meat axe as dull as "east versus west." Environmental risks in the west are not uniform; nor is the balance of those risks with resource values. Interior should face the true complexities of its leasing responsibility and not oversimplify the problem.

In the long run, the environmental movement will be better served by balancing than by the more rigid no-significant-damage view. Since passage of NEPA, Interior's leasing behavior has changed substantially for the better; environmental values carry much greater weight than they did even a few years ago. The lever of change, however, has hardly been a moral revolution; it has been the threat of successful suit under NEPA. In leasing, that threat is now on the wane. The Interior Department has had a remarkable record of success in the courts against NEPA suits.

Despite repeated and spirited attacks, the OCS program has been almost injunction-proof. Coal is off to a bad start with a weak environmental statement on resumption of leasing, but it is only a question of time until the administering agencies learn how to avoid court losses, as they have on the OCS. Unfortunately, because of the way NEPA is written, even this waning threat only addresses the procedure, not the substance of leasing decisions; and as the threat fades, it is far from clear what if anything will push Interior further toward substantive environmental concern. One possibility is balancing, which is good public policy and, if well executed, would produce major improvements in leasing decisions. Mechanisms for balancing should be incorporated at each successive stage of the leasing process: tract selection, setting of lease terms, bid evaluation, approval of development plans, regulation of operations, and lease cancellation in case of unexpected environmental hazards. The problem is complex, requiring difficult analysis and careful understanding of both the economics and the environmental effects of leasing; but the need is real, and Interior is not yet close to proper balancing.

THE ROLE OF THE STATES

The administration's 1974 proposal to extend OCS leasing to frontier areas brought a storm of protest from governors of coastal states. The reaction came partly from states that had experienced no previous offshore development, but much more than unfamiliarity was involved. Leasing on the OCS presents in virulent form one of the classic problems of federalism: how to reconcile the views of the federal government and the states on a program that affects them differently.

The Submerged Lands and Outer Continental Shelf Lands Acts of 1953 together struck one of the great compromises of American federalism by giving states control, in most places, over the first three miles of ocean floor and its resources, with the federal government taking control beyond that limit. For Louisiana and California, the states mainly concerned at the time, the compromise must have been a sweet one, because the prior trend of court decisions had made it clear that control of all ocean lands would be federal, and those states already knew about the valuable oil and gas resources present inside the three-mile limit. But however sweet, the compromise unfortunately was flawed in major ways.

When an OCS lease is sold, competition tends to force the high bid up to a level approximating the difference between the market value of the oil and gas and the cost of extracting it. That is to say, most of the benefits of oil and gas development go directly into the federal Treasury. The direct financial costs of development are, of course, paid by the lessees, who hire the labor and make the development investments; but much of the resultant economic activity takes place onshore within the boundaries of the adjacent states, and if this activity has unfavorable impacts, the states and their localities must deal with them. In short, states get none of the benefits, but they do suffer some of the problems. The impacts of accelerated OCS development were not seen by all states as "problems," particularly those states with high unemployment. The recession of 1974-1975 undoubtedly saved the program from even more severe opposition than it actually received. To the extent that environmental damages are involved, these are not only problems, they are, in fact, part of the true cost of development itself. This situation generates very different attitudes toward OCS leasing as between a governor and a president: a president sees benefits and costs, but a governor sees only costs.

There are two basic approaches to ameliorating the inevitable resulting conflicts. Under the Mineral Leasing Act of 1920, a share of onshore federal leasing revenue is awarded to the state (50 percent in the lower forty-eight, 90 percent in Alaska). This revenue sharing in effect gives the state an ownership stake in development similar to that of the federal government, and should tend to give them similar perceptions of benefits and costs. Alternative to revenue sharing is impact aid, under which federal assistance goes to states to compensate for the adversity caused by federal activity. Impact aid is compensation, not an ownership stake, and even under perfect conditions it would produce only indifference on the part of the states, rather than the enthusiasm that might result from joint ownership.

The debate beginning in 1974 between advocates of revenue sharing and impact aid for the OCS ended in 1976 in victory for the latter. An amendment to the Coastal Zone Management Act instituted a program of impact loans providing for construction of public facilities where federal energy developments (offshore or on) will cause population growth. The loans are forgivable if the developments (and hence the associated tax base to support repayment) fail to materialize.

It is doubtful whether this program will bring acceptance of OCS leasing by coastal states. As written, it will probably not be financially important to any state but Alaska (admittedly the state for which leasing impacts, relative to the present economic base, will be greatest). A major Ford administration motive was to keep down the budgetary effect of the program, and to do so it adamantly refused (despite initial arguments by Interior) to consider revenue sharing. Revenues from OCS leasing are large (several billion dollars per year), and a sharing formula comparable to that in the Mineral Leasing Act would have involved far more money than did impact aid. Environmentalists generally agreed with the administration in opposing revenue sharing; they tended to characterize it as a "bribe" to buy state acquiescence, and presumably they preferred to see states remain allied with them in opposition to accelerated leasing.

The Political Problem

States attitudes toward OCS, and the doubtful adequacy of impact aid to change them, are parts of a broader problem— perhaps the most intractable faced by federal energy proprietorship. Leasing on the OCS has huge benefits to the nation as a whole—$5 to $10 per barrel of oil produced, the difference between the cost of imports and the cost of OCS production. Few government programs can boast such large and unambiguous national gains; yet to the extent that these gains are realized in the form of direct Treasury revenues, no political constituency forms around them. The national benefits are real, but they are not tangible for any pressure group. The political structure of the debate over OCS is therefore that the president and the oil companies tend to be alone in favoring the program; most of Congress, representing as it does a collection of narrower interests, tends to be opposed. Contrasting the federal water project programs of the Corps of Engineers and the Bureau of Reclamation is instructive. For a dam, the *costs* are largely national, but the *benefits* are local, the exact opposite of OCS. The political lineup reverses itself accordingly; the Congress proposes, and the president opposes. This is the fundamental reason that OCS leasing has been so slow in responding to the need for acceleration: there were few if any concrete political advantages to the administering agencies and their congressional patrons in faster leasing because of the way the program's benefits are realized. By failing to support general OCS revenue sharing in order to protect the budget in the short run, the Ford administration lost a major chance to create a broader constituency for the program, and in the long run may have sacrificed substantial benefits for the nation as a whole.

AMENDMENT AND REORGANIZATION

Major changes for energy leasing are not imminent as a result of amendments to the OCS Lands Act and the president's energy reorganization. The OCS amendments came within a hair of passing in the 94th Congress, and will almost surely do so in the 95th. President Ford opposed them, but President Carter is expected to sign. The bill is enormously complex—over a hundred pages amending a law that is barely a tenth as long. As might be expected, given the congressional origin of the bill and the politics of OCS leasing, it is a collection of slaps at aspects of the program which irritate one constituency or another. Environmentalists have their innings, anti-oil company populists have theirs, governors get in some licks, and in the wake of Watergate suspicion of executive discretion, many procedures which for years have been governed by Interior Department regulations are written into statute to restrict the administration's freedom to change them. Only the operators of the program find little in the bill that they want.

One exception is authority to try a number of new bidding systems for selling leases, but even this is soured by the requirement that half of future frontier area acreage be devoted to experimental, untested bidding systems, some of which may well prove disastrously inferior to the present one. Experimentation, carefully designed and limited, would be useful; blind risk-taking on a massive scale is something else.

But perhaps the most important thing to say about the OCS amendments is that they make no fundamental change in the way the program operates. There would be longer delays, confusing new multiple lines of authority, ambiguous new language to be interpreted, greater vulnerability to delaying court suits, more paper work to be done; but in the end, though the program will be messier, slower, and more costly to administer, it will not have changed very much. Perhaps the Congress should be praised—at least faintly—in that, after hearing both the chorus of complaints and the administration's answers, it has responded with largely symbolic changes and has not seriously crippled what is a basically sound system.

One can only hope desperately for as harmless an outcome from the president's first major reorganization, the formation of the Department of Energy. In a ghastly misplay of Solomon's judgment in which, for some reason, neither mother offered to save the child, responsibility for energy leasing was split between the Interior and the Energy departments. Energy is to set leasing goals and write regulations pertaining to production rates, competitive bidding and alternative bidding systems, rentals and royalties, and "fostering competition for leases"; Interior is to write the other regulations and enforce them all. No one knows yet what this means. The terms of the split are so vague that a drawn-out fight over authority seems inevitable, and no administrative logic whatever is apparent. It would have been far better for the leasing programs to have been transferred totally to Energy than to have been given two bosses at the same time. The mistake seems so gross and so obvious that one feels a remedy must magically appear, but of course it may not.

Barring reversal or repair of the reorganization, improvements that should be made in the leasing programs (some of them outlined here) are unlikely to be able to compete for attention with turf fights and the unproductive wheel-spinning known euphemistically in Washington as "coordination." This perhaps is part of the price we pay for a political system in which administrations periodically change. One imagines that this particular case is the outcome of bargaining between a forceful new Energy Department reaching for any available authority, and an inexperienced Interior Department that did not understand what was being given away. It is unfortunate that the reorganization urge strikes administrations when they are so new and when they may not avoid its pitfalls. This particular aspect of the energy reorganization scheme seems a colossal mistake, and the quality of federal energy proprietorship may suffer deeply from it.

Accelerating OCS leasing, installing environmental balancing procedures at key stages of the leasing process, experimenting with profit-share leases, beginning limited government OCS exploration, moving up the release time for geologic down-hole data to six months, and legislating meaningful OCS revenue sharing—this is the policy agenda on which the new administration should be working. The items on it are complex—difficult jobs under the best of circumstances—and unfortunately the energy reorganization may make the circumstances next to impossible.

IX

FRED S. HOFFMAN   RICHARD NEHRING

OIL AND GAS SUPPLY IN THE NATIONAL ENERGY PLAN: ENERGY POLICY IN A CLOUDY CRYSTAL BALL*

Basic concepts. Known and future oil and gas availability. Current estimates. Estimating methods. Policy implications. Treatment of resource depletion in the National Energy Plan. Prudent policy and analysis of costs and benefits. The myopic market case. The responsive market case. Conclusion.

INTRODUCTION

Expectations about future oil and gas availability play a major role in the National Energy Plan ("the Plan") presented by President Carter on 20 April 1977. The Plan gives much greater weight

*Views expressed in this chapter are those of the authors, and are not necessarily shared by The Rand Corporation or its research sponsors. Rodney T. Smith has contributed helpful suggestions for the analysis presented, but bears no responsibilitsy for its errors or limitations.

to the threat of resource depletion on a global scale than did its predecessors in the Nixon or Ford administrations. This emphasis is indicated by the following excerpt:

> . . . there are physical and economic limits on the world's supply of oil. There is considerable uncertainty and debate about the size of the world's oil resources. A widely used geological estimate of total recoverable oil resources, past and present, is about 2 trillion barrels. More than 360 billion barrels have already been consumed. . . . Despite the uncertainty about the exact size of recoverable world oil resources and about the exact size of recoverable world oil resources and about the rate of increase in productive capacity, this fundamental fact is clear: within about four generations, the bulk of the world's supply of oil, created over hundreds of millions of years, will have been substantially consumed. . . . recent experience suggests that, from the perspective of world oil consumption, future discoveries will be small or moderate in size, will occur in frontier areas, and will yield oil only at very high cost. Obviously, continued high rates of growth of oil consumption simply cannot be sustained. (Plan 1977:15-16)

There are several ways by which adjustment to this forthcoming depletion could occur. As oil and gas become more scarce, their prices would increase, encouraging the development of other sources of supply and the more efficient use of oil and gas. However, the Plan implies that adjustment by market forces, even at the current OPEC-determined price of oil and an equivalent price of natural gas, would occur too late, the current price being too low to provide the necessary incentives to conserve. According to the Plan, the national interest requires further reductions in oil consumption, to be achieved through a combination of taxes, subsidies, and government regulation.

In order to provide a basis for evaluating this aspect of the Plan, in this chapter we will review several key resource concepts, survey estimates of both known and ultimate world and national oil and gas resources, and consider the possible policy implications of each.

Our review of resource estimates indicates that knowledge about recoverable oil and gas resources beyond those included in reserve estimates leaves a large range of uncertainty with important implications for energy policy. Estimated reserves, worldwide, amount to about 600 billion barrels of oil and 2,200 trillion cubic feet of gas. The level of reserves, however, is dictated by economic conditions and by the projected production needs of the industry. Estimates of resources remaining to be recovered are considerably larger and less certain, ranging from over 1,000 billion to over 3,000 billion barrels of oil, and from over 4,000 trillion to over 14,000 trillion cubic feet of gas. The amount of oil and gas that will ultimately be recovered and its rate of production depend on the associated costs and the future path of oil and gas prices, information generally absent from existing estimates. The absence of such information is a serious limitation on the usefulness of existing estimates for policy purposes.

The design of prudent energy policy under such uncertainty requires analysis of the implications of alternative resource estimates. An illustrative analysis of this sort for policy respecting oil indicates that, under reasonable assumptions about market behavior, the usefulness of government energy conservation measures to reduce consumption from the level that would result from market prices depends on assumptions about resource availability. At the mid-value or upper end of the range, such measures would result in misallocation of resources. At the pessimistic end of the range, appropriate conservation measures might improve the situation, but so would efforts to ensure that public policy did not inhibit the availability of substitute fuels. These results should be tested in more detailed calculations than those presented, and for sensitivity to key assumptions. Under optimistic assumptions about resource availability, there may still be important public policy issues related to political and institutional impediments to commercial efforts to explore for and develop currently unknown resources.

BASIC CONCEPTS

The analysis of future oil and gas availability is plagued by the failure to keep several fundamental conceptual distinctions clearly in mind. Consequently, both popular and governmental discussion of the question is characterized by considerable confusion. The first basic distinction is that between *in-place* and *recoverable* resources. In-place resources are the oil and natural gas calculated to be in the pore-space of the reservoir rock in which the oil and gas is trapped. Recoverable resources are the proportion of in-place resources which can be economically extracted.

At the end of 1976, the American Petroleum Institute estimated that between 147.2 billion barrels or 33.0 percent of the 446.3 billion barrels of oil-in-place discovered to date in the United States were recoverable. The rate of recovery varies considerably among fields and regions, ranging from 80 percent in the east Texas field to 7 percent in the Spraberry Trend in west Texas. It has slowly increased. During the past decade the recovery rate nationwide has grown an average of 0.16 percent annually from 119.7 billion barrels (31.4 percent) of the 380.9 billion barrels in-place discovered by 1966, primarily because of increases in west Texas and California, the two major producing areas with lower recovery than the national average. Because 50 to 75 percent of the gas associated with oil and 80 to 90 percent of non-associated gas is estimated to be recoverable, the difference between in-place and recoverable gas is not normally considered to be significant. In some cases, however, high prices have made increased recovery from known gas fields possible.

A second basic distinction is between *proved reserves* and *potential resources*. Proved reserves consist of the oil and gas calculated to be recoverable from known reservoirs given current economics, technology, and operating practices. Total potential resources consist of proved reserves plus oil and gas which is estimated to be ultimately discovered and recovered, assuming in principle improved economics of exploration and production, technological advance, and optimum operating practices. The former are known with reasonable certainty; parts of the latter are highly speculative. A commonly used third and intermediate category, *probable reserves,* consists of expected additions to reserves from the growth of known fields.

A third distinction is between reserves as a *physical* concept and reserves as an *economic* concept. Reserves are often thought to be the total amount of oil and gas remaining to be recovered from known fields. Economists have suggested that they be viewed instead as working inventories, noting that the estimates of the total recoverable oil and gas in a field or producing province increase over time as the areal and vertical limits of the field are extended and there is more intensive development within the limits of a field. Because this additional development requires additional investment, it is undertaken only when necessary to support additional production.

The idea of reserves as working inventories is particularly applicable to large fields which are not fully developed because of the lack of a market (e.g., the Middle East into the 1960s and 1970s), to fields subject to regulatory limits on production (e.g., the large Texas fields from the 1930s to the early 1970s), or to fields where reserves are taxed. At any given price, reserve growth eventually reaches geologic and technical limits; with increasing prices, reserve growth eventually reaches a limit where it is no longer economically desirable. (In some fields, estimates of the total recoverable oil and gas may decrease as cumulative production increases because of greater than anticipated declines in reservoir pressure or poorly designed production policies which impair ultimate recovery.)

Estimates of potential resources have traditionally been limited to the amounts of oil and gas obtainable from *additional discoveries*. In recent years, estimators have also emphasized the amounts, particularly of oil, obtainable from *additional recovery* of known in-place resources. Both are important and need to be considered explicitly in determining future oil and gas availability. There are no *a priori* means for deciding which of the two will prove to be more important for future oil availability.

Discussion of oil and gas resources has typically focused on *ultimate recoverable resources,* the total amount likely to be discovered and recovered over the centuries. For policy purposes, medium-term *resource availability* is a more relevant concept. It is more important to have a reasonable idea of the amounts which could be available during the next twenty to forty years, their costs, and the rate at which reserves could be added. Medium-term resource availability of oil and gas, the level of ultimate resources, defines the need for substitution, whether that be the replacement of existing uses of oil and gas with more efficient means of using them or with alternative sources of energy.

Popular discussion of remaining oil and gas resources revolves around the comparison of single values of total recoverable resources. Such estimates obscure more than they enlighten. At best, any single estimate of remaining oil and gas resources indicates the judgment of the estimator about the expected value; that is, the value for which it is equally likely that the actual value will be greater or less. Resource estimates, particularly of resources remaining to be discovered, are more appropriately expressed as *probability distributions,* expressing the range of uncertainty about the potential. Resource estimates, particularly of additional recovery of known in-place resources, can also be expressed as a *cost curve*, indicating the additional amounts likely to be available at a given cost of recovery. Both geologic uncertainty and the economics of exploration and production need to be explicitly incorporated in a resource estimate if it is to be used with confidence.

Traditionally, resource estimation has focused on the so-called *conventional* supplies of oil and gas. The *nonconventional* supplies (heavy oil sands or tar sands, oil shale, and natural gas in low-permeability formations, coal beds, or geopressured zones) have been considered separately. This distinction can be misleading, particularly in suggesting a more pessimistic outlook than is warranted. From the viewpoint of energy consumers, there is no distinction between conventional and nonconventional sources of oil and gas. Geologically, there is a clear continuity between conventional sources and at least some of the nonconventional ones (for example, heavy oil sands and low-permeability gas formations). Economically, there is an overlap. Some proportion of the nonconventional sources can be produced and delivered to consumers at a lower cost than some proportion of the conventional ones. Separating the two is a legitimate part of the disaggregated analysis which goes into making any well-reasoned resource estimate. However, both types belong to any total estimate of future oil and gas availability.

A final distinction which is particularly important for estimates of resource availability is that among *prices, resource costs,* and *risk*. Higher prices are normally considered to provide incentives for additional exploration and recovery. However, it is not higher prices *per se* which provide the incentive, but the prospect of higher revenues to the individuals and organizations who make exploration and production decisions. A large proportion of the market price for oil and gas can consist of various taxes and transfer payments to government and other owners of the mineral rights. These can increase, as they have substantially in the OPEC countries since 1973, without providing any additional incentive for additional exploration and recovery in a given area. An incentive exists only if the additional discounted revenues are expected to exceed the additional resource costs. Moreover, there must be some degree of continuity in that expectation. Because the revenues are accrued only after most of the costs have been incurred, operators need to consider how long incentives may persist in determining an adequate return on their investment.

KNOWN FUTURE OIL AND GAS AVAILABILITY

Estimating oil and gas availability is inevitably a numbers game. But how those numbers are developed, what they really mean, and the uncertainties associated with them are essential in drawing the appropriate policy implications. In order to provide a skeletal background for understanding resource estimates, in this section we will (1) summarize current estimates of known oil and gas resources and several key characteristics of them, and (2) discuss briefly approaches to estimating future availability, recent estimates of availability (for both the world and the United States), and several basic shortcomings of these estimates.

The existence of petroleum (oil and natural gas) in commercially viable accumulations depends upon several essential conditions. First, sufficient organic material must have existed, been buried, and preserved. The organic material must then have been subjected to sufficient temperature and pressure to be converted to petroleum. Secondly, permeable carrier rocks must be present adjacent to the source rocks in which the conversion from organic material to petroleum occurs to receive the petroleum when it is expelled from the source rocks. Third, an effective closed trap must have existed where the migrating petroleum could accumulate. Fourth, this trap must be preserved intact once filled so that the petroleum in it is neither destroyed, dispersed, nor decomposed. Some of these conditions, particularly the first, appear to have been common. The combination of all four, particularly in the appropriate temporal relationship, appears to have been relatively rare on any large scale.[1]

The relative rarity of the appropriate temporal combination of the geologic conditions necessary for large accumulations of petroleum is indicated by the known spatial distribution of petroleum. By the end of 1975, an estimated 960 billion barrels of oil and 3,000 trillion cubic feet of gas had been discovered worldwide (Table 1). (Estimates vary from 950 to 1,100 billion barrels of oil and 2,800 and 3,200 trillion cubic feet of natural gas, the range both depending upon the extent to which probable reserves are included and resulting from uncertainty about reserves in the Middle East, the Soviet Union, and China.) Most of this is still remaining to be produced. Current world reserves are roughly thirty times annual world production. Moreover, because of the exponential growth in world oil production (which doubled every ten years from the early 1860s to the early 1970s), half of cumulative world production has occurred only in the past fifteen years.

Both oil and gas are distributed unevenly over the earth's surface. Nearly half of the total oil discovered to date is in the Middle East; another 25 percent is in the United States and the Soviet Union. Roughly 75 percent of the natural gas discovered to date is in the Soviet Union, the United States, and the Middle East, each having around 25 percent of the world total. Petroleum accumulations are also unevenly distributed within the United States. The crude oil discovered to date has been found primarily in the Gulf

Table 1

Current Estimated Recovery of Crude Oil and Natural Gas in the World by Region as of December 31, 1975

Region	Crude Oil (billion barrels)			Natural Gas (trillion cubic feet)		
	Cumulative Production	Reserves	Total	Cumulative Production	Reserves	Total
United States	109.0	37.7	146.7	499	224	723
Canada	7.4	7.8	15.2	26	71	97
Latin America	46.4	25.6	72.0	40	111	151
Western Europe	2.9	27.1	30.0	38	175	213
Africa	20.6	55.4	76.0	18	207	225
Middle East	85.2	374.8	460.0	50	643	693
Asia/Pacific	10.0	20.0	30.0	10	120	130
Soviet Union	50.0	50.0	100.0	105	700	805
Eastern Europe	4.5	3.6	8.1	17	24	41
China	3.0	20.0	23.0	8	25	33
World Total	339.0	622.0	961.0	811	2180	2991

Source: American Petroleum Institute; Central Intelligence Agency; *Oil and Gas Journal;* U.S. Bureau of Mines; *World Oil.* (Various dates of publication.)

Coast, west Texas, California, Oklahoma, and Alaska. Most of the gas has been found in the five adjacent states of Louisiana, Texas, Kansas, Oklahoma, and New Mexico.

The worldwide geographic distribution of petroleum is the consequence of the fact that most of the oil and gas discovered to date has been discovered in a relatively small number of very large fields. An estimated 30,000 oil and gas fields have been discovered. Nearly half of the crude oil discovered to date is contained in only 0.1 percent of these fields, the super-giants with 5 billion barrels or more each. Roughly 75 percent is contained in the 300 or so giant fields, fields with 500 million barrels or more. Another 15 percent is found in major fields, fields of 100 to 500 million barrels. Most of the giant fields, particularly the super-giants, are found in the Middle East. The nearly 200 giant gas fields (3 billion cubic feet or more each) contain 87 percent of the natural gas discovered worldwide to date, with approximately 20 super-giant gas fields (30 billion cubic feet or more) containing 40 to 45 percent of the world total. The giant gas fields found to date, particularly the super-giants, are concentrated in the Middle East and Western Siberia. The concentration of known oil and gas in very large fields in the United States is less, but nonetheless still prominent. The roughly 100 giant oil and gas fields discovered to date contain about 45 percent of known crude oil and 30 percent of known natural gas. Approximately 95 percent of the oil and natural gas discovered to date is in fields with more than 10 million barrels or 60 billion cubic feet.[2]

Estimates of proved and probable reserves of oil and natural gas only provide an extremely conservative estimate of how much oil and gas is remaining. The interesting question for policy purposes is how much will ultimately be available, when, and at what cost. This is the fundamental question of energy resource estimation.

Two basic approaches with several variants have been used to estimate the amount of oil and gas remaining to be discovered. One, essentially that of geologic analogy, considers the various geographic variables affecting petroleum accumulation. The geologic approach can be methodologically simple, for example, estimating discoverable resources by applying some recovery factor to the volume of unexplored sedimentary rock in a basin. It can become very complex, for example, using probability distributions of the values of several geologic variables related to petroleum accumulation to estimate the likely range of the amount remaining to be discovered. The other approach is the mathematical-statistical one, extrapolating trends in production and reserves or in the discovery rate per unit of drilling effort to obtain ultimate production and discovery curves. Many recent efforts at estimating ultimate U.S. and world resources have used a combination of these approaches, using projections based on the mathematical-statistical approaches to check the estimates derived from probalistic geologic analysis. Additional amounts which may be recovered from existing fields have been estimated by calculating future reserve growth, using trends of past reserve growth, and by economic-engineering calculations of the amounts which may be recovered from enhanced recovery operations.

From 1910-1920 when estimates of world and U.S. ultimate recoverable oil and gas resources were first made, assessments of ultimate potential have grown substantially. During the 1960s these estimates reached their peak. Since then they have been scaled down, partly because of a lack of significant discoveries in previously promising areas and partly because of the use of more sophisticated, reproducible approaches to resource estimation.

Recent detailed estimates of ultimate recoverable conventional petroleum liquids in the United States, adjusted by us to include enhanced recovery at prices up to $25 per barrel, have mid-values between 300 and 320 billion barrels, with a range from 240 to 260 at the low end and between 370 and 400 billion at the upper end. (The mid-values include 30 to 35 billion barrels of natural gas liquids and 25 billion barrels of crude oil from enhanced recovery.) Recent estimates of ultimate recoverable conventional from 1,100 to 1,400 trillion cubic feet, and a range from 950 to 1,250 trillion cubic feet at the low end to between 1,475 and 1,700 trillion cubic feet at the upper end.[3] By comparison, 1976 production and cumulative production respectively were 3.5 and 129 billion barrels of petroleum liquids and 19.5 and 519 trillion cubic feet of natural gas.

Estimates of recoverable nonconventional oil and gas resources vary widely, primarily because of cost and technological uncertainties. Large amounts of in-place resources are known (hundreds, if not thousands of billion barrels of shale oil and hundreds of trillion cubic feet in each of the nonconventional gas resources). The amounts recoverable at acceptable economics are highly disputed.

As the National Energy Plan indicates, estimates of ultimate world oil recovery (including past production) cluster around 2,000 billion barrels (possibly higher, if adjusted for enhanced recovery). The range, adjusted for enhanced recovery, is from 11,500 to 3,600 billion barrels. (The higher bound depends upon the discovery of many super-giant fields in the Middle East, the Soviet Union, and China, a possibility which is not strongly supported by currently available evidence.) During the past twenty years, estimates of conventional ultimate world recoverable natural gas resources have ranged from 5,000 to 15,000 trillion cubic feet. The best supported current estimate is at the low end of that range, roughly 5,000 to 6,000 Tcf.[4] Comprehensive estimates of nonconventional world oil and gas resources have not, to our knowledge, been made. There are several known heavy oil or tar sand deposits in the world, each with 100 to 1,000 billion barrels of oil-in-place.

The quality of resource estimates has increased substantially during the past decade. During this time, estimates have become more detailed, and disaggregated; estimators have become more explicit about their methods, sources of data, coverage, assumptions, and the like; multiple approaches have been more commonly used, permitting greater confidence in the results; and uncertainty has been explicitly incorporated in the estimates. Despite the substantial improvements which have occurred, there are still several shortcomings which preclude them from being a fully reliable guide to policymaking.

Recent estimates of U.S. oil potential are considered to have reached a basic consensus, given the high degree of overlap in their range and the near agreement of expected values. Yet this consensus is more apparent than real. Although the totals are similar, the components differ sharply, particularly in their assessments of U.S. onshore potential. This agreement extends to estimates of U.S. natural gas potential as well. These substantial differences at the disaggregated level indicate that reiteration of these estimates would be desirable. The assumptions used earlier, particularly if they differ from estimate to estimate, need to be explicitly compared and tested against the full range of relevant evidence.

A second, more debilitating, shortcoming is the general lack of economic information in current resource estimates. Only estimates of oil obtainable from enhanced oil recovery have been published in the form of a cumulative cost curve. At best, estimates of remaining discoverable resources have incorporated the economic limit, beyond which the potential resource was considered to be nonrecoverable. This lack of economic information obscures an important transition which is occurring in the exploration for and production of oil and gas.

Most of the oil and gas made recoverable to date has been in large, relatively accessible, and low-cost deposits. Because both the number and the average size of giant oil fields discovered since the early 1960s have declined markedly, and because the more accessible areas have been intensively explored, the oil and gas discovered in the future is likely to come from smaller, less accessible, and thus more costly deposits. The costs of additional recovery will be significantly higher than those of primary recovery.

The costs of any increment of potential oil and gas resources are important because they indicate the extent to which the resource is likely to be used. They indicate whether sufficient incentives exist to explore and produce for those who make those decisions, and they indicate the extent to which substitutes, whether they be means of using oil and gas with greater efficiency, nonconventional sources of oil and gas, or other sources of energy, are competitive. During the next twenty-five to fifty years, these considerations will become increasingly important.

To illustrate the information which economically oriented resource estimates could provide, we have developed the conventional world oil cost curves shown in Figure 1 for known recoverable resources and for alternative assumptions about ultimate world resources (using the estimates of Mobil [Moody and Esser 1975], adjusted for enhanced recovery). The cost curves are based on known resource costs of production for different areas of the

Figure 1

**Estimated Cost Curves
of Conventional Oil Production in the World
for Different Estimates of Ultimate Resource Availability**

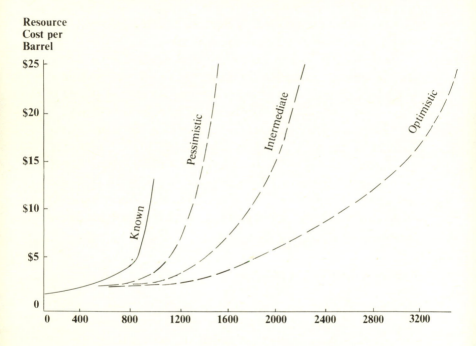

Ultimate Recovery (billion barrels)

world and of different operating environments, including transportation costs to major refining centers, and on the estimated resource costs of enhanced recovery. The known cost curve ranges from Middle East oil, with its very low production costs, to oil produced from stripper wells in the United States. Resource costs are projected to increase with further discoveries, because some proportion will occur in expensive operating environments (Arctic and sub-Arctic regions, deep water) and some will occur from fields with low productivity per well. The costs of additional recovery from known fields will also be higher than primary recovery. Most additional conventional oil is expected to be available at a range of resource costs between $3 to $15 per barrel. A cut-off level of $25 is assumed, based on the cost of known substitutes and the costs of current recovery technology. These curves should, however, be considered to be illustrative only. Although suggested by currently available information, the information is insufficient to verify them.

The curves, particularly for the intermediate value or less, indicate an abrupt economic transition. Most of the resources which are estimated to be available are expected to be available at resource costs less than $15 per barrel. By comparison, heavy oil (including tar sands) deposits only become available in significant quantities at resource costs between $10 and $20 per barrel, and shale oil becomes available at resource costs above $20 per barrel (neither are incorporated in the cost curves of Figure 1). These cost differences between conventional and nonconventional oil resources indicate the policy problem which is the subject of the remainder of our discussion.

POLICY IMPLICATIONS

Nonconventional sources are likely to be commercially unavailable in significant quantities until sufficient information exists to indicate that the probability of extensive additional supplies of low resource cost oil is very low. However, once that information is available, the time available to make the necessary transition may be too short to develop other sources of supply if demand has grown to high levels. In principle, this problem can be eased substantially by a combination of measures including conservation to reduce the peak of conventional production, and to obtain a larger transitional period, the discovery and development of remaining potential, and the improvement of estimates about ultimate recovery. Uncertainty about reserve availability is a central issue in determining the proper role for government in dealing with resource depletion problems. The remainder of this discussion outlines an analysis to help in identifying that role, and applies it illustratively to government policy issues concerning oil.

Treatment of Resource Depletion in the National Energy Plan

The Plan's emphasis on conservation has been almost universally approved both at home and abroad. Like those who love humanity but can't stand people, much of the public, the press, and the Congress show more affection toward conservation as a general philosophical concept than towards the specific measures required to achieve it, let alone the instruments of government policy proposed to induce those measures. The tendency for consensus to evaporate as we move from precept to practice suggests the need for clarity about the underlying rationale for conservation programs to enact—and even more to carry out a program of government-induced energy conservation. This is nowhere better illustrated than in the Plan's treatment of natural gas, and both gas and oil in the residential sector.[5]

Popular usage identifies energy conservation as consisting of reductions in energy use induced by government action or by changes in individual views of proper social behavior, and as distinct from reductions motivated by market determined price increases. We follow this usage. Clarity about the reasons for conserving is difficult to achieve because of the variety of problems adduced as reasons for government intervention in energy production and use, the complexity of their interrelations, and the uncertainty associated with them.

Several reasons for government intervention have been widely discussed. The one of primary concern in this chapter is the prospect that the depletion of global oil and gas resources is imminent. However, we also list several of the others as a context for the discussion (they are analyzed in several of the other chapters):

> Government ownership of energy resources and production facilities.
>
> Regulation of monopoly power in energy-related industries.
>
> Avoidance of windfall gains and socially unacceptable loss of economic well-being resulting from the sharp rise in energy prices.

Protection of the environment against spillover effects of energy production and use.

Political vulnerability arising from high oil import levels.

Macroeconomic problems arising from high oil prices.

National security problems arising from the diffusion of sensitive energy technologies, notably nuclear fuel cycle technology.

The legitimacy of some of these motives, and the desirability of the means chosen to deal with the problems, comprise the bulk of the debate over energy policy; the present discussion will concentrate on the issue of resource depletion, and will comment selectively on some of the other issues that are particularly closely related to it.

Anxiety about imminent depletion of nonrenewable oil and gas resources is an important element of the rationale in the Plan for government intervention to slow the rate of consumption and stretch the availability of these resources. Such anxiety about socially important resources is hardly a new phenomenon. In retrospect, it is quite clear that previous exhortations to conserve vital resources in danger of exhaustion have been mistaken, either because the threatened exhaustion did not materialize, or because adequate (or preferable) substitutes were sought and found, or both (see Rowen, Chapter I). Nevertheless, there can be no guarantee that past experience will be repeated, and the weight of expert opinion with respect to available oil and gas resources suggests that depletion is likely to become a significant factor within the foreseeable future—certainly within a century, and possibly within two decades. At the pessimistic end of the range, some appear to be saying that resource depletion will force drastic adjustments in energy use by the mid-1980s. (It is not always clear in these statements whether the problem in view is resource exhaustion or OPEC market power [CIA 1977a].[6] The distinction will be discussed further in what follows.) The inherent uncertainty surrounding resource availability has given rise to demand for government action to insure that private markets do not adopt an excessively myopic view of oil and gas supply. This motive for government intervention, and its reflection in the Plan, constitute the major issue for the remainder of this chapter.

It is true, as suggested in the excerpt from the Plan, that viewed from the perspective of the geologic time over which oil deposits have been formed, and from the perspective of the generations over which we wish human life and society to flourish, insistence on the importance of uncertainties in estimates of nonrenewable resources appears trivial and niggling. But the proposals in the Plan will not extend the oil and gas era by eons or even generations. If they work as intended, they would extend oil and gas use by some years. If they are to be considered as the first steps in a "journey of a thousand miles," their timing and pace have little to do with when and how journey's end is reached. And timing and pace are at the heart of the issues raised by the Plan.

Clearly, market adjustments in the absence of the Plan would also slow growth in oil and gas demand as resource depletion made it physically impossible to maintain a constant growth rate in their production and resulted in higher costs to find, develop, and produce them. The Plan implies that without government intervention, market forces would react too late and too slowly; that private decisions (even as motivated by high OPEC prices) inadequately reflect the imminence of oil and gas depletion, and uncertainty about the timely availability of substitutes for them. The issues of resource depletion raised by the Plan pertain principally to events in the next ten to twenty years; their resolution has little to do with the quality of life a millenium from now. Within this time frame, uncertainties about resource availability are neither trivial nor niggling; they are critical to policy determination. The failure of the Plan to treat them explicitly is a major shortcoming.

Prudent Policy and the Analysis of Costs and Benefits

Earlier discussion in this chapter has indicated the nature and rough magnitude of uncertainty about oil and gas resources. To assess the importance of that uncertainty, and evaluate the actions proposed in the Plan, it is necessary to estimate the costs and benefits of the actions under alternative assumptions within the range of uncertainty. Analyzing the results can suggest prudent courses of action—those that insure us against disaster if pessimistic forecasts prove to be correct, but that do not prevent enjoyment of good fortune under optimistic outcomes, and do not involve excessively high insurance premiums whatever the outcome. Measuring costs and benefits accurately and reliably is difficult both conceptually and in terms of available data, and is beyond the scope of this discussion. The nature of the needed analysis is outlined in what follows, with calculations that should be regarded as illustrative only.

The Plan seeks to defer consumption of oil and gas. It is important to recognize that we are not proposing, as a society, to sacrifice benefits from current oil and gas consumption to establish a permanent heirloom to be handed down from generation to generation. The Plan would shift consumption of oil and gas saved between now and say, 1985 to some unspecified future time. The cost of such shifting would be the loss of goods and services during the period when government policy is restraining demand for oil and gas. In principle the amount of this loss can be estimated if we know the amount of oil and gas "saved," the current price level, and the relevant supply and demand curves. The benefits of the shift depend on how soon we assume the oil and gas will finally be consumed and by how much its value at that time will exceed its present value. Timing of benefits is important, because resources currently in hand are worth more than the same resources available at some time in the future.[8] Both the timing of future consumption of oil and gas saved and its value when consumed depends, among other things, on assumptions about the size and nature of remaining oil and gas resources, particularly those yet to be discovered.

Unfortunately, estimates of oil and gas resources like those presented earlier are not generally translated into future rates of production, costs, or prices. This is understandable, given the complexity of the subject. Where experts have feared to tread, we will venture—to clarify the problem, not to solve it. In the analysis to follow, we will consider the world oil market; the option to increase imports of foreign oil is a clear alternative to rapid development of new U.S. fuel resources on one hand, and to conservation efforts on the other. Since 1973 we have been pursuing the import option assiduously. Without substantial conservation efforts or development of indigenous U.S. resources like shale, or coal liquefaction, such imports will continue to increase rapidly. The issue considered in our discussion is the ability of world resources to support growing demand by the U.S. and others. Our analysis largely ignores the question of production restraint through exercise of OPEC cartel power, except insofar as it does not include cases in which the price of oil falls in the near future. The omission of cases in which prices fall from their present level signifies neither that we regard such outcomes as impossible nor as socially undesirable. As will be seen below, for significant ranges of estimates about resource availability and discount rates, market conditions would be consistent with a fall in conditions, and such a fall would be consistent with the efficient use of oil resources. We excuse the omission of such cases on grounds of the difficulty of predicting cartel behavior, and the fact that our central purpose is to focus on uncertainty about how fast the world is running out of oil and gas. Further, since our purpose is illustrative, we restrict the analysis to oil alone.

Like other commodities, the quantity of oil produced and its price were influenced by the conditions of supply and demand, at least until about 1970. The nature of the industry and the existence of strong government influences, such as tax policy and the import quota system in the United States, set it apart from many other commodities even before that date. Since then, the rise of OPEC market power has been a dominant influence on price and quantity. A central issue of the present discussion is whether and how considerations of depletion of a nonrenewable resource are or should be affecting price and quantity. To deal with that issue, however, it is necessary to make assumptions about the nature of demand for oil.

Like other commodities, the quantity of oil demanded is responsive to its price, quantity declining as price increases relative to other commodities (assuming that the prices of other commodities remain unchanged in relation to each other). In addition to changes in prices,[9] the quantity demanded is affected by growth in the level of economic output, generally measured by the Gross National Product (GNP). Other factors that may also affect oil demand are changes in technology such as the introduction of the automobile, and changes in life style and tastes such as those inherent in the suburbanization of metropolitan areas in the United States. Although technology and tastes change independently of the relative prices of oil and other commodities, there is evidence that large and long-term changes in relative prices may induce technical and life-style changes that are useful in adapting to the price changes.

There have been many analyses of energy demand to estimate the degree of its responsiveness to price changes and growth rates in GNP. The subject is complex, and the range of variation among the estimates considerable. For the purposes of this discussion we have chosen estimates that lie in the range, but the midpoint is difficult to determine. Specifically, we assume that a 10 percent increase in world price for crude oil will result in a 5 percent reduction in the amount of crude oil demanded. We also assume that a 10 percent rise in GNP will lead to an increase in quantity demanded of somewhat less than 9 percent. If we assume a growth rate in output of 4 percent per year, and constant real prices, these assumptions imply a growth rate in the quantity of oil demanded of 3.5 percent per year. This is in contrast to the historical trend of growth of between 6 and 7 percent per year for total world consumption.

The Myopic Market Case

To begin, we assume that the world oil market behaves in what might be described as a myopic fasihon, seeing only what is, so to speak, under our noses, and ignoring the possibility of future resource depletion. It might take the form, for example, of allowing real oil prices to remain constant, and production to grow to meet the growing demand, for so long as the resource base will support such behavior. We assume that production will keep pace with the amount demanded at constant prices for so long as reserves can be maintained at least twelve times annual production. In effect, we assume that this is a necessary working inventory for the industry. Additions to reserves, to replace production, are limited to the lesser of annual production or 3 percent of unknown recoverable oil remaining in undiscovered fields or unproven in known fields. This assumed connection between reserve addition and production is related to the fact that reserves are analogous to working inventories. Subject to geological vagaries and assuming a continuing exploratory effort, capital is invested in increasing them only as much as necessary to support expected production. The connection between the quantity of unknown recoverable oil and the rate of additions to reserves is a gross simplification of the interplay of geology, technology for exploration, political accessibility, costs, and the expected path of market prices for oil. In addition to their complexity, all involve great inherent uncertainties that cannot be eliminated or perhaps even substantially reduced.[10]

Under our assumptions, unknown recoverable resources will decline as additions to reserves are withdrawn from the unknown category. Sooner or later reserve additions will be unable to keep pace with production, and reserves will begin to decline. As production continues to rise and reserves decline, the reserves will approach the level of twelve years of current production, at which we assume available reserves will begin to constrain production. That will be the point of maximum production, and production will decline thereafter at a rate determined by the decline in reserves and additions to reserves. Prices will rise after that point, as determined by the demand relationship.

Table 2 shows our assumptions and some results of our calculations for two alternative cases of myopic market behavior, chosen to display the effects of uncertainty about unknown recoverable oil resources. Our assumptions are based on the earlier discussion, but we have chosen a more modest upper limit than the one

Table 2

Myopic Market Behavior

	Resource Assumption	
	Pessimistic	Optimistic
Amount ultimately recoverable*	1,500	3,000
Unknown recoverable resources in 1977*	500	2,000
Rates of change before peak production:		
Price (percent per year)	0	0
Production (percent per year)	3.5	3.5
Maximum annual reserve additions:		
Date	1978	1996
Amount*	15	42
End of growth in production:		
Date	1988	2000
Annual production*	32	49
Subsequent rates of change:		
Price (percent per year)	23	23
Production (percent per year)	- 8	- 8

*Billions of barrels.

presented there. Experts will not need to be warned against taking the results of Table 2 too seriously. The large annual production and reserve addition figures in the optimistic case look unrealistic in relation to experience to date. Referring to a much lower figure than the one shown for the optimistic case, the Plan makes the following comments:

> The world now consumes over 20 billion barrels of oil per year. To maintain *even that rate of consumption* and keep reserves intact, the world would have to discover another Kuwait or Iran roughly every 3 years, or another Texas or Alaska roughly every 6 months.

Although some large discoveries will be made, the likelihood of a continuous flow of large discoveries is small. . . . future discoveries will be small or moderate in size, will occur in frontier areas, and will yield oil only at very high cost. (Plan 1977:16; italics in original)

The optimistic estimate in Table 2 may turn out to be wrong. It is, however, consistent with a range of estimates of total recoverable resources made by reputable geologists. If the projection goes far beyond our experience with the rate of reserve additions, so do the levels of production assumed; and, to repeat, there is a strong economic nexus between the two. Assuming that the oil is in fact in place, waiting to be discovered, levels of production like those shown would, subject to qualifications discussed below, call forth resources for exploration and development and possibly new technology also beyond our experience.[11]

As Table 2 indicates, the additional resources available in the optimistic case postpone the date of peak production by about twelve years from 1988 to 2000. Following peak production in each case, there is an extremely rapid increase in the demand price as the quantity of oil begins to diminish. The inability to expand or even maintain production would cause prices to increase much faster than costs. In neither case would cumulative production exceed half of ultimately recoverable resources as of 1977, by the date of peak annual production. Figure 1 suggests that at these levels of cumulative production, the resource cost of finding and producing oil might still be below $5 per barrel when prices begin their precipitous climb, and that costs will move upward much more slowly than price. Given the abrupt decline in production shown and the consequent rate of price increase, GNP would not continue to increase smoothly at 4 percent. Although the linkage between any particular fuel or energy in general and economic output appears to be weak in the long term, there would clearly be some transitory effects and the period of adjustment might be substantial. The results might be akin to those experienced in the 1973 to 1975 period in which we had an abrupt increase in crude oil prices. The 1973-1974 OPEC price increases, however, did not, unlike the pattern posited in Table 2, continue indefinitely.

Figure 2 displays the resulting paths of price increases in the two cases of Table 2. The differences between the two cases is that the date of peak production and rapid price increases in the optimistic case occurs twelve years later than in the pessimistic case. If that were all to be said, the significance of uncertainty about resource availability might indeed be trivial. But so would be conservation efforts, which at best would postpone the inevitable crisis for a few years.

A key part of the solution is the possibility of substituting other liquid fuel in plentiful supply for crude oil. Shale oil and oil

Figure 2

Oil Prices-Myopic Market Behavior

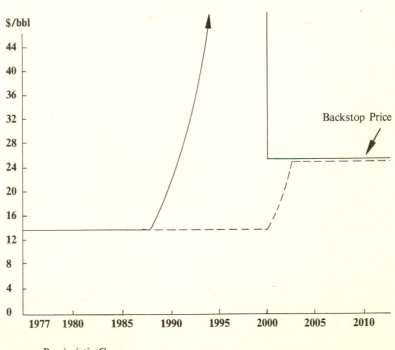

——— Pessimistic Case
- - - - - Optimistic Case

derived from coal liquefaction are candidates for this function. Both rely on resource bases that are large relative to the range of oil resources available. But neither is available now in large quantities, and neither is prospectively available at prices competitive with the 1977 price of petroleum. Both the price and time of availability of these synthetic substitute forms of oil are uncertain.

Technology for production of shale oil is in hand, though its cost would be high, its environmental effects troublesome, and the amounts of water required for large production levels might raise political problems in the Rocky Mountain states. Less troublesome and less expensive methods for using shale resources are currently under development, but their ultimate costs and availability are unclear. Coal liquefaction also requires additional development. Currently identified approaches appear to involve costs higher than those for shale.[12] We assume conservatively that beginning in the year 2000, synthetic liquid fuels can be available as substitutes for petroleum in quantities large enough to meet the difference between petroleum production and demand for crude oil at constant real prices—that is to say, at the rate of growth of 3.5 percent per year in total liquid fuels consumed. We assume that such synthetics will be available at a price of $25 per barrel and could play the role of a backstop technology.[13] Under the myopic market assumption, however, there is no reason to believe that private initiative would begin building up the needed productive capacity until after prices began their precipitous climb. To avoid this situation, earlier government incentives would be necessary.

Figure 2 shows the effects of the backstop technology assumptions on the course of oil prices in the myopic market case. In the optimistic case, there is a brief period of rapidly rising prices, whose effects would be less severe than the 1973-1974 price increases, ending at the $25 level, after which prices are assumed to remain constant and oil use resumes its growth at 3.5 percent. The situation is quite different in the pessimistic case. Under our assumptions, the backstop technology could not be available in sufficient quantities when prices begin their precipitous climb in 1988, and they would rise to an extremely high level, with the probability of serious disruptions. The range of uncertainty about oil resources leads to significant differences in the seriousness of the problem.

There are also differences with respect to the need for additional efforts to restrict oil use before peak production is reached. The fact that oil prices rise much faster than any reasonable social discount rate after peak production is reached indicates that there would be net benefits to shifting consumption of oil from the period of constant prices to the period of rising prices. Conservation measures, including an early rise in oil prices, might accomplish such shifting. To illustrate the magnitude of the benefits, consider that in the pessimistic case the present value in 1977 of an additional barrel of oil in the year 2000 would be over $40 per barrel, discounted at 6 percent.[14] In this case, conservation efforts would confer benefits from 1977 on. In the optimistic case, however, even at a discount rate of 3 percent, the present value in 1977 of an additional barrel of oil in 2004 (the year at which the backstop technology begins to govern the price) would be $11, which is less than the current price of oil. Immediate conservation measures would be desirable only at discount rates below 2.5 percent. Conservation efforts would be indicated by the mid-1980s if the discount rate were 3 percent, or the mid-1990s if it were 6 percent. The timing of conservation measures in the Plan roughly coincides with the 3 percent discount case.

Thus, in the case just discussed, a myopic market requires a farseeing government to provide incentives for the development of a large-scale synthetic fuel industry to avoid a precipitous price rise even in the optimistic case; both production incentives and immediate conservation incentives are needed in the pessimistic case.

The Responsive Market Case

The problem calling for a government-provided remedy resulted from the failure of the market to make any adjustment in prices until production peaked due to depletion, and falling production forced price increases at a rapid rate. Markets need not behave in this fashion, however, and there is good reason to believe that they will be more responsive than we have assumed. Without assuming that markets will behave optimally, based on perfect foresight about matters that are uncertain now and likely to remain so, we might make a modest allowance for responsiveness. Specifically, we assume that market prices will begin to rise after annual additions to reserves fall below annual production, producing a decline in reserves; and that they will rise fast enough to delay peak production until after the year 2000, when the backstop technology is assumed to be available, but no faster than the rate of return on investment in the private sector.

After those involved in the oil market have become convinced that declines in reserve additions are resulting from resource depletion, the prospect of rapid future price rises will cast its shadow backward to the present, and sellers will hold for higher future prices, driving current prices up. Available data suggest that there has, in fact, been a decline in known reserves. However, before concluding that the market is ignoring a signal of impending resource depletion, it is necessary to consider several other factors that may be masking the actual relevance of these changes to the underlying resource availability. The simplest of these is the chance element involved in resource exploration. Simple bad luck might depress reserve additions for a period of years. Another factor is the excessively high current ratio of reserves to production. A ratio as high as the present one might be producing an oil glut in the absence of OPEC restrictions. Finally, there are the changes in the environment for exploration and its effect on incentives to invest in exploration, particularly abroad. These changes and their implications are briefly discussed in the concluding section of this chapter and in other chapters of this volume. The precise pattern of price rises in the actual market situation will therefore be the result of factors too complex to predict with precision. We can, nevertheless, illustrate the effect of particular patterns of responsiveness for various assumptions about resource availability.

Table 3 presents results for various assumptions about resource availability under conditions of greater market responsiveness

Table 3

Responsive Market Behavior*

	Resource Assumption			
	Pessimistic		Inter-mediate	Optimistic
	Conservative Backstop	Early Backstop		
Amount ultimately recoverable**	1,500	1,500	2,200	3,000
Unknown recoverable resources in 1977**	500	500	1,200	2,000
Prior to peak annual reserve additions (percent per year):				
Rate of change in prices	-	-	0	0
Rate of change in production	-	-	3.5	3.5
Date of peak annual reserve additions	1978	1978	1986	1996
Prior to peak annual production (percent per year):***				
Rate of change in prices	5.4	3.4	3.8	5.9
Rate of change in production	0.8	1.8	1.6	0.6
Date of peak production	2000	1995	2002	2006
Price at peak production (per barrel)	$47	$25	$25	$25

*Degree of precision shown in results is to permit approximate reproduction of calculations.
**Quantities in billions of barrels.
***Rates of change shown are for period from peak annual reserve additions to peak production.

than in the case of Table 2. In the pessimistic case, we are already in the period of declining reserve additions, and the table displays results for alternative assumptions about market behavior. In the "conservative backstop" case, the market consensus is consistent with the assumption about timing of the backstop in the earlier discussion. The market initiates a pattern of price increases calculated to make the date of peak production coincide with the date of backstop availability. In this case, however, the market has already overshot, and the necessary price increases bring the price of crude oil to the level of $47, above the backstop price. The path of prices in the pessimistic case is shown in Figure 3.

While the path of prices is much less abrupt than that shown for the pessimistic case of Figure 2, under the conservative backstop assumption the rapid price increase would result in misallocation of resources if the discount rate were less than the rate of price increase.[15] The situation could then be improved by initiating larger price increases immediately.

Figure 3

Responsive Market Behavior: Pessimistic Resource Assumption

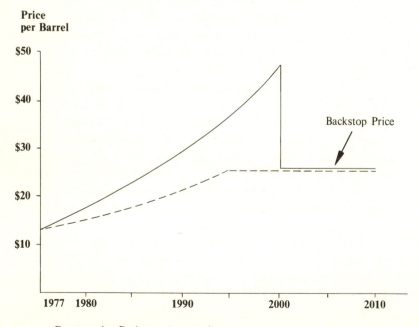

Conservative Backstop Assumption
Early Backstop Assumption

This, therefore, is a case in which government conservation measures might be indicated on grounds of resource depletion if the market failed to increase oil prices rapidly enough. The Plan, of course, employs a variety of measures, some that actually do increase prices to users through taxes, and others that work through subsidies or regulatory restraints on fuel use. The attractiveness of government action to induce conservation depends not only on whether market performance is optimal, but on the specific means chosen by government to remedy its failures. Grounds for believing that government policies can be designed to work perfectly to achieve their objectives are no stronger— probably weaker—than those for believing that markets work perfectly. Actual, as opposed to ideal, government interventions involve some misallocation of resources, administrative costs, and inequities, just as actual markets do. Usually, the more detailed the intervention, the greater the divergence between intent and actuality. Also it must be remembered that dealing with global resource depletion calls for measures on a global scale.

Before reaching conclusions about conservation in the pessimistic case, however, we should consider the "early backstop" variant of it. Here the market takes a more optimistic view of the backstop availability date. Aiming for the transition in 1995 rather than in 2000 permits satisfaction of the two conditions that peak production not be reached before backstop availability, and that price not rise above the backstop price; and it also makes unnecessary the large immediate price increase of the "conservative backstop" variant. If, however, the optimism proves to be unfounded, there would be a very rapid price increase between 1995 and 2000 which would bring the price far above the level of the "conservative backstop" case.

On the other hand, the assumption might be validated through government efforts to accelerate the availability of substitute fuels. The comparison of the two variants of the pessimistic case suggests how government efforts to bring on alternative fuels earlier can substitute for conservation efforts. The preferred combination depends not only on the specific conservation measures contemplated, but on the specific nature of the bottlenecks limiting the availability of backstop technologies. To the extent that the bottlenecks are related to noncommercial factors such as uncertainty about public policy, government regulation, leasing decisions on the public domain, or technical uncertainty, government action to remove the impediments may be indicated.

When we turn from the pessimistic case of Table 3 to the other two cases, the situation changes substantially. If the market adjusts to make the date of peak production coincide with the date on which the price reaches $25 at any time after the date of availability of the backstop technology, the patterns shown in Figure 4 emerge for the intermediate and optimistic cases. The

Figure 4

Responsive Market Behavior: Various Resource Assumptions

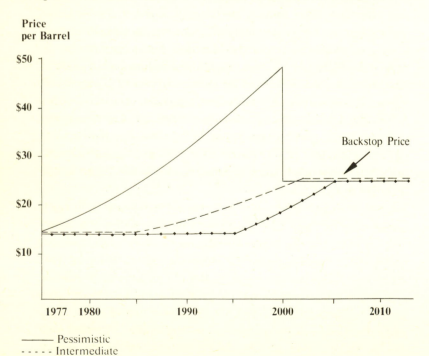

Price per Barrel

———— Pessimistic
- - - - - Intermediate
—•—•— Optimistic

pattern shown for the intermediate case would be very close to optimal for a 3 percent social discount rate, and that shown for the optimistic case, for a 6 percent rate. There would be very little room for improvement in the allocation of crude oil resources over time by government action in these cases, and efforts to change these patterns markedly would waste resources. Neither case requires a price increase in the very near term.

CONCLUSION

Our review of estimates of oil and gas availability reveals that they imply a large measure of uncertainty for energy policy because the range of estimates of ultimate volumes of oil and gas remaining to be recovered is large, the empirical and theoretical basis for making such estimates is unclear, and the relationship of the estimates to future rates of production, costs, and prices is not specified. Our illustrative analysis of oil suggests that assumptions about both resource availability and market behavior make a substantial difference in the indicated policy approaches to energy problems. Under pessimistic assumptions, our analysis suggests that there is a case for early government policy intervention to reduce current rates of consumption. However, under reasonable assumptions about market behavior, and for all but the pessimistic part of the range of uncertainty, the present OPEC-determined oil price level is too *high* and further government restriction of near-term consumption would make a bad situation worse.

Under conditions of great uncertainty, prudence becomes a major criterion for policy. To design a prudent policy it is necessary to compare the expected gains and losses under various policy options and assumptions about the uncertainties we have discussed. To do that goes well beyond the objectives of this discussion, which are only to outline the problem and to illustrate an analytic approach to it. A first step, however, would be to determine whether an analytic approach similar to that presented here is appropriate, and to test the results for sensitivity to key assumptions. Among those to which we have called attention, in addition to the resource estimates and market price response, are the shape of the demand function and the assumption that reserve additions are limited to a constant proportion of remaining unknown resources. If the rate of reserve additions were limited to a rate other than the 3 percent per year assumed in our analysis, the results might be significantly different, particularly if the rate were responsive to the price of oil, as it well might be. Variation in the price responsiveness of demand for oil would also affect the results significantly. Lower responsiveness would extend the range of situations in which market performance is unsatisfactory, and higher responsiveness would diminish that range. Finally, we repeat that our analysis has been restricted to the issue of resource depletion as a motive for government intervention. Clearly, the issue of economic and political vulnerabilities arising from dependence on imported oil is an important subject for government policy and is discussed elsewhere in this volume (see Wright, Chapter II). Several factors related to availability of imported oil are closely related to our discussion.

Although there are large resources remaining to be recovered under our intermediate and optimistic cases, it is unlikely that a large fraction of them will be found within U.S. territory. Further, the discovery of many large new fields in these cases may take levels of exploration hitherto unknown, using technologies yet to be developed. Yet the current environment for the conduct of such activities is distinctly less favorable than that of the past, when technical expertise and the financial resources to support exploration were united under the control of the multinational companies that expected to benefit from success.

Expropriation of equity interests in large oil finds is now the expectation for private firms operating internationally—in those increasingly infrequent cases when they are not simply operating as the agent for a nationally owned firm. The odds against success are still long, but the expected rewards are much more limited. The cash flow in oil has clearly changed its channel too, and the policies of OPEC countries with regard to reinvestment in oil exploration are unclear, as is their skill and efficiency in the allocation of resources for this purpose. Other national governments controlling promising areas for exploration may lack both financial resources and managerial skills to sponsor exploration in their territories. Suitable prices, and the availability of resources to be recovered, will not be sufficient to lead to growing production unless the international political and institutional environment is also suitable. Since the U.S. is, and will continue to be, a major importer, the improvement of that environment should be a major objective of government policy.

The political geography of remaining recoverable oil is also a matter of substantial policy interest. In the pessimistic case, a very large fraction of the oil yet to be produced will be located in the territories of the major OPEC producers and the Soviet Union. These countries own a very large part of known reserves, and known reserves are large relative to ultimate oil production in the pessimistic case. The situation is far less clear in the more optimistic cases. In those cases, large resources may exist in new areas, perhaps in a number of less-developed countries as well as in the Soviet Union, China, and offshore areas. Such a widespread distribution might both provide the basis for increasing reserves rapidly and increase the number of producing countries. And increasing the number of producers is the surest limitation on the market power of a cartel (Moorsteen 1975:3-11).

The previously mentioned impediments to international exploration would have to be overcome, however. So would a number of political problems, particularly if a large part of the resources were in countries like China or the Soviet Union that have closed their territories to exploration by foreigners for political, ideological, or economic reasons. Disputes among countries in East Asia also have at least temporarily closed offshore areas of high interest.

In addition to its direct role in determining whether we will enjoy the benefits of large oil resources, if they exist, the environment for oil exploration may also mask signals that might indicate the amount of oil remaining to be added to reserves. The rate of reserve additions was taken as such a signal in our analysis, but several factors may make it an ambiguous indicator.

The high current ratio of known reserves to production may lead to concern that substantial additions to reserves may either be unnecessary if OPEC restrictions persist or may lead to a break in prices if the number of producers expands substantially. This might depress the level of investment in exploration outside the major consuming countries, as might those other aspects of the international environment for oil exploration discussed above.

Some of the distortions that mask the underlying resource availability by affecting the level of exploration might be penetrated by analysis of changes in the returns to exploratory effort rather than in the gross rate of additions to reserves. Presumably, the private firms that now conduct oil and gas exploration perform such analysis for areas in which they have data. Since, however, these data are largely subject to proprietary restrictions, neither public nor private decision makers have a comprehensive basis for drawing global conclusions about the trend of reserve additions per unit of exploratory activity. Other distortions that affect the choice of areas for exploration, such as denial of access to promising areas, could not be analyzed readily.

Policy development would clearly be assisted by better information on the amounts, geographic distribution, and costs of oil and gas resources available for recovery. The issues are centered, not on information about *known* reserves for its own sake, but on data that may serve as indicators of the availability of unknown resources, such as the rate of additions to reserves per unit of exploratory effort. Such indicators are likely to remain fragmentary, inconclusive, and expensive to improve. Still, efforts to improve them may be worth considerable expense because of the benefits in providing enough warning of the impending resource depletion to permit market or public policy adjustments, given the lead times involved in changing consumption patterns or bringing substitute fuels into large-scale production.

The cases in the relatively optimistic parts of the range of resource availability offer the possibility, but not the assurance, of more attractive alternatives than restrictions of demand for oil and gas by government intervention. It appears likely at this point that the supply of oil and gas will be restricted by the failures of institutional arrangements before a world wide lack of resource availability is felt. The opportunities provided by resource availability may not be realized without a number of initiatives by government to remove politically imposed obstacles to resource development. Our conclusion for policy, therefore, is not a counsel of passivity.

X

EDWARD J. MITCHELL

ENERGY POLITICS: THE IRRELEVANT DEBATE

The decline of traditional political interest groups, and the rise of ideology. The dominance of "liberal" ideology over energy policy. Ideology and natural gas deregulation: examining voting records. Comparing votes on other issues. The irrelevance of price controls to consumer prices. Ideology and the Carter proposals.

From the 1920s to the mid-1960s U.S. energy policy was dominated by the economic interests of the petroleum industry. In the 1920s special tax breaks, including the depletion allowance, were granted to producers of oil. Since the 1930s market demand prorationing statutes enabled producing states to withhold production and support prices under the banner of "conservation" (a motherhood word even then). In the 1950s and 1960s domestic producers were sheltered from cheaper foreign oil by import quotas. Energy policy was not in the national interest, but it was definitely in someone's interest.

By the late 1960s, with Sam Rayburn, Lyndon Johnson, and other oil state powers gone, the influence of the oil industry on

public policy waned. It remains to this day a collection of orga-
nized interests, but not powerful interests.[1] The power to create
policy passed to consuming state politicians. Unfortunately, there
was no well defined and articulated consumer interest to rally
around. Because of the inherent diffusion of consumer interests,
no group or corporate body has had the incentive, the credibility,
and the capability to organize a consumer interest bloc. So-called
"public interest groups" or "consumer groups" have thus far
been able to organize only on ideological or "civic balance" principles, thus degenerating into little more than anti-producer coali-
tions. Outside the producing states, even regional and local
economic interests have been poorly thought out, with the result
that regional blocs, like the bipartisan New England coalition, as
often as not vote against their own economic interests.

With no clearly defined consumer interest at the national,
regional, or local level, the politican and the voter have had no
choice but to fall back on ideology. By ideology I mean simply
that body of general beliefs you consult when you have to make a
decision on something you know little or nothing about. Thus,
with a precision that is frightening to behold, "liberals" (more
sensibly labeled democratic socialists in the rest of the world) have
voted for state control, and "conservatives" (called liberals in the
rest of the world) have voted for the free market on issue after
issue.

That the new administration has followed an ideological
approach is somewhat out of character. In other fields of economic regulation, such as trucking and the airlines, it has
proceeded rather pragmatically. The sharp departure in energy
probably can be explained by the particular advisers chosen—and
the independence given them—by the president.

The purpose of this chapter is to show that in fact ideology
dominates energy policy, that abstract opinion overwhelms real
public interests, and that the energy debate is for the most part
unrelated to questions of the public interest. In characterizing
energy policy as largely ideological, I do not mean to denigrate
ideology in general or the "liberal" ideology that holds front
stage in particular. People, and especially politicians, cannot

function without general opinions on matters of which they have little understanding or first-hand knowledge. Politicians must vote on hundreds of public issues, but can only hope to gain expertise in a few subjects. Employing instincts or ideology on most issues is simply an economical way of using the limited amount of working hours available.

If a public issue is not generally well understood, perhaps because of its inherent complexity, ideology will tend to dominate public choice. If the prevailing ideology happens to correlate well with the pragmatic answer, the nation is fortunate; if not, the public is poorly served. In energy policy, the prevailing "liberal" ideology does not correlate well with pragmatism. This is rather easy to show. The dominant issue in the energy debate is whether or not to control oil and natural gas prices. The last five chairmen of the President's Council of Economic Advisers, spanning the Johnson to Carter administrations, have, within earshot of me and in public, supported decontrol of both oil and natural gas prices. These are all pragmatic men. While two are "liberal" and three "conservative" in their ideological leanings, their economic advice is rooted in a common discipline based on logic and experience. On occasion they would undoubtedly make different value judgments and thus be led to different positions on public issues. But when the issue is not heavily "valueloaded," and the control of petroleum prices is not "valueloaded," the advice is likely to be the same and broadly reflective of their profession.[2]

The divergence of ideology, on the one hand, and fact and pragmatism on the other, is always very hard to close. Energy as a major social issue has been before the public since, at the latest, October of 1973. Yet the public overestimates the profits of oil companies per dollar of sales by a factor of twelve to fifteen. Journalists persist in beliefs about the petroleum industry that run directly counter to the vast majority of experts. For example, in a recent opinion survey a majority of journalists agreed with the statement that "the major, integrated U.S. oil companies currently possess monopoly power in one or more stages of the oil business," while more than three-fourths of the academic economists specializing in the petroleum industry disagreed.[3] Whether it is the complexity of the issue or the robustness of ideology, there does not seem to be any noticeable convergence between ideology and reality.

To this point I have merely asserted the power of ideology in the energy debate. Let us now take a look at how energy politics actually work. Take the issue of natural gas deregulation. Table 1 shows you all you have to know about natural gas deregulation politics.

Table 1

ADA Ideological Rating and Congressional Vote on Natural Gas Deregulation, 1976

ADA Rating	Votes against Deregulation	Votes for Deregulation
95-100	26	0
85-90	31	0
75-80	41	4
65-70	33	2
55-60	30	3
45-50	19	10
35-40	8	18
25-30	7	20
15-20	1	37
5-10	3	69
0	0	37

Source: *ADA Legislative Newsletter* (Washington, D.C), 1 January 1977; *Congressional Record* 122, 14 (5 February 1976):H 771.

It groups congressmen into eleven classes using the liberal-conservative ratings of the Americans for Democratic Action (ADA). Inspection of the table shows extraordinary correlations between the deregulation vote and these ratings. (The vote is on the Smith substitute amendment to the Natural Gas Act of 5 February 1976, a crucial vote on deregulation by the full House of Representatives. The amendment passed, which is to say deregulation failed, 205-201.) A simple prediction rule that says if a congressman's ADA rating is 45 percent or higher he will vote against deregulation, and if under 45 percent he will vote for deregulation, would be correct in 361 out of 399 cases, or better than 90 percent of the time. (Six congressmen who voted on deregulation voted so seldom on other issues that a meaningful liberal-conservative rating could not be computed.) The symmetry of the vote was almost perfect: the liberal half voted 180 to 19 against deregulation, while the conservative half voted 181 to 19 for deregulation.

More recently, the House Commerce Committee voted 22-21 in favor of the president's plan to continue price regulation, thereby reversing a subcommittee decision to deregulate. Of the 43 committee members voting, 35 had ADA ratings from the previous session of Congress. The votes of 32 members were predicted correctly by my simple model. And of the three "deviant" members, one, Metcalf of Illinois, waited until all other votes had been cast and might have followed true to form if his vote had been decisive. Thus, even at the committee level, the ideological model is 90 percent accurate. Furthermore, this was a true *ex ante* forecast, the rule having been developed prior to the actual vote.

A more technical econometric analysis (Mitchell 1977) shows that state-to-state variation in economic interest factors, such as gas shortages, gas consumption, and gas production explain little or nothing about voting patterns. This is especially true and rather evident in consuming states. For example, according to FPC pipeline curtailment data, both New Jersey and North Carolina had huge shortages of natural gas during the winter the House vote was taken. The North Carolina delegation voted 9 to 2 *for* deregulation; the New Jersey delegation voted 14 to 1 *against* deregulation. Michigan and Georgia were among the states least affected by pipeline curtailments. The Georgia delegation voted 7 to 3 *for* deregulation; the Michigan delegation voted 11 to 5 *against* deregulation.

If this pattern holds, the reality of gas shortages will exert little influence on the course of events: conservatives will become more convinced that regulation is folly, and liberals will be more convinced that the oil industry is evil incarnate. Whether we deregulate or not will depend overwhelmingly on the philosophical complexion of the Congress. The fact that deregulation was voted down in Congress after the dismal failure of regulation was evident, but was passed in two earlier Congresses under Truman and Eisenhower before regulation had even begun, illustrates the small bearing that reality and experience have on energy politics. The earlier Congresses were simply more conservative and that is all there is to it.

The natural gas case is no exception. Many energy policy votes reflect the same ideological polarization. To show how ideological they are, I collected data on a number of energy and non-energy votes of the House of Representatives during 1976. The non-energy votes were selected from those chosen by the ADA or the Americans for Constitutional Action (ACA), a conservative counterpart to ADA, to form their ideological ratings. From these votes I selected a variety from those that sounded to me most ideologically polarizing. The energy votes were selected on an essentially random basis, with the sole condition that they be a relatively important vote.

To measure ideology I used the following index: Divide the House of Representatives into two equal parts based on the ADA ratings. All those with ratings below 45 percent are conservatives; all those 45 percent or above are liberals. Calculate for each vote the percentage of yeas that are liberals and the percentage of nays that are liberals. The absolute value of the difference is the measure of ideology. (Note that using conservatives instead of liberals in the calculations gives the same answer.) If liberals (or conservatives) represent the same percentage of the vote on each side of the issue, the index is zero. If liberals (or conservatives) represent all the votes on one side and none on the other, the index is 100. As an example, if liberals represented 60 percent of the yea vote on an issue and 40 percent of the nay vote, the score would be 20. If liberals represented 80 percent of the yea vote and 10 percent of the nay vote, the score would be 70. The latter vote would be much more ideological.

Of the thirty-odd issues I examined, Table 2 displays a representative group of ten votes (Mitchell 1977) with emphasis on the highest scores from both the energy and non-energy issues. I would stress again that all the non-energy issues are supposed to be highly ideological. I have not attempted to estimate what the average score would be of all House votes to get a feel for the degree of ideology in a normal or more typical vote. These calculations are tedious and time-consuming, and I leave to further researchers the exhausting job of comprensively researching this problem. We are dealing here only with what appears to be "high ideology."

Several points are suggested in the table. First, the energy votes are among the most ideological. In fact, of the eight votes I chose from the ADA list of twenty, two were energy votes (Gas Deregulation and Uranium Enrichment), and their scores were the highest of all. Second, the most ideological of the non-energy votes was the B-1 bomber, which, like energy, involved a highly complex subject. (As a non-expert in defense matters but one who follows the debate in the press, I could not have voted on that bill personally in any way other than ideologically. It thus becomes easier for me to understand why non-experts in energy vote as they do.) Third, some issues, like abortion, that would seem extremely ideological because they are so "valueloaded," did not score as high as expected.

Fourth, it is easy to find energy issues, like the Synthetic Fuel Subsidy, that have relatively low scores. The reasons are obvious. Many votes have several aspects, with the ideology running in one direction for one aspect and in the other direction for another aspect. Loans of federal money to private energy firms obviously are helpful to those "private enterprises" and encourage the supply of domestic energy. It is in that sense pro-U.S. business, and was supported by many business leaders and some conservative congressmen. On the other hand, it is not a "free market" policy. It biases the allocation of capital to certain firms and introduces a larger government role in the energy industry. On these grounds, many conservative congressmen—and fewer businessmen—opposed it. On the liberal side, the same ambivalence showed. At once the bill increased the federal presence in the industry, but did so by benefitting the large energy companies that are so poorly regarded in liberal circles. Incidentally, the bill was defeated 193-192, with conservatives favoring the bill about two to one and liberals opposing it by about the same ratio. The *Congressional Quarterly* (1976:2672) characterized the opposition as an "unusual coalition of fiscal conservatives and environmentally sensitive liberals," suggesting further crosscurrents. My guess is that the pragmatic conclusion of most economists would be that the liberals were right on this one.

Throwing out bills with obvious ideological crosscurrents, we are led to believe that energy policy is probably among the more ideological issues of contemporary public policy.

When political choice is mainly philosophical rather than pragmatic, debate, if it can even be called that, has a way of degenerating into a series of cliches and countercliches. No doubt the greater use of high-flown rhetoric is appealing to some, but not to anyone concerned with its consequences. The daily newspaper is filled with this extraneous cant, but I can only hope to touch on a few examples here.

As we have seen in Table 2, the vote on oil price controls in the House of Representatives was very much along ideological lines. The ideological score for the Krueger amendment to HR 7014 was 68.5, well up there in a list of highly ideological bills. It is a fact that I could have chosen other votes on other oil price control amendments to the same bill showing equally high ideological scores. (An apparent exception is the Heinz amendment, which was ideologically ambiguous, opposed by leading conservatives, and defeated overwhelmingly.) Oil price control must be viewed as a highly ideological issue.

Postured on one side of this issue are liberals who, among other things, argue they are defending the consumer, especially the poor. (Never mind that the poor consume little energy.) On the other side are conservatives arguing for the free market, greater oil production, and less bureaucracy. The key assumption of liberals in this debate is that oil price controls keep oil prices down to consumers. But there is precious little evidence that they do!

It is of course not easy to predict exactly what oil prices would be here if we decontrolled them. I suppose the simplest thing to do is to see what they are in other countries where they are not controlled, where refiners must purchase all their oil at the high world price. Let us look at some of those prices.

The closest foreign competitors of the major U.S. Gulf Coast refineries are the Caribbean refineries, which are equidistant from the big U.S. east coast market. Price quotations are reported monthly for both refinery sources, although by separate agencies.[4] I am not confident that these price data are accurate to the mill, but there is reason to believe they are in the ball park. At any rate the price difference that should result from the low U.S. crude oil prices, if they were passed through, is enormous. Typically, the subsidy implied to U.S. refiners by cheap domestic oil has been on the order of $2.50 to $3.00 per barrel, or 6 to 8 cents per gallon. These are big numbers compared to the average level of prices, and we must suppose that differences much smaller than that would be picked up by the data.

Looking at the figures for 1975 and 1976, there is very little difference for the U.S. Gulf Coast and the Caribbean. A barrel of regular gasoline averaged $13.74 in the U.S. Gulf Coast refinery in 1975. During the same period it averaged $13.07 in Caribbean refineries, 67 cents per barrel or 1.5 cents per gallon *less*. In 1976 the figures were $14.91 per barrel in the U.S. Gulf Coast and $14.92 in the Caribbean, for all practical purposes identical. Thus, for what is by far the most important product in the United States, prices were at most equal at refineries that purchased completely uncontrolled crude oil.

For premium gasoline the comparisons are essentially the same as for regular gasoline. The only products that appear to have lower prices in the United States are kerosene and gasoil, but these price differences are still only on the order of about one-third of the difference in crude oil costs.

Explaining why the Federal Energy Administration (FEA) presides over a price control program with no or little price consequence is not easy, and the reader is referred elsewhere for the details (Mitchell 1977; Phelps and Smith 1977). What is worth knowing is that the low U.S. crude oil costs wind up in higher U.S. refinery costs and higher U.S. refinery profits. In fact, the FEA seems to be primarily in the business of taking profits away from some oil companies and giving them to others through its so-called "entitlements" program. This program involves nothing more than some refiners writing out checks to the FEA which are then turned over to other refiners.

The sums involved in the program are staggering. I found thirteen companies who had always received checks from the government under the program and who also reported their profits to the public. In 1976 the total after-tax profits of these companies was $1,350 million. The checks they received from the FEA amounted to $960 million, or 71 percent of total profits. All of this money came from their competitors.

The likelihood that price controls have not controlled prices and that the FEA is really a welfare agency for refiners has not been a deep dark secret. The sins of the FEA have been heard right from the horse's mouth. The former head of the FEA, Frank Zarb, who co-chaired the Presidential Task Force on Reform of the Federal Energy Administration Regulations, reported in December 1976: "FEA regulations as they now exist confer few, if any, benefits on the public" (Presidential Task Force 1976:33).

The report goes on to argue specifically that current FEA regulations impose large costs on society in the form of a lack of new domestic refining capacity, inefficiencies in product distribution, barriers to the importation of cheap foreign oil products, overuse of domestic refining capacity, plus annual FEA administration costs of at least $47 million and industry compliance costs of $500 million. Furthermore, the report concedes that the compliance program is ineffective and "exceptions" have become the rule.

While evaluations of most government economic control programs tend to sound like this, the fact that this is the government
describing itself is somewhat refreshing.

What is significant for our purposes is that the debate—
consumerism, the poor, inflation, and all that—is a sham. Here
are 87 percent of the liberals voting for a program that has
apparently little or no effect on its rhetorical beneficiaries. Unless
liberals secretly have a preference for Standard of Ohio over
Sunoco, or Standard of California over Shell, they know not what
they do.

While the Congress is undoubtedly the richest source of
ideological irrelevancy, the new administration is rapidly gaining
ground. The president's National Energy Plan adopts the view of
Congressional liberals with regard to price controls on oil and gas,
even extending gas price controls to the heretofore unregulated
intrastate market. In addition, the president introduces a bewil-
deringly complex collection of taxes and subsidies on various
energy products. Simplifying this Rube Goldberg system, it
appears that if crude oil winds up in your car, you pay a high price
for it; if it ends up in the basement as heating oil, you pay a low
price for it; and if it ends up embodied in almost any of the manufactured products you buy, you pay something in between. I
don't think there is anything in a straight economics book that
explains any of this. The message you get is that the energy architects dislike cars as compared to houses.

If you heat your house with solar energy, the government pays
for part of it; but if you heat with oil or gas, you pay your own
way. If you keep warm by insulating, you are subsidized; if you
use oil or gas, you pay your way.

At times the president's energy advisers argue for a tax on
domestic oil because it would reduce the windfall profits of oil
companies. But there is no tax on coal to capture the windfall
profits of coal companies, or on uranium to capture the windfall
profits of uranium companies, and prices of those commodities
have soared right along with oil prices. Furthermore, the Carter
program itself will create windfall profits for suppliers of solar
energy and insulation through the subsidy plan. The president's

own Council on Wage and Price Stability points out that the demand for fiberglass insulation could increase as much as 50 percent as a result of the subsidy, and the industry is currently operating near capacity (Wage and Price Stability 1976). Windfall prof-

Table 2
Indexes of Ideology for Selected House Votes, 1975-76

House of Representatives Bill No.	Brief Name	Issue	Index	ADA or ACA Issue
HR 9464 (Smith substitute amendment)	Gas Deregulation	Deregulating natural gas prices	81.0	ADA, ACA
HR 7014 (Moss amendment)	Oil Industry Audit	Authorizing GAO to audit required oil industry government reports	75.7	
HR 8401 (Bingham amendment)	Uranium Enrichment	Private industry role in uranium enrichment	71.4	ADA
HR 14262 (Addobbo amendment)	B-1 Bomber	Deferring spending of funds on B-1 bomber	70.2	ADA
HR 10799	Legal Services Corporation	Allowing grants for research in poverty law	68.8	ACA
HR 7014 (Krueger amendment)	Oil Decontrol	Gradually decontrolling oil prices	68.5	
HR 11963 (Harrington amendment)	Chile	Prohibiting military sales to Chile for human rights violations	63.1	ADA
HR 14232 (Hyde amendment)	Abortion	Barring use of federal funds for abortions	43.6	ADA
HR 12112	Synthetic Fuel Subsidy	Authorizing federal loans and price supports for development of synthetic fuels	33.5	

its are inevitable. Indeed, windfall profits and losses are created every time there is an unforeseen change in the economy, which of course is a regular occurrence in a free economy. Why are windfall profits on oil to be singled out?

The preference of houses over cars, non-energy over energy, solar energy over oil, indeed, almost any other source of energy over oil, is what leaps out at you when you read the National Energy Plan. You will not find these preferences explained in any economics book. The answer is to be found in political philosophy. When only 72 congressmen were willing to vote for a gasoline tax, 78 percent of them were liberals. Eighty-eight percent of the liberals favored a rapid depreciation of solar heating equipment. Ninety-seven percent of the liberals favored an audit of confidential petroleum industry data. Ninety-three percent of the liberals favored funding an electric car. Ninety-two percent of the votes for maintaining low natural gas prices were liberal. And 87 percent of the liberals favored keeping controls on oil prices (Mitchell 1977). What makes the Carter program hang together, what makes the seeming hodgepodge of taxes, subsidies, directives, requirements, and cliches a whole, is ideology.

If we grade the Carter program as we judge women's clothing, that is, on the basis of style or fashion, liberals will give it high marks and conservatives low marks. If we judge it on the basis of its likely consequences for human welfare, both liberals and conservatives must turn thumbs down.

XI

HENRY S. ROWEN

POSTSCRIPT

Several themes emerge from these essays.

Our ignorance on important matters.   We lack scientific knowledge on the amount and distribution of oil, gas, uranium; the health and ecological effects of SO_2 and trace elements in coal and oil; and the seriousness of the CO_2 "greenhouse" effect, among others. We lack *technical* knowledge on the efficiency, safety, and likely proliferation effects of the plutonium breeder in comparison with other nuclear reactor fuel cycles, the means of efficiently extracting oil from shale, natural gas from deep geopressured methane deposits, and so on. We are short on *behavioral* data on such matters as the response of suppliers to an environment which has both higher prices and extensive—and changing—government regulation, the behavior of the OPEC cartel, the energy prospects of the Communist countries, and long-run changes in the economy that might be brought about by sharply higher energy prices.

The more we can reduce our ignorance on these matters, the less likely we are to make serious mistakes.

There is also *lack of agreement on what ails us and the efficacy of various remedies.* The patient has symptoms, but the doctors have not agreed on a diagnosis. Is the real problem the oil sheiks, the prospect of the world running out of oil, the profligacy of American consumers, the power of oil firms, the incompetency of government, or all of the above? Until our political leadership settles on a diagnosis which seems to correspond to reality as perceived by consumers and producers (who are not as short-sighted as often represented), confusion and divisiveness will continue.

We should get our priorities straight, and *some problems seem more compelling than others.* Two stand out: 1) the risk of importing oil from the Middle East (because of the international political costs of growing U.S., European, and Japanese dependency, possible Arab wielding of the "oil weapon," and the contingency of interruption of supply during the next Middle East war); and 2) the spread of nuclear explosives made possible by the diffusion of nuclear technology.

In contrast, these essays do not provide much support for the proposition that we should stay awake nights worrying about the world running out of oil soon, or how the world will obtain energy in the 21st century. We or our descendants may have great difficulties with energy in that century, but they are not visible through the fog of time. Carrying out basic research is about the best we can do for future generations now.

It is much easier to get into the energy control business than to get out of it. Controls beget more controls beget. . . Government intervention of the past several years has already caused a number of interests in the control system to be vested, and more people are acquiring a stake in the maintenance and extension of this system every month. How much more comfortable and secure it is to be protected from the winds of competition by having a paternalistic government fending off disruptive players.

The power of ideology. Particularly energy-related interests are certainly evident in the political marketplace these days; many are strongly represented in the halls of Congress. The legitimacy of this process can hardly be questioned, but the efficiency of the political marketplace in producing equity and in limiting economic waste in this domain is doubtful. So is the social utility of the ideology in which many current proposals are embedded. It is a kind of demagoguery to pretend that taxes on gas-guzzling cars are imposed on the energy profligate and the rich, and that preventing "windfall" gains will not affect the supply of energy. This populist rhetoric is satisfying to many, but not helpful with the most serious of our problems.

Confusion exacts a price. Political victories can be won in the short run. A sense of community interest and willingness to sacrifice can sustain political support for a while. Interests vested in the control system will defend it. But broad public support has not existed since the early months of 1974. The Carter administration begins with a large capital stock of goodwill and it has the advantage of a relatively friendly Congress. These assets will be dissipated if the sacrifices people are being called on to make do not seem, as time passes, to correspond well to reality. Alienation, already evident on many fronts in our society, may grow with time. If it appears that our energy policy has only made things worse, then a backlash may occur.

The message is concentration on a few essentials: reducing our ignorance, sorting out the problems, getting straight our priorities, being more cautious about extending the control system, and lowering the ideological temperature.

NOTES

I. Henry S. Rowen: "Comprehensive Energy Policy: King Stork?"

1. The view that the U.S. government contributed importantly to the strengthening of OPEC during the 1970-1973 period and to the oil crisis in 1973 is supported by a good deal of evidence. See Akins (1973), Vernon (1974), and *Forbes Magazine* (1976).

2. Report of the President's Material Policy Commission, widely referred to as the "Paley Commission," June 1952.

3. The optimum price and consumption rate of nonrenewable resources presents problems in forecasting that are not present in renewable resources. However, the assumption that this is sufficient cause for government intervention assumes, without adequate basis, that government decision makers will do better than the interaction of private ones in approximating these optima.

4. Here is a case where a tax on energy consumption makes sense. A tax per kwh of electricity or deregulation combined with a stiff excess profits tax would largely remove this distortion by bringing the price facing consumers up to the cost of adding capacity.

5. The *locus classicus* of the analysis of confused reasoning on energy and the environment, and of the paternalist approach to consumer behavior, is Alchian (1975). See also Mitchell (1974*b*).

6. Observed behavior in the past few years is consistent with the estimates of long-term energy demand price elasticity of around .5 for the end uses of energy, and around .25 for primary uses.

7. For instance, today the cost of electricity from solar cells is 20-40 times greater than that from conventional electricity sources. Yet we should not rule out the possibility that this technology, if vigorously pursued, may be competitive and start coming into widespread use within a decade.

8. Chapter IX by Fred Hoffman and Richard Nehring discusses long-run oil and gas supplies.

9. According to Phelps and Smith (1977), because oil products are being imported into the United States, the domestic price for products is arguably not less than the world price, despite our price controls. Who, then, is receiving the difference between that price and the controlled domestic price of crude oil? Evidently not entirely consumers. The difference allegedly is accruing to refiners and distributors. On this view, "windfall" gains are not being prevented by the price controls after all, but are merely being shifted largely from resource owners to "downstream" firms.

10. Moreover, because a large part of the delivered price of natural gas is fixed pipeline cost, consumers end up paying almost as much for less gas. For example, the average

wellhead price on interstate gas this year is $0.78, while the average price facing interstate consumers is $2.23. The difference is largely transportation cost. It has to be paid no matter how much gas is shipped. Because the pipelines have a guaranteed rate of return, the consumers pay a good deal more for less. See *Wall Street Journal,* 21 June 1977.

11. The Council of Economic Advisors has estimated a potential growth rate for the economy of 3.5 percent through 1980; Data Resources, Inc., has estimated 3.35 percent, and George Perry (1977) of Brookings, 3.9 percent.

12. This estimate assumes the price elasticities noted in Note 6, and economic growth from now to 1985 at 3.25 percent annually.

13. In contrast with the CIA (1977) estimate, the OECD (1977) estimates only a 3.4 percent increase in OECD consumption between 1974 and 1985. WAES (1977) assumes an average annual global economic growth rate for 1977-1985 of 3.4 percent to 5.2 percent (and 2.8 percent to 4 percent for 1985-2000). It does not deal explicitly with price elasticities, but instead assumes (or concludes from country team judgments) that the ratio of energy growth to GNP growth will be about .82/.87 instead of the historical ratio of 1.02. This produces annual increases in global energy consumption to 1985 from 1972 from 2.8 percent to 3.4 percent. The range predicted for oil demand growth is 2.5 percent to 3.4 percent per year. WAES estimates a non-Communist world oil demand (presumably at something like today's real prices) of around 60 million B/D in 1985 in contrast to CIA's estimate of about 70 million B/D.

WAES assumes that world oil production will peark at between 65 and 85 million B/D between 1990 and shortly after 2000, assuming no government limits on production. With OPEC production limits, non-Communist world production might he held to as low as 55 million B/D, causing an earlier crisis.

14. This argument is developed in Moorsteen (1975).

15. The Soviet Union, which now produces more oil than the United States, produces only about half as much natural gas. There is scope for a large increase in natural gas usage, and a large increase is planned. The rate of growth of output is hindered by high costs of development in remote parts of Siberia and by limits in pipeline construction capacity. Even so, a large push to expand natural gas exports to Western Europe is to be expected.

16. Given that it is expensive to move the gas to the factories, one response is to move gas-utilizing factories to the gas. This is now beginning to happen to a noticeable extent. This will have the effect of reducing energy demand in consuming countries.

17. See Chapter VI by Robert Pindyck.

The president has been reported as saying that gas decontrol would produce only an extra 1.1 TCF at an additional cost to consumers of $70 billion (*New York Times,* 13 July 1977). One of his senior energy advisors has been quoted as saying that the transfer from consumers to producers more likely would be $100-$150 billion, apparently over the next decade (ibid., 24 July 1977). These are the lowest bids so far in the demand elasticity sweepstakes.

Energy Daily (2 June 1977) reports that 1977 FEA draft National Energy Outlook Report, the American Gas Association, the Institute for Gas Technology, and WAES estimate that gas production could be 3-4 TCF higher in 1985 with decontrol, at a price between $2.00 and $2.90/MCF.

The Market Oriented Program Planning Strategy (MOPPS) study of ERDA (3 June 1977), using methods which are unclear, estimates that gas reserves at a price of $2.50 (the BTU equivalent price for the close substitute of gas, distillate oil) are at least 350 TCF. At a production cost of $4/MCF, the conjectured resources of gas from devonian shale, coal seams, tight western sands, and geopressured methane range from 300 to 1800 TCF. In addition, there is the "backup" technology of coal gasification (generated *in situ* or aboveground) alleged to be producible at around this cost.

A rebuttal to the administration position by two members of Congress asserts that decontrol will save $48 billion by 1990, allowing for the costs of substitute fuels (Brown and Stockman 1977).

Although there are large uncertainties on future gas production, the administration assumption of near zero price elasticity over $1.75/MCF is extraordinary.

18. Some commentators suggest that OPEC's prices are not at the monopolist level; i.e., that further real increases today would be in the financial interest of its members. In contrast, the analysis here suggests that Saudi Arabia is not doing the West a favor in holding down price increases, but rather is restraining the more imprudent and shortsighted members of the club. Saudi Arabia has been in the happy position of (more or less) maximizing its economic interest and those of its partners, and at the same time earning political credit by assuming a stance of responsible restraint. For an analysis of the optimal pricing of cartels and of OPEC, see Pindyck (1976), a paper which supports the proposition that OPEC's current price is near the monopoly price.

19. This assumes that the world price of oil today in a competitive market would be around $5/Bbl rather than $12.50. There are also additional social costs from the cartel-maintained high price.

20. Fred Hoffman has suggested that individuals be given incentives to stockpile at no cost to the taxpayer by guaranteeing that private stocks would be exempt from future price controls and allocations.

21. Any such scheme would have to take account of agreements for crisis oil-sharing among consuming countries.

22. See Chapter IX by Fred Hoffman and Richard Nehring.

23. This subject is discussed in Chapter III, "Nuclear Power and Nuclear Proliferation," by Albert Carnesale.

II. Arthur W. Wright: "Energy Independence: Insuring against Disruptions of Supply"

1. It might be argued that the risk premium should vary with the reliability of the source of supply—higher for more risky sources, lower for less risky; thus domestic supplies would have the lowest premium (zero), and imports from a "hostile" country like the USSR the highest. This argument ignores the point that the dislocation caused by the disruption of some supplies would make all remaining supplies more valuable. In addition, "reliability" is difficult to define (for example, the USSR paid lip service to the Arab oil embargo but increased its shipments of oil to the West in late 1973 and early 1974), and the fungibility of crude oils makes price discrimination virtually impossible to enforce.

2. The quota limited imports to about one-eighth of U.S. domestic oil production (with certain exceptions) and thereby protected a price differential between the U.S. market (about $3.00 a barrel) and the world market (about $1.75 a barrel delivered to the U.S. East or Gulf Coast). Thus U.S. oil imports were restricted when world oil prices were relatively low, and then allowed to increase rapidly just as world prices were beginning their sharp rise.

3. Curiously, public discussion has focused mainly on possible increases, not declines, in world oil prices. The periodic pricing conferences of the Organization of Petroleum Export-

ing Countries (OPEC) are monitored closely by the press, and official Washington and others are wringing their hands over the imminent exhaustion of world oil resources (e.g., CIA 1977a). True, markets are ill-equipped to cope with political events like OPEC conferences, but with the cartel (a subset of OPEC) apparently having achieved its major price goals, future increases are likely to be comparatively modest. Markets are quite capable, however, of taking into account progressive resource exhaustion. In the case of oil, higher finding costs will raise the prices of new reserves; the increase in the cost of this major capital input will in turn raise crude oil prices (Adelman 1972). At present, it is the cartel's restricted output, not finding costs, that is setting world oil prices, and this will continue to be the case for the indefinite future. Thus hand-wringing, official or otherwise, over how soon the world will "run out of oil" is silly.

4. Another source, Phelps and Smith (1977), argues that the entitlements program does not reduce any refined product price; however, their argument can be questioned on statistical grounds.

5. The plan envisioned 5-cent annual increases in the federal gasoline excise tax, up to a maximum of 50 cents a gallon by 1989. This particular proposal is dead, at least in the current session of Congress, although there is talk of a 4-cent increase in the tax.

6. This policy recommendation is developed at length in Tyner and Wright (1977). It represents an idea implicit in an earlier paper coauthored by Cox and Wright (1975: 29-42).

7. For simplicity, I assume here that domestic crude oil prices would be decontrolled. It is probable that decontrol would pose thorny equity issues involving windfall profits to crude oil producers and some consumer price increases. If crude oil prices were not decontrolled, the present policy proposal would have to include a differentiated excise tax on domestic crude oil.

8. I am indebted to Gerard M. Brannon of Georgetown University for first pointing this out to me.

III. Albert Carnesale: "Nuclear Power and Nuclear Proliferation"

1. Isotopes of a given element cannot be separated by chemical means. Sophisticated physical techniques which exploit the minute differences in the masses of the isotopes are required. For the foreseeable future, the important methods of enrichment are: gaseous diffusion, which accounts for most of the enrichment performed to date for weapons and reactor fuel; gas centrifuge, which is just reaching commercialization and which is under active development in a number of countries; aerodynamic processes, which have been demonstrated in West Germany and South Africa, but are far from commercialization; and laser techniques, which are in the laboratory research stage.

2. The form of plutonium preferred for weapons is plutonium-239. Special reactors designed and operated for a weapons program produce "weapons-grade" plutonium which is almost pure plutonium-239. But the "reactor-grade" plutonium produced in the normal operation of light-water power reactors contains only about 60-70 percent plutonium-239; the remainder is dominantly plutonium-240. (By operating a power reactor "abnormally" and uneconomically, plutonium containing much higher concentrations of Pu-239 can be produced.) Plutonium-240 is non-fissile and its presence in a nuclear weapon adversely affects both the yield and the reliability. Despite these difficulties, reactor-grade plutonium is "weapons-usable"; that is, it can be used to make workable weapons with explosive power equivalent to thousands of tons of TNT. For more detailed discussions of the use of reactor-grade plutonium in weapons, see Greenwood et al. (1976), and Wohlstetter (1976-77: 88-179).

3. In fairness to the reader, the author notes that the principal elements of the president's program resembles strongly in substance the recommendations set forth by Nuclear Energy (1977), and that the author was a member of that group.

IV. Stanley M. Greenfield: "Environmental Problems with Fossil Fuels"

1. Currently underway in EPA is a regulatory effort, under the water pollution laws, to control the emission of toxic substances. When promulgated, these may further restrict the handling and disposal of processing wastes from fossil fuels due to the trace elements present.

2. Additional reasons are the development of major electric utility facilities in the west, and the accompanying desire to reduce fuel transportation costs.

3. What are described as oil shale environmental problems are equally applicable to tar sands, but at a somewhat lower scale, the differences occurring primarily in the waste disposal associated with each process.

4. I am indebted to my colleague, Dr. E. L. Husting, for his contribution to the analysis of the potential health effects of coal gasification and liquefaction.

5. In partial support of the above contention, Table 12 has been extracted from a recent paper on "Environmental Aspects of Coal Liquefaction" (Forney et al. 1974), and it expresses the need for research to determine the environmental impact of this process.

VI. Robert S. Pindyck: "Prices and Shortages: Evaluating Policy Options for the Natural Gas Industry"

1. In fact, the FPC found production to be 3.7 percent below demand in 1971. Among those consumers who were curtailed were farmers who used natural gas to dry their newly harvested gain. The result of the curtailment was that grain could not be dried quickly enough, and it rotted.

2. This case against the Phillips Petroleum Company, brought by the Attorney General of Wisconsin, was based on the argument that although the pipelines were regulated, wellhead price increases by large petroleum companies could be passed through as "costs" in pipeline wholesale prices, thereby increasing retail prices to the consumers. The Supreme Court, although not claiming that gas producers had monopoly power, did find that the FPC should regulate wellhead prices. For further discussion, see MacAvoy and Pindyck (1975a:12-14).

3. For discussion of these decisions, and estimates of what free market new contract prices would likely have been, see MacAvoy and Pindyck (1975b:15-19; 1975a:17-21).

4. A House bill and a related administration proposal would have allowed interstate pipelines to purchase gas in intrastate markets if the consuming areas served by those pipelines were expected to have significant curtailments. In the administration proposal, pipelines would have paid whatever free market prices prevailed in the intrastate market, and this higher price gas would be "rolled in" with the lower interstate prices. The House bill (H.R. 9464) would have placed a ceiling on the intrastate price. For estimates of the probable impact of such a plan on interstate and intrastate gas markets, see Pindyck (1975).

5. *American Public Gas Association et al. vs. FPC,* Decision 76-2000. The Consumer Federation of America may appeal the decision further, but except for the Phillips decision, the Supreme Court has in the past supported FPC authority and methodology in establishing natural gas prices.

6. This markup is regulated by state regulatory commissions, and is usually based on an allowed rate of return on undepreciated capital. Unless there are major changes in supply,

capital requirements are not likely to change much in the future. Assuming that labor costs and nominal interest rates reflect the aggregate rate of inflation, it seems reasonable to assume that the markup will remain constant in real terms, as it more or less has in the past.

As an alternative means of forecasting retail prices, we fit a regression equation relating retail prices to average wellhead prices over data from 1960 to 1976. For the residential retail price, the resuting regression equation is:

$$P_r = 0.7224 + 2.1218P_w, \ R^2 = .984 \ \text{(Standard errors in parentheses)}$$
$$(.0419) \quad (.1359)$$

For the industrial retail price, our equation is:

$$P_i = 0.0421 + 2.0722P_w, \ R^2 = .999$$
$$(.0123) \quad (.0399)$$

With these equations, retail prices would be somewhat higher in 1980 and 1985. For example, in 1980 the residential retail price could range from $2.57 to $3.48 under the alternative policies, while the industrial price could range from $1.84 to $2.74.

7. "New" gas includes new discoveries "from onshore wells more than 2 1/2 miles from an existing well, or 1000 feet deeper than any existing well within a 2 1/2 mile radius," and offshore gas "produced from wells on new Federal leases granted on or after April 20, 1977, or old leases which had been abandoned and are subject to re-leasing" (Plan 1977:53).

8. These prices are in nominal (undeflated) terms, and based on an assumed 6.5 percent rate of general inflation.

9. Fact sheet on president's energy program issued by White House Energy Staff; and Plan (1977).

10. Obtained using our econometric model.

11. These retail prices are again based on the markup forecasts described earlier.

12. The model was constructed by P. W. MacAvoy and R. S. Pindyck, and various versions are described in MacAvoy and Pindyck (1973; 1975a; 1975b). In 1976 the model was structurally revised and reestimated using an updated data base. The most recent version of the model is described in Pindyck (1977).

13. Although exploratory drilling is about the same under FPC and Carter, under the president's plan more of that drilling would be directed toward higher risk and higher return areas, so that discovery sizes would be larger.

14. We could have computed this cost by summing over a longer time horizon, but there is too much uncertainty over natural gas supply and demand after 1985 to make such a calculation meaningful.

15. We have made the assumption that, in the short term, consumers of gas switch to oil and coal only if they are unable to purchase gas (i.e., the effective price of gas to them is infinite), but not if the price of gas increases. This assumption of near zero cross-price elasticity in the short term was necessary since we do not have a complete econometric model of inter-fuel substitution.

16. The actual elasticities are probably smaller, and the use of larger elasticities will give us an *underestimate* of the induced expenditure on oil and coal. Again, we choose the larger elasticities in order to obtain as conservative an estimate of the induced expenditure as possible.

17. The winter of 1976-1977 was an unusually cold one, so that using that winter's shortage induced unemployment as a basis for predicting future shortage induced unemployment might tend to bias the predictions upwards. On the other hand, larger shortages are likely to have greater than proportional unemployment effects, since there is less

room to use allocation schemes to shift available supplies to those industrial consumers with no short-term substitution possibilities.

18. For a recent empirical estimate of Okun's Law, see Perry (1977:1).

19. If higher prices in fact shift exploratory effort to the extensive margin, one would have certain *a priori* expectations regarding the signs of the coefficients of price terms in the success ratio and size of find equations. Estimation of the latest version of the model gives no evidence of clear-cut shifts toward the extensive or intensive margin in response to price increases. Much of the variation in success ratios, for example, was found not to be caused by changes in price, but rather by regional differences and depletion effects. Although the size of find for gas does show a clear positive dependence on the price of gas, the size of find for oil shows no dependence. Thus the impact of changes in price on new discoveries occurs largely through the level of exploratory activity.

VII. James L. Sweeney: "Energy Regulation—Solution or Problem?"

1. These prices equal $1.39 and $0.51 per million BTU, respectively. This compares to the average refiner's acquisition cost for crude oil of $2.05 per million BTU.

2. The retail price of natural gas sold to residential consumers for heating use was $1.15 per million BTU in March 1977, while the average residential heating oil price was $3.30 per million BTU (FEA 1977).

3. This average price equals the total of electricity revenues from ultimate customers divided by the total sales of electricity to ultimate customers. Edison Electric Institute, *Statistical Yearbook* (New York), is the source for these data.

4. In the past, however, the government did not sell or auction off import rights, but rather assigned them—somewhat arbitrarily—to those firms already importing oil. Thus a significant amount of wealth was transferred to those firms. Such a scheme is equivalent to a tariff system in which all governmental revenues are divided among the firms importing oil at the time of the system's initiation.

5. For simplicity, business use of gasoline is ignored here. However, some provision would normally be made for this class of user.

6. This is not say that there are no difficulties associated with the penalty formula legislated under the EPCA. The current formula provides incentives for market segmentation either by size, class of automobile, or by geographic changes. However, these difficulties could be solved by simple changes in the penalty formula. See Sweeney (1978) for a more complete discussion.

VIII. William R. Moffat: "Federal Energy Proprietorship: Leasing and Its Critics"

1. Remarks here about bidding are based on theories developed in recent years by company explorationists and by decision theorists. See, for example, Vickrey (1061), Wilson (1969), and Capen et al. (1971).

2. *Calvert Cliffs' Coord. Com. v. AEC,* 449 F. 2d 1109 (1971).

3. *Sierra Club v. Morton,* decided by the U.S. Court of Appeals for the D.C. Circuit on 16 June 1975.

4. *Kleppe v. Sierra Club,* decided by the Supreme Court on 28 June 1976.

5. 42 U.S.C. 4332.

IX: Fred S. Hoffman and Richard Nehring: "Oil and Gas Supply in the National Energy Plan: Energy Policy in a Cloudy Crystal Ball"

1. For a detailed discussion of the origin, migration, and accumulation of petroleum, see Levorsen (1967), and Hobson and Tiratsoo (1975).

2. For data and analysis on giant petroleum fields worldwide, see Halbouty (1970), Holmgren et al. (1975), and Meyerhoff (1976:536-41). For comprehensive data on significant petroleum fields in the U.S., see Nehring (1977).

3. For summaries of three recent detailed estimates of ultimate petroleum liquids and natural gas in the United States, see Miller et al. (1975), Langston (1976), and Moody and Geiger (1975:39-45). For estimates of enhanced oil recovery, see National Petroleum Council (1976). For a fourth estimate of U.S. gas resources, see Potential Gas Committee (1977).

4. For estimates of world oil and gas, see Moody and Esser (1975), and Adams and Kirkby (1975).

5. The Plan's proposals regarding natural gas and residential energy use reflect more than unclarity about the motives for conservation; they reflect the dominance of concern about the distribution of costs and benefits over considerations of economic efficiency.

6. While the CIA report (1977) appears to emphasize OPEC unwillingness to increase production to meet demand at current prices, much of the press reaction emphasized the prospect of running out of world oil resources.

7. Problems like the greenhouse effect from increasing CO_2 concentrations in the atmosphere might ultimately require us to limit the rate at which we burn fossil fuels. We are just beginning to learn about the nature and implications of these problems and the relevant time scale appears to be decades or centuries, so they do not seem to be a major factor in decisions about the rate and pattern of energy use over the next ten to twenty years. In any case, if such considerations finally affect the total amount of fossil fuel burned over the lifespan of the earth, it is likely that the reductions they imply will be in the use of fossil fuels other than oil and gas from conventional sources. The oil and gas saved by the Plan, therefore, is saved to be used another day.

8. The relevance of discounting is not in serious dispute. The specific discount rate to be applied, and the rationale for it, is still the subject of some disagreement. We will consider two alternative values of the discount rate in the discussion that follows—3 percent and 6 percent, both net of inflation. These are at the low end of the range of values, and favor arguments for conservation.

9. Unless otherwise stated, "price changes" will refer to changes relative to the general price level, sometimes called "real" price changes or "constant dollar" prices. Where prices are given, they will be in terms of 1977 price levels as reflected in the GNP implicit price deflator.

10. Clearly, additions to reserves follow no such smooth pattern, particularly since the bulk of oil reserves discovered so far have been found in large fields. In fact, it appears that a major problem for the oil industry throughout the post-World War II period has been the overhang of reserves resulting from the Persian Gulf discoveries, which have led to reserve ratios far greater than the level we posit as a target. Associated with these large reserve ratios, we believe, was the threat of glut. OPEC has so far poven better able to deal with this "problem" than the oil companies. Apart from geologically induced randomness, the rate of reserve addition relative to remaining unknown resources can be affected by the rate of resource allocation to exploration. A more complete analysis than the present one would test for sensitivity to different ratios of reserve additions to unkown resources, perhaps relating this figure to the rate of change in oil prices.

11. Any comparison with recent levels of reserve additions must also take account of the very high ratio of known reserves to current production. Even at current OPEC prices, this ratio may be a restraining influence on world-oil exploration. Probably even more serious are changes in the politico-economic environment for international resource exploration, discussed below.

12. For estimates on shale, see Whitcombe et al. (1976). For estimates on synthetics from coal, see Detman (1976).

13. This is similar to the "backstop technology" notion introduced by Nordhaus (1973: 529-70). Nordhaus defines a backstop technology as one without limitations on its resource base. Shale and coal combined do not satify this, but come close enough for the purposes of this discussion. To simplify our calculations, we make the artificial assumption that the backstop technology is not available at all until its assumed date of introduction; thereafter, it is available in quantities sufficient to supply the difference between total demand for liquid fuels and petroleum production.

14. Oil at that date would command a price of about $170 per barrel under our artificial assumptions about market response and backstop availability. A slightly more realistic calculation would recognize that substitute liquid fuels would be available in limited quantities, perhaps at higher prices than the assumed $25, before the industry reaches full maturity.

15. The artificiality of the discontinuity of prices at the transition to the backstop was discussed in note 14.

X. Edward J. Mitchell: "Energy Politics: The Irrelevant Debate"

1. For a brief political-economic history of the petroleum industry, see Mitchell (1974: 27-69).

2. That the economics profession tends to favor decontrol of natural gas prices is shown in Senate Interior Committee (1973).

3. See Hobbie and Mancke (1977). The survey finds statistically significant differences between expert and journalistic opinion on every issue of substance.

4. The U.S. Gulf Coast prices come from *Platt's Oilgram Price Service,* while the Caribbean prices are from *Petroleum Intelligence Weekly.*

REFERENCES

ACDA. 1976. Moving Toward Life in a Nuclear Armed Crowd? ACDA/PAB-263, PH 76-04-389-14, Final Report (April). Prepared for U.S. Arms Control and Disarmament Agency by Pan Heuristics. Los Angeles, California.

Adams, T. D., and Kirkby, M. A. 1975. Estimate of World Gas Reserves. *Proceedings, Ninth World Petroleum Congress* 3. London: Applied Science Publishers, Ltd.

Adelman, M. A. 1972-1973. Is the Oil Shortage Real? Oil Companies as OPEC Tax Collectors. *Foreign Policy* 9 (Winter).

———. 1972. *The World Petroleum Market.* Baltimore, Md.: Johns Hopkins Press for Resources of the Future.

Agria, Susan. 1969. Special Tax Treatment of Mineral Industries. In *The Taxation of Income from Capital,* ed. Arnold Harberger and Martin Bailey. Washington, D.C.: The Brookings Institution.

Akins, James E. 1973. The Oil Crisis: This Time the Wolf Is Here. *Foreign Affairs* (April).

Alchian, Armen. 1975. An Introduction to Confusion. In *No Time to Confuse.* San Francisco: Institute for Contemporary Studies.

American Academy of Political and Social Science. 1977. *The Annals* 430 (March).

American Gas Association. 1977. Economic Impact of Winter 1976-77. Statistics Directorate (10 May).

American Petroleum Institute. 1974. *Petroleum Taxation and Energy Independence.* Washington, D.C.: American Petroleum Institute.

Atomic Energy Commission. 1975. *Reactor Safety Study: An Assessment of Accident Risks in U.S. Commercial Nuclear Power Plants.* WASH-1400 (NUREG-75/014) (October). Washington, D.C.: U.S. Nuclear Regulatory Commission.

BLM. 1976. *Projected Coal Production for Six Western States* (June). Washington, D.C.: U.S. Department of the Interior, Bureau of Land Management.

———. 1973. *Public Land Statistics.* Washington, D.C.: U.S. Department of the Interior, Bureau of Land Management.

British Royal Commission on Environmental Pollution. 1976. *Nuclear Power and the Environment.* Sixth Report (September). Sir Brian Flowers, Chairman. London: Her Majesty's Stationery Office.

Brown, Clarence, and Stockman, Dave. 1977. The Cost of Natural Gas Deregulation: A Re-estimate. Processed (11 July).

Bua, B., and Snekvik, E. 1972. Klekkeforsøk med rogn av laksefisk 1966-1971. Virkning av surhet og saltinnhold i klekkevannet. Direktoratet for vilt of ferskvannsfisk, Norway. *Vann* 7:86-93.

Cabinet Task Force on Oil Import Control. 1970. *The Oil Import Question.* Report (February). Washington, D.C.

Capen, E., Clapp, R., and Campbell, W. 1971. Competitive Bidding in High Risk Situations. *Journal of Petroleum Technology* (June).

Carter, Jimmy. 1976a. Nuclear Energy and World Order. Address at the United Nations, 13 May. Washington, D.C.: The White House.

———. 1976b. Remarks on Nuclear Energy Policy. San Diego, California, 25 September. Washington, D.C.: The White House.

———. 1977. Statement by the President on Nuclear Power Policy. 7 April. Washington, D.C.: The White House.

CBO Analysis. 1977. Congress of the United States, Congressional Budget Office. *Staff Working Paper* (June). Washington, D.C.: U.S. Government Printing Office.

Central Intelligence Agency. 1977a. *The International Energy Situation: Outlook to 1985.* ER 77-10240 U (April). Washington, D.C.

———. 1977b. *Prospects for Soviet Oil Production* (April). Supplemental Analysis (July). Washington, D.C.

Cohen, B. L. 1976. *American Scientist* 64 (September-October):550-59.

Combes, F. C. 1954. *Coal Tar and Cutaneous Carcinogenesis in Industry.* Springfield, Ill.: Charles C. Thomas, Publishers.

Congressional Quarterly. 1976 (25 September).

Cox, James C., and Wright, Arthur W. 1977. The Effects on Refined Product Prices and Energy Independence of Decontrolling Crude Oil Prices. Mimeo (February).

———. 1975. A Tariff Policy for Independence from Oil Embargoes. *National Tax Journal* 28, 1 (March).

Dahlem Konferenzen. 1976. *Global Chemical Cycles and Their Alterations by Man.* Ed. Werner Stumm. Berlin.

Dance, K. L. 1975. High Level Radioactive Waste Management: Past Experience, Future Risks and Present Decisions. Report by Teknekron, Inc., to the Ford Foundation (1 April).

Darmstadter, Joel, and Landsberg, Hans H. 1974. The Economic Background. In *The Oil Crisis,* ed. Raymond Vernon. New York: Norton.

Davis, P., and Ozburn, G. W. 1969. The pH Tolerance of *Daphnia pulex. Canadian Journal of Zoology* 47.

Detman, Roger. 1976. Factored Estimates for Western Coal Commercial Concepts. Interim Report, ERDA, FE-2249-5 (October). Prepared by C. F. Braun & Co.

Dochinger, L. S., and Seliga, T. A. 1976. *Proceedings of the First International Symposium on International Rain and the Forest Ecosystem.* USDA Forest Service General Technical Report NE-23.

Environmental Policy Center. 1974. *Facts about Coal in the United States* (April). Washington, D.C.

Epstein, William. 1977. Why States Go—and Don't Go—Nuclear. In American Academy of Political and Social Science, *The Annals* 430 (March).

Erdahl, C. A., and Keeling, C. D. 1973. Atmospheric Carbon Dioxide and Radiocarbon in the Natural Carbon Cycle. In *Carbon and the Biosphere*, U.S. AEC Conf-721510.

Executive Office of the President, Council on Wage and Price Stability. 1976. *The Insulation Market*. Washington, D.C.

FEA. 1977. *Monthly Energy Review* (March). Washington, D.C.: Federal Energy Administration.

———. 1976. *National Energy Outlook* (February). Washington, D.C.: Federal Energy Administration.

———. 1974. *Project Independence Report*. Washington, D.C.: Federal Energy Administration.

Forbes Magazine. 1976 (15 April).

Ford Foundation. 1977. *Nuclear Power Issues and Choices—Report of the Nuclear Energy Policy Study Group*. Cambridge, Mass.: Ballinger Publishing Co.

Ford Foundation Energy Policy Project. 1974. *A Time to Choose America's Energy Future*. Cambridge, Mass.: Ballinger.

Ford, Gerald. 1976. Statement by the President on Nuclear Policy, 28 October. Washington, D. C.: The White House.

Forney, A. J., et al. 1974. *Analyses of Tars, Chars, Gases and Water Found in Effluents from the Synthane Process*. Technical Progress Report 76 (January). Pittsburgh Energy Research Center.

Gerarde, H. W. 1960. *Toxicology and Biochemistry of Aromatic Hydrocarbons*. Amsterdam: Elsevier Publishing Company.

Greenfield, S. M. 1957. Rain Scavenging of Radioactive Particulate Matter from the Atmosphere. *Journal of Meteorology* 14, 2 (April).

———, Husting, E. L., and Peyton, T. O. 1976. *Environmental Research to Support the Development of Fossil Energy Technology Options*. TR-11300-2 (31 October). San Rafael, Cal.: Greenfield, Attaway & Tyler, Inc.

Greenwood, Ted, Rathjens, George W., and Ruina, Jack. 1976. Nuclear Power and Weapons Proliferation. *Adelphi Paper* 130 (Winter).

Halbouty, M. T., ed. 1970. *Geology of Giant Petroleum Fields*. Tulsa, Okla.: American Association of Petroleum Geologists.

Hall, R. E., and Pindyck, R. S. 1977. The Conflicting Goals of National Energy Policy. *The Public Interest* 47 (Spring).

Hamilton, L. D., ed. 1974. *The Health and Environmental Effects of Electricity Generation: A Preliminary Report*. BEAG-HE/EE 12/74 (20 July). Biomedical and Environmental Assessment. Brookhaven National Laboratory.

Hendrey, G. R., Baalsrund, K., Traaen, T. S., et al. 1976. Some Hydrobiological Changes. *AMBIO* 5:5-6:224.

Hobbie, Barbara, and Mancke, Richard B. 1977. Oil Monopoly Divestiture: Media versus Expert Perceptions. *Energy Policy* (September).

Hobson, G. D., and Tiratsoo, E. N. 1975. *Introduction to Petroleum Geology*. Beaconsfield, England: Scientific Press, Ltd.

Hogan, William W., and Manne, Allan S. 1977. Energy-Economy Interactions: The Fable of the Elephant and the Rabbit ? *The Energy Modeling Forum* (July). Stanford, Cal.: Stanford University.

Holmgren, D. A., Moody, J. D., and Emmerich, H. M. 1975. The Structural Settings for Giant Oil and Gas Fields. *Proceedings, Ninth World Petroleum Congress* 3. London: Applied Science Publishers, Ltd.

Keesing's Research Report 7. 1972. *Disarmament: Negotiations and Treaties, 1946-1971.* New York: Charles Scribner's Sons.

Krishna, D. 1953. Effect of Changing pH on Developing Trout Eggs and Larvae. *Nature* 171:434.

Langston, J. D. 1976. A New Look at the U.S. Oil and Gas Potential. Paper presented in Dallas (10 March).

Lave, Lester B., and Siskin, Eugene P. 1977. *Air Pollution and Human Health.* Baltimore, Md.: Johns Hopkins University Press for Resources for the Future, Inc.

Levorsen, A. I. 1967. Geology of Petroleum. 2d ed. San Francisco: W. H. Freeman and Company.

MacAvoy, Paul W., ed. 1977. *Federal Energy Administration Regulation: Report of the Presidential Task Force.* Washington, D.C.: American Enterprise Institute.

————, and Pindyck, R. S. 1973. Alternative Regulatory Policies for Dealing with the Natural Gas Shortage. *The Bell Journal of Economics and Management Science* 4, 2 (Autumn).

————. 1975a. *The Economics of the Natural Gas Shortage (1960-1980).* Amsterdam: North-Holland Publishing Company.

————. 1975b. *Price Controls and the Natural Gas Shortage.* Washington, D.C.: American Enterprise Institute.

McDonald, Stephen L. 1971. *Petroleum Conservation in the United States: An Economic Analysis.* Baltimore, Md.: Johns Hopkins Press for Resources for the Future.

Machta, L. 1973. Prediction of CO_2 in the Atmosphere. In *Carbon and the Biosphere,* U.S. AEC Conf-720510.

Magee, E. M., Hall, H. J., and Varga, G. M., Jr. 1973. *Potential Pollutants in Fossil Fuels.* EPS-Rs-73-24-9 (June). Esso Research and Engineering Co.

Malmer, N. 1976. Chemical Changes in the Soil. *AMBIO* 5:5-6:231.

Mancke, Richard B. 1975. *Performance of the Federal Energy Office.* Washington, D.C.: American Enterprise Institute.

Mead, Walter J. 1968. Economic Analysis of Leasing Experience under the OCS Lands Act. In *Study of the Outer Continental Shelf Lands of the United States,* ed. Robert E. Krueger et al. Washington, D.C.: Public Land Law Review Commission.

————. 1977. An Economic Appraisal of President Carter's Energy Program. *Science* (22 July).

Meadows, Dennis; Meadows, Donella; Ronders, J.; Behrens, W. W. 1972. *The Limits to Growth.* New York: Potomac Associates.

Meyerhoff, A. A. 1976. Economic Impact and Geopolitical Implications of Giant Petroleum Fields. *American Scientist* 64.

Miller, Betty M., et al. *Geological Estimates of Undiscovered Recoverable Oil and Gas Resources in the United States.* Geological Survey Circular 725. Washington, D.C.

Mitchell, Edward J. 1977. *Energy Policy and Ideology.* Washington, D.C.: American Enterprise Institute.

———. 1974*a. U.S. Energy Policy: A Primer.* Washington, D.C.: American Enterprise Institute.

———. 1974*b. U.S. Energy Policy.* Washington, D.C.: American Enterprise Institute.

Montgomery, W. David. 1977. *A Case Study of Regulatory Programs of the Federal Energy Administration.* Social Science Working Paper No. 147 (January). Pasadena, Cal.: California Institute of Technology.

Moody, J. D., and Esser, R. W. 1975. An Estimate of the World's Recoverable Crude Oil Resource. *Proceedings, Ninth World Petroleum Congress* 3. London: Applied Science Publishers, Ltd.

Moody, J. E., and Geiger, R. E. 1975. Petroleum Resources: How Much Oil and Where? *Technology Review* (March/April).

Moorsteen, Richard. 1975. OPEC Can Wait—We Can't. *Foreign Policy* 18 (Spring).

Morgan, J. D. 1976. *Availability of Conventional Energy Resource Materials—Coal.* U.S. Bureau of Mines (21 June).

Nacht, Michael. 1977. The United States in a World of Nuclear Powers. In American Academy of Political and Social Science, *The Annals* 430 (March).

National Academy of Sciences. 1975. *Air Quality and Stationary Source Emission Control.* Prepared for the Senate Committee on Public Works.

———. 1977. *Report of Committee on Nuclear and Alternative Energy Systems.* From information supplied by W. E. Grimes, Oak Ridge National Laboratory.

National Energy Plan. 1977. Washington, D.C.: Executive Office of the President (April).

National Petroleum Council. 1976. *Enhanced Oil Recovery.* Washington, D.C.

Nehring, Richard. 1977. *The Discovery of Significant Oil and Gas Fields in the United States.* Santa Monica, Cal.: The Rand Corporation.

NIOSH. 1973. *Criteria for a Recommended Standard. Occupational Exposure to Coke Oven Emissions.* Washington, D.C.: National Institute for Occupational Safety and Health.

———. 1974. *Criteria for a Recommended Standard. Occupational Exposure to Sulfur Dioxide.* Washington, D.C.: National Institute for Occupational Safety and Health.

Nordhaus, William. 1973. *The Allocation of Energy Resources.* Brookings Papers on Economic Activity 3. Washington, D.C.: The Brookings Institution.

Nuclear Energy Policy Study Group. 1977. *Nuclear Power Issues and Choices. Report* (March). Spurgeon M. Keeny, Jr., Chairman. Cambridge, Mass.: Ballinger Publishing Company.

OPA. 1976. *Joint Bidding for Federal Onshore Oil and Gas Lands, and Coal and Oil Shale Lands* (June). Washington, D.C.: Department of the Interior, Office of Policy Analysis.

Organisation for Economic Cooperation and Development (OECD). 1977. *World Energy Outlook.* Paris.

———/IAEA. 1975. *Uranium.* A Joint Report (December).

Overrein, Lars N. 1976. Report from International Conference on the Effect of Acid Precipitation [Telemark, Norway], 14 -19 June 1976. *AMBIO* 5:5-6: 201- 48.

Parker, N. A., and Thompson, B. C. 1976. *U.S. Coal Resources and Reserves.* FEA/B-76/210 (May).

Perry, G. L. 1977. Potential Output and Productivity. *Brookings Papers on Economic Activity* 1. Washington, D.C.: The Brookings Institution.

Peyton, T. O. 1975. The Input and Distribution of Aerially Deposited Heavy Metals in an Urban Aquatic Ecosystem. Doctoral thesis, Purdue University.

————, McIntosh, A., Anderson, V., et al. 1976. Aerial Input of Heavy Metals into an Aquatic Ecosystem. *Water, Air and Soil Pollution* 5:443-51. Dordrecht-Holland: Reidel Publishing Company.

Phelps, Charles E., and Smith, Rodney T. 1977. *Petroleum Regulation: The False Dilemma of Decontrol.* R-1951-RD (January). Santa Monica, Cal.: The Rand Corporation.

Pindyck, R. S. 1975. Emergency Proposals to Deal with the Natural Gas Shortage. Testimony before the House Committee on Interstate and Foreign Commerce, Subcommittee on Energy and Power, 24 September.

————. 1976. Gains to Producers from the Cartelization of Exhaustible Resources. MITEL 76-012WP. MIT Energy Laboratory Working Paper.

————. 1977. Higher Energy Prices and the Supply of Natural Gas. *Energy Systems and Policy* (Autumn).

Potential Gas Committee. 1977. *Potential Supply of Natural Gas in the United States as of December 31, 1976.* Golden, Colorado.

Ranger Uranium Environmental Inquiry. 1976. *First Report* (October). Mr. Justice R. W. Fox, Presiding Commissioner. Canberra: Australian Government Publishing Service.

Report of the Presidential Task Force on Reform of Federal Energy Regulations. 1976 (December). Washington, D.C.

Rose, D. J., Walsh, P. W., and Leskovjan, L. L. 1976. *American Scientist* 63 (May-June).

Russell, Milton. 1977. Energy. In *Setting National Priorities: The 1978 Budget.* Washington, D.C.: The Brookings Institution.

Schipper, L., and Lichtenberg, A. J. 1976. Efficient Energy Use and Well-Being: The Swedish Example. *Science* (3 December).

Senate Interior Committee. 1973. *Natural Gas Policy Issues and Options.* Serial No. 93-20 (92-55). Washington, D.C.

Sweeney, James L. 1978. U.S. Gasoline Demand: An Economic Analysis of the EPCA New Car Efficiency Standard. In *The Structure of Energy Markets,* vol. 1 of *Advances in the Economics of Energy and Resources,* ed. Robert S. Pindyck. Greenwich, Conn.: JAI Press (forthcoming).

Tamm, C. O. 1976. Biological Effects in Soil and Forest Vegetation. *AMBIO* 5:5-6:236.

Tyner, W. E., and Wright, Arthur W. 1977. U.S. Energy Policy and Oil Independence: A Critique and a Proposal. *Materials and Society* 1, 4.

U.S. Bureau of Mines. 1974a. Land Utilization and Reclamation in the Mining Industry, 1930-71. USBM IC8642. *Engineering and Mining Journal* (August).

—————. 1967. *Mass Spectrometric Analysis of Coal Tar Distillates and Residues.* TN-U7-7000. Report of Investigations 7000 (August).

—————. 1974*b*. *Mass Spectrometric Analysis of Product Water from Coal Gasification.* Technical Progress Report 86 (December).

U.S. Department of Health Education and Welfare. 1969. *Air Quality Criteria for Sulfur Oxides.* National Air Pollution Control Administration (January).

—————. 1975. *Request for Information on Certain Chemical Agents. Suspected Carcinogens.* Federal Register 40, 121:26389-496 (23 June). Center for Disease Control.

U.S. House of Representatives. 1977. Clean Air Act Amendments of 1977. Report No. 95-564 (August), 95th Congress, 1st Session.

U.S. Senate. 1956. Committee on Foreign Relations. *Disarmament and Security: A Collection of Documents, 1919-1955.* Washington, D.C.: U.S. Government Printing Office.

Vernon, Raymond, ed. 1974. *The Oil Crisis.* New York: Norton.

Vickrey, W. 1961. Counterspeculation, Auctions, and Competitive Sealed Tenders. *Journal of Finance* (March).

Walske, Carl. 1977. Nuclear Electric Power and the Proliferation of Nuclear Weapon States. *International Security* 1, 3 (Winter).

Whitcombe, John A., Vawter, R. Glenn, and Nutter, J. F. 1976. Shale Oil Production Costs and the Need for Incentives for Pioneer Plant Construction. Paper prepared for the American Chemical Society, Division of Industrial Engineering Chemistry, Symposium on the Commercialization of Synthetic Fuels (February). Colorado Springs, Colorado.

Wilson, R. 1969. Competitive Bidding with Disparate Information. *Management Science* (March).

Wohlstetter, Albert. 1976-77. Spreading the Bomb without Quite Breaking the Rules. Foreign Policy (Winter).

—————. 1977. The Spread of Nuclear Bombs: Predictions, Premises, Policies. *Pan Heuristics.*

Workshop on Alternative Energy Strategies. 1977. *Energy: Global Prospects 1985-2000.* New York: McGraw Hill.

Wright, R. F., and Gjessing, E. T. 1976. Changes in the Chemical Composition of Lakes. *AMBIO* 5:5-6:219.

ABOUT THE AUTHORS

ALBERT CARNESALE, Associate Director of the Program for Science and International Affairs and lecturer in Public Policy at Harvard University, is a nuclear engineer whose research and teaching activities focus on nuclear energy policy, nuclear arms control, and the relationships between them. He served as a member of the U. S. delegation to SALT (1970-1972), and on the Nuclear Regulatory Commission's special hearing board on the use of plutonium as fuel for nuclear power reactors (1976-1977). Mr. Carnesale is presently consultant to the Arms Control and Disarmament Agency, the Department of Defense, the Department of State, and the Nuclear Regulatory Commission. He is the author of "The Nuclear Fuel Cycle and Nuclear Proliferation," published in *International Arrangements for the Nuclear Fuel Cycle* (1977), is one of the authors of *Nuclear Power Issues and Choices* (1977), is a coauthor with P. Doty and M. Nacht of "The Race to Control Nuclear Arms," *Foreign Affairs* (1976), and is coeditor of the quarterly *International Security.*

STANLEY M. GREENFIELD is president of Greenfield, Attaway & Tyler, Inc., a firm involved with the social, economic, and environmental problems affecting society. A former assistant administrator of the U.S. Environmental Protection Agency concerned with the ecological effects of pollution and with the development of control technology, Dr. Greenfield previously headed the Environmental Science Department of The Rand Corporation, conducting research programs in such fields as weather modification, ionospheric physics, and infrared radiation. He has published a number of technical articles and reports, and is the author of *The Responsible Role of the Atmospheric Sciences in Determining the Future Quality of Man's Environment* (1969).

FRED S. HOFFMAN, economist and Director of Rand's Energy Policy Program, served in the 1960s as Deputy Assistant Secretary of Defense for Systems and Analysis, responsible for the analysis of requirements for nuclear offensive and defensive forces and of regional force requirements to meet alliance commitments. From 1967 to 1969 he was an Assistant Director, U.S. Bureau of the Budget, concerned with national security, international affairs, atomic energy, space, and with the introduction of the Planning, Programming, and Budgeting System to the domestic agencies of the federal government. With The Rand Corporation, he has been the principal investigator of an NSF-sponsored project on energy regulations and technology change, on an analysis of Japanese energy research and development for ERDA, and on policy planning and evaluation for the FEA. He is a member of the Chief of Naval Operations Executive Panel.

EDWARD J. MITCHELL, Professor of Business Economics at the University of Michigan, is a member of the Energy Finance Advisory Committee of the FEA, and of the National Petroleum Council's Subcommittee on Conservation Policy to the Committee on Future Energy Prospects. An economist with The Rand Corporation and member of the Institute for Advanced Study at Princeton University in the 1960s, he was Executive Director in 1972 of the Energy Subcommittee of the President's Domestic Affairs Council. He has written extensively in the fields of international affairs, energy, and fuel problems, is the author of *U.S. Energy Policy* (1974), and the editor of *Vertical Integration in the Oil Industry* (1976).

WILLIAM R. MOFFAT, director of the Public Management Program in the Graduate School of Business at Stanford University, obtained his Ph.D. in Economics from Harvard University in 1968 after some years of practical experience in the business community. He served in the U.S. Department of Health, Education, and Welfare (1971-1973), and as Director of Policy Analysis in the U.S. Department of the Interior (1973-1976). Among his publications are "The Dominant Firm," *Public Policy* (1954), and "Taxes in the Price Equation," *Review of Economics and Statistics* (1970).

RICHARD NEHRING, a social scientist, spent 1971-1972 in the Office of Economic Analysis, Department of the Interior, where he made an analysis of the Alaskan pipeline and other natural resource issues and was a consultant to the Natural Resources Defense Council. In 1973 he joined The Rand Corporation, where he has worked on studies of U.S. oil imports, disruptions in fossil fuel supplies, and federal offshore leasing proposals. His Rand publications include *Oil and Gas Supplies for California* (1975); and he is coauthor of *Protecting the U.S. Petroleum Market against Future Denials of Imports* (1974) and *Coal Development and Government Regulation in the Northern Great Plains: A Preliminary Report* (1976).

ROBERT S. PINDYCK, Associate Professor of Economics in the Sloan School of Management at MIT, is Senior Research Advisor, Institute for Applied Economic Research (Montreal), and consultant to the Federal Energy Administration and to the Development Research Center of the International Bank for Reconstruction and Development. He is coauthor with P. W. MacAvoy of *Price Controls and the Natural Gas Shortage* (1975), and is editor of the forthcoming two-volume work, *Advances in the Economics of Energy and Resources*. His articles have appeared in many technical journals, and include "The Econometrics of U.S. Natural Gas and Oil Markets," *Energy Policy* (1974), "Should the Federal Government Enter the Oil Business?" *Challenge* (1976), "Pricing Policies for a Two-Part Exhaustible Resource Cartel: The Case of OPEC" (with E. Hnyilicza), *European Economic Review* (1976), and "The Conflicting Goals of National Energy Policy" (with R. E. Hall), *The Public Interest* (1977).

NORMAN C. RASMUSSEN heads the Department of Nuclear Engineering at MIT. His experience in the field of radiation detection has led to a concern with nuclear safety and the environmental impact of nuclear power, and to his appointment by the U.S. Nuclear Regulatory Commission as director of an evaluation of the overall risks from reactor accidents. The report, "Reactor Safety Study: An Assessment of Accident Risks in U.S. Commercial Nuclear Power Plants" (WASH 1400), was completed in November 1975. As consultant to government and industry, Dr. Rasmussen's clients include the U.S. Nuclear Regulatory Commission, ERDA, and the insurance pool that insures nuclear reactors, NELPIA. In 1974 he was appointed to the Defense Science Board, and the following year he headed a task force to review the basic research program of the Department of Defense. He is a member of the Presidential Advisory Group on Contributions of Technology to Economic Strength.

DAVID J. ROSE, Professor of Nuclear Engineering at MIT, has spent many years in the study of national laboratory, energy, and environmental policy. At Oak Ridge National Laboratory he was a visiting staff member in 1967 and 1968, and he later spent two years there as director of long-range planning and initial program director of the National Science Foundation's Interdisciplinary Research Relevant to Problems of Society. He has been a visiting staff member at the United Kingdom Atomic Energy Authority's Culham Laboratory, where he directed an international workshop on fusion reactors in 1974. Professor Rose is consultant to the U.S. and other governments, and to a number of private industrial firms. He has published widely in the fields of electronics and plasma physics, controlled nuclear fusion, nuclear power, and energy policy, and is coauthor with M. Clark, Jr., of *Plasmas and Controlled Fusion* 1971).

HENRY S. ROWEN, president of The Rand Corporation from 1967 to 1972, is Professor of Public Management at the Graduate School of Business, Stanford University. As Deputy Assistant Secretary of Defense from 1961 to 1964, he was primarily responsible for European policy issues, and he continues as member of the Scientific Advisory Group on Effects for the Nuclear Defense Agency; he is also a member of the Board of Trustees of The Rand Corporation, the Council on Foreign Relations, and the International Institute for Strategic Studies. Among his many publications are "The Role of Cost-Benefit Analysis in Policy Making" in *Cost-Benefit Analysis and Water Pollution Policy* (1975), "Policy Analysis as Heuristic Aid: The Design of Means, Ends, and Institutions" in *When Values Conflict—Essays on Environmental Analysis, Discourse, and Decision* (1976), and (with Gregory Jones) "Influencing the Nuclear Technology Choices of Other Countries: The Key Role of Fuel Recycling in the U.S."(1976).

JAMES L. SWEENEY is Associate Professor in the Department of Engineering-Economic Systems at Stanford University and a consultant to the Federal Energy Administration. Until 1976 he was director of the FEA Office of Energy Systems, and headed the analysis of numerous proposed energy policy options and the development of forecasts for the 1976 *National Energy Outlook*. A graduate of MIT and the author of several articles on the demand and consumption of gasoline, he is coauthor with William W. Hogan and Michael H. Wagner of the forthcoming "Energy Policy Models in the National Energy Outlook" to be published in *Management Science*.

ARTHUR W. WRIGHT, Associate Professor of Economics, Purdue University, is Associate Director/Economics of the National Science Foundation Project on "The Soviet Union in World Commodity Markets." As a specialist in comparative economic systems and in fuel and energy policies of the U.S. and Eastern Europe, he has been a recent consultant to the U.S. Congress Office of Technology Assessment, the Federal Energy Administration, and Resources for the Future. He has written extensively, and is coauthor (with James C. Cox) of "The Determinants of Investment in Petroleum Reserves and Their Implications for Public Policy," *American Economic Review* (1976), and "The Impact of the Tax Reduction Act of 1975 on the Petroleum Industry," *Boston College Industrial and Commercial Law Review* (1976). His article (with Wallace E. Tyner) on "Taxes and Energy Policy: What Are the Alternatives?" is forthcoming in the House Ways and Means Committee hearings on President Carter's energy tax proposals.

SELECTED PUBLICATIONS FROM
THE INSTITUTE FOR CONTEMPORARY STUDIES
260 California Street, San Francisco, California 94111

Catalog available upon request

NO TIME TO CONFUSE—A Critique of the Ford Foundation's Energy Policy
   Project: *A Time to Choose America's Energy Future.*
   $4.95. 156 pages. Publication Date: 2/25/75. ISBN 0-917616-01-4
   Library of Congress #75-10230
Contributors: Morris A. Adelman, Armen A. Alchian, George Hilton, M. Bruce
   Johnson, Walter J. Mead, Arnold Moore, Thomas Gale Moore, William
   Riker, Herman Kahn, James DeHaven.

NO LAND IS AN ISLAND: INDIVIDUAL RIGHTS AND GOVERNMENT
   CONTROL OF LAND USE
   $5.95. 190 pages. Publication Date: 11/19/75. ISBN 0-917616-03-0
   Library of Congress #75-38415
Contributors: Benjamin F. Bobo, B. Bruce-Briggs, Connie Cheney, A. Lawrence
   Chickering, Robert B. Ekelund, Jr., W. Philip Gramm, Donald G. Hag-
   man, Robert B. Hawkins, Jr., M. Bruce Johnson, Jan Krasnowiecki, John
   McClaughry, Donald M. Pach, Bernard H. Siegan, Ann Louise Strong,
   Morris K. Udall.

GOVERNMENT CREDIT ALLOCATION: WHERE DO WE GO FROM
   HERE?
   $4.95. 208 pages. Publication Date: 11/20/75. ISBN 0-917616-02-2
   Library of Congress #75-32951
Contributors: Karl Brunner, George Benston, Dwight Jaffee, Omotunde
   Johnson, Edward Kane, Thomas Mayer, Allan H. Meltzer.

THE POLITICS OF PLANNING: A REVIEW AND CRITIQUE OF
   CENTRALIZED ECONOMIC PLANNING
   $5.95. 352 pages. Publication Date: 3/3/76. ISBN 0-917616-05-7
   Library of Congress #76-7714
Contributors: B. Bruce-Briggs, James Buchanan, A. Lawrence Chickering,
   Ralph Harris, Robert B. Hawkins, Jr., George Hilton, Richard Mancke,
   Richard Muth, Vincent Ostrom, Svetozar Pejovich, Myron Sharpe, John
   Sheahan, Herbert Stein, Gordon Tullock, Ernest van den Haag, Paul H.
   Weaver, Murray L. Weidenbaum, Hans Willgerodt, Peter P. Witonski.

THE CALIFORNIA COASTAL PLAN: A CRITIQUE
$5.95. 192 pages. Publication Date: 3/31/76. ISBN 0-917616-04-9
Library of Congress #76-7715

Contributors: Eugene Bardach, Daniel Benjamin, Thomas Borcherding, Ross Eckert, H. Edward Frech, M. Bruce Johnson, Ronald N. Lafferty, Walter Mead, Daniel Orr, Donald M. Pach, Michael Peevey.

NEW DIRECTIONS IN PUBLIC HEALTH CARE: AN EVALUATION OF PROPOSALS FOR NATIONAL HEALTH INSURANCE
$5.95. 265 pages. Publication Date: 5/17/76. ISBN 0-917616-06-5
Library of Congress #76-9522

Contributors: Martin S. Feldstein, Thomas D. Hall, Leon R. Kass, Keith Leffler, Cotton M. Lindsay, Mark V. Pauly, Charles E. Phelps, Thomas C. Schelling, Arthur Seldon.

PUBLIC EMPLOYEE UNIONS: A STUDY OF THE CRISIS IN PUBLIC SECTOR LABOR RELATIONS
$5.95. 295 pages. Publication Date: 6/23/76. ISBN 0-917616-08-1
Library of Congress #76-18409

Contributors: Jack D. Douglas, Raymond Horton, Theodore W. Kheel, David Lewin, Seymour Martin Lipset, Harvey C. Mansfield, Jr., George Meany, Robert Nisbet, Daniel Orr, A. H. Raskin, Wes Uhlman, Harry Wellington, Charles Wheeler, Ralph Winter, Jerry Wurf.

THE CRISIS IN SOCIAL SECURITY: PROBLEMS AND PROSPECTS
$5.95. 214 pages. Publication Date: April 1977. ISBN 0-917616-16-2
Library of Congress #77-72542

Contributors: Michael J. Boskin, George F. Break, Rita Ricardo Campbell, Edward Cowan, Martin Feldstein, Milton Friedman, Douglas R. Munro, Donald O. Parsons, Carl V. Patton, Joseph A. Pechman, Sherwin Rosen, W. Kip Viscusi, Richard J. Zeckhauser

DEFENDING AMERICA: A NEW INTERNATIONAL ROLE
AFTER DETENTE
$13.95 (hardbound only). Publication Date: April 1977 by Basic Books (New York). ISBN 0-465-01585-9
Library of Congress #76-43479

Contributors: Robert Conquest, Theodore Draper, Gregory Grossman, Walter Laqueur, Edward M. Luttwak, Charles Burton Marshall, Paul H. Nitze, Norman Polmar, Eugene V. Rostow, Leonard Schapiro, James R. Schlesinger, Paul Seabury, W. Scott Thompson, Albert Wohlstetter.

PARENTS, TEACHERS, AND CHILDREN: PROSPECTS FOR CHOICE IN AMERICAN EDUCATION
$5.95. 336 pages. Publication Date: June 1977. ISBN 0-917616-18-9
Library of Congress #77-79164

Contributors: James S. Coleman, John E. Coons, William H. Cornog, Denis P. Doyle, E. Babette Edwards, Nathan Glazer, Andrew M. Greeley, R. Kent Greenawalt, Marvin Lazerson, William C. McCready, Michael Novak, John P. O'Dwyer, Robert Singleton, Thomas Sowell, Stephen D. Sugarman, Richard E. Wagner.

ONCE IS ENOUGH: THE TAXATION OF CORPORATE EQUITY
  INCOME
  $2.00. 32 pages. Publication Date: May 1977. ISBN 0-917616-23-5
Author: Charles E. McLure, Jr.

OPTIONS FOR U.S. ENERGY POLICY
  $5.95. 300 pages. Publication Date: September 1977. ISBN 0-917616-20-0
  Library of Congress #77-89094
Contributors: Albert Carnesale, Stanley M. Greenfield, Fred S. Hoffman, Edward J. Mitchell, William R. Moffat, Richard Nehring, Robert S. Pindyck, Norman C. Rasmussen, David J. Rose, Henry S. Rowen, James L. Sweeney, Arthur W. Wright.

The Institute for Contemporary Studies, founded in 1972, is a publicly supported, nonpartisan research and educational foundation. Its purpose is to distribute research and information on national and international issues to the opinion-making institutions, especially the mass media. Views expressed in the Institute's publications are those of the authors and do not necessarily reflect the views of the staff, officers, or directors of the Institute.

Cover Design by Douglas A. Deluchi

89

"The preference
of houses over cars, non-
energy over energy, solar energy
over oil, indeed, almost any other source
of energy over oil, is what leaps out at you
when you read the National Energy Plan.
You will not find these preferences explained in
any economics book.... What makes the Carter
program hang together... is ideology."
—**Edward J. Mitchell**

"The Carter administration begins with a large capital stock of good will and... a relatively friendly
Congress. These assets will be dissipated if the
sacrifices people are being called on to make
do not seem, as time passes, to correspond
well to reality. If it appears that our energy
policy has only made things worse, alienation [now] evident on many fronts
in our society, may grow."
—**Henry S. Rowen**